D1498400

ENGLiSH to GCSE

Geoff Barton

Oxford University Press 1996

Oxford University Press, Walton Street, Oxford OX2 6DP

Oxford   New York
Athens   Auckland   Bangkok   Bombay
Calcutta   Cape Town   Dar es Salaam   Delhi
Florence   Hong Kong   Istanbul   Karachi
Kuala Lumpur   Madras   Madrid   Melbourne
Mexico City   Nairobi   Paris   Singapore
Taipei   Tokyo   Toronto

and associated companies in
Berlin   Ibadan

Oxford is a trade mark of Oxford University Press

First published 1996

ISBN 0 19 831289 X School edition
ISBN 0 19 831298 9 Bookshop edition

For acknowledgements see page 224

Printed in Italy

Introduction

English to GCSE is aimed at students who want to do well in English Language and Literature at GCSE. To these students, English can frequently prove frustrating. Whereas in Science or Maths you can see exactly what you're getting right or wrong, in English it's harder to tell. In other subjects you can hope to get 100% in a test or exam; whilst in English that can seem impossible. It isn't that English lessons feel much more difficult than other subjects - they may even seem easier and more enjoyable - it's just that it isn't always clear what you need to do next to improve your work. There are so many layers to think about - basic punctuation, spelling, sentence structure and vocabulary; writing clearly but not too simplistically; giving detail; creating atmosphere; responding to texts; reading between the lines... the list can seem unending.

If English sometimes feels like that to you, then you're the kind of student the book was written for. It isn't a 'How to Pass English at GCSE' set of crib notes; nor a book of potted plot-summaries. Instead it is an attempt to map out all of the important elements in the new GCSE courses and to give a clearer sense of what is required, what you need to know, which skills you will need to practise, and what the examiners are looking for. The book is not written for any single examining board, but it is based on the core requirements of all of them, so that whichever syllabus you are studying, the material here will have relevance.

The most important dimension to *English to GCSE* is that it is based firmly in students' own experience of English. Throughout the book you will see comments, questions, problems, and samples of work from pupils in Years 10 and 11. They made clear what they felt they needed to know to do better at GCSE, and the book is therefore written in collaboration with those pupils. I am grateful to all of them for their suggestions and for allowing me to present their work.

Examiner's comments...

Another key element of *English to GCSE* is the presence of Martyn Thorpe, an experienced GCSE examiner and English teacher. At the end of each section we have included a sample of pupils' examination or coursework, and Martyn has provided detailed comments based on his knowledge of the requirements of the examination boards. He has also answered questions posed by GCSE students about the exact nature of assessment in speaking and listening, language and literature work.

Active preparation

The book is intended to be read actively. There are plenty of activities and questions to get you involved in the challenge of preparing for GCSE. There is also plenty of reading material in order to develop your familiarity with a variety of styles and genres.

Simply reading through *English to GCSE* won't automatically earn you a grade A. But I hope that it will build your confidence in English Language and Literature, and give you a clearer understanding of what the courses require. Armed with those two assets – confidence and understanding – you should be in a much stronger position to succeed in both the coursework and final examinations. I hope also, of course, that you will enjoy both this book and the challenge of your GCSE course.

Geoff Barton

Contents

INTRODUCTION

SECTION 1 : LANGUAGE SKILLS

06   The Tools of English
08   Starting Point: Sam's Report
10   Grammar Grounding
12   Simple Sentences
14   Compound Sentences
16   Complex Sentences
18   Standard English
22   Basic Punctuation
25   Advanced Punctuation
28   Apostrophes
31   Spelling Matters I
32   Spelling Matters II

SECTION 2 : SPEAKING AND LISTENING

36   Self-assessment
38   Storytelling
42   Rules of Conversation
45   Chairing Meetings
48   The Language of Speeches
52   Writing a Speech
56   Formal v Informal Speech
58   Dialects
61   Attitudes to Accents
64   Received Pronunciation
66   Speech v Writing
68   Assessing Speech

SECTION 3 : READING FOR INFORMATION

70   Non-fiction: Autobiography
74   Non-fiction: Reportage
78   Non-fiction: Diaries
82   Non-fiction: Travel Writing
86   Reading for Meaning I
88   Reading for Meaning II
90   Advice Column
91   Advanced Reading Skills
95   Fact v Opinion
98   Examining Data
99   Examiner's Comments: Reading Paper

SECTION 4 : PRACTICAL WRITING

104 Writing to Inform: Presenting Information
108 Conventions of Letters
110 Creative Writing
114 Writing Dialogue
116 Writing Journalism
118 Discursive Assignments
122 Drafting Skills
124 Note-making
127 Assessing Writing
128 Examiner's Comments: Imaginative Writing

SECTION 5 : READING LITERATURE

130 Keeping a Reading Diary
132 Influential Texts I
136 Influential Texts II
140 Shakespeare's Language
144 Imagery
148 Reading Poetry
150 The Short Story
154 Reading Drama
158 Building Tension
162 Assessing the Reading of Literature
163 Examiner's Comments: Literature Unseen

SECTION 6 : WRITING ON LITERATURE

166 Creative Responses to Literature
170 Writing About Literature
174 Studying Character
178 Studying Plot
182 Poetry Unseens
186 Comparing Texts
189 Planning Coursework
191 Revision Advice
193 Examiner's Comments: Literature Essay

REFERENCE SECTION

196 Examiner's Question & Answer
198 Literature Timeline: 15th/16th/17th/18th/19th/20th Centuries
216 Wider Reading List
218 Glossary
222 Feedback

The Tools of English

Getting Down to Basics

For some people, good English seems a simple matter of being able to use punctuation marks accurately, to spell well, and to have a clear written style. Of course these are very important. But you also need to have something to say. Other spreads in this book will help you get your tone and style right. This one is concerned with the basics of English.

For many students of English at GCSE, writing is like a game of snakes and ladders – with too many chances of getting caught out. Every piece of writing means trying to climb the ladders and avoid the snakes.

Seen like this, every essay can be something of a battlefield – you try to get through it, head spinning in all directions!

Know Your Enemy

The key to writing clear, accurate English is to see grammar rules, punctuation, and spelling advice as tools to help you write well, rather than as obstacles. That means knowing precisely what purpose they serve, and how they can help you.

LANGUAGE SKILLS

Activity

How much do you understand about the different rules and conventions of English? Use this self-assessment quiz to explore your knowledge, and then compare your responses with the comments of some Year 10 pupils...

Spend around 10 minutes on this activity. Write your answers in note-form on a piece of paper. The more you think about your current knowledge, the more you will be able to develop your language skills.

THE BASICS OF ENGLISH

1 What is PUNCTUATION for?
2 Which are the most important punctuation marks?
3 What do we need full stops for?
4 What do we need commas for?
5 Which punctuation marks are you unsure about?

6 Is correct SPELLING important? Why? Why not?
7 What spelling rules do you know?
8 Which words do you always forget how to spell?
9 What techniques do you use to help you spell a new word you're unsure about?

10 What do you understand by the word GRAMMAR?
11 When you are writing, how much is your mind on CONTENT (what you are saying), how much on ACCURACY (getting spellings right, etc.), and how much on STYLE (writing in an interesting, clear, lively way)? Express your answer in a ratio – e.g. 20:60:20.
12 When do you enjoy writing? When do you strongly dislike it? What would help you to be better at writing?

Working on

What do your answers reveal about your attitude to English? Analyse your strengths and weaknesses.

Questions 1 to 5

How clear are you about the purpose of punctuation marks? If you were unsure about questions 2 and 3, you probably need to sharpen your understanding. See 'Basic Punctuation' on page 22.

Questions 6 to 9

What is your attitude to spelling? Do you have clear strategies for learning how to spell words? If you had no answer for question 9, see 'Spelling Matters II' on page 32.

Questions 10 to 12

What is your attitude to writing generally? Do you have a sense of how to structure and shape your work, to give it clarity and precision? Are you able to think about *how* you write as well as *what* you write? The spreads on sentences (pages 12 to 17) might give you ideas about how to liven up your style.

Follow-up

- To see how one Year 10 pupil used basic rules to improve her English, see 'Starting Point: Sam's Report' on page 8.
- To learn more about grammar basics, see 'Grammar Grounding' on page 10.

Starting Point: Sam's Report

English at Work

This spread gives practical advice for taking the rules of grammar, punctuation, and spelling, and applying them to a coursework assignment.

GCSE students are often asked to write reports or accounts of personal experiences. Sam, in Year 10, was asked to write about her two-week work experience placement at a wine bar in central York.

Activity   Read through the first part of her assignment on page 9, and make notes using the headings provided below. For each one, give a grade 1 to 5 (top) to indicate how successful you think the assignment is.
- How interesting do you find it? (1–5) How might it be improved?
- How clear is it to follow what is going on? (1–5)
- How accurate is it? (1–5)

The essay is reprinted in its first draft form, without any corrections. Make a note of any grammar, punctuation, and spelling mistakes you spot.

Feedback to Sam

The report succeeds in telling the reader what you did on work experience and how much you enjoyed it. It simply isn't very interesting to read. By keeping the content the same but paying attention to your style, you could really make us want to read on. Here are some specific suggestions:

Grammar
You write in sentences, but there isn't enough sentence variety. The result is that your work lacks sparkle: it doesn't make us want to read on. Some sentences seem to drift a bit. The assignment needs tighter structuring.

Punctuation
You use full stops to indicate the ends of sentences, but that's about all the use of punctuation you make. Your meanings could be clearer in places if you used a greater variety of punctuation. You need to revise apostrophes.

Spelling
You spell basic words well, but there are some fairly obvious errors (*I choose* instead of *I chose*; *weather* for *whether*).

Style
You concentrate too much on the events that took place, without giving us enough sense of the atmosphere or the people. Your style needs to be more lively and ambitious. More unexpected vocabulary would also pep up the overall effect – such as 'Christian was furious' instead of 'Christian went mad'.

How would you react to these comments if you were Sam? Do they seem helpful, or too critical? To see how the advice works when put into practice, see the rest of the Language Skills section.

Work Experience Report

For my work experience placement I choose Oscars Wine Bar. The reason for choosing this was because when I left school I wanted to go into catering. I wasn't absolutely sure so going on this placement helped me decide weather this was the career for me or not.

When I went for my interview I got to meet the people I'd be working with, this helped me because when I got there on my first day I new who most of the people were so I wasn't as nervous. The place was down a small back street which was quite out of the way of other shops.

The first day of work soon arrived and I began to get really nervous, loads of questions were going through my head. "What if I was late." I had to start work and 9.30 so I decided to get to the bus stop at 9.00.

But I thought that if I got their and a bus had just gone by I would be late so I got there at 8.45 and caught the bus straight away. The bus was half empty so I sat on my own. The journey seemed to go by well so quite soon I arrived in town it was only 5 past 9. I went for a walk round. I saw a couple of my friends stood talking so I went to join them, they too were very nervous so I knew I wasn't alone. I walked back slowly to Oscars and peered down into the courtyard where a young looking lad about the same age as me was sweeping up.

I walked down and said "Hello", I knew I'd seen him from somewhere before and he recognized me too. It was a boy called Sam. He explained what he was doing there and what I would have to do. He was on a youth training scheme but he had to start work at 9.00 as he helped to clear up. We were locked out because Matt hadn't got the keys. Matt worked in the Bar. I met him next we were sat...

Everything was a mess. When we went into the kitchen Christian went mad, food was left all over the place so I had to tidy it up. It soon came to diner time and this is what I dreaded most. People piled into the place so there were lots of meals to take down.

Finish making your notes and then look at 'Feedback to Sam' on page 8.

Follow-up
- To see Examiner's comments on students' assignments, see the end of each section.
- To find out more about the requirements of GCSE, see 'Examiner's Question & Answer' on page 196.

Grammar Grounding

Objectives:
- to clarify your sense of how sentences are structured
- to show that grammar and punctuation are tools rather than obstacles

As a Rule

We learn most of the rules of English grammar before our sixth birthday... so why do people still get so worried by the word 'grammar'? It's partly because many people don't actually know what grammar is! Which of these descriptions do you think is right?

Grammar is:
1 the dos and don'ts of English
2 accurate spelling and punctuation
3 structuring words in the best order
4 correct English

The most accurate answer is probably number 3. Grammar is simply a system which allows us to communicate clearly and effectively. These sentences, for example, are ungrammatical:

> cat the on chair is the
> sister my decided to not go to town

They break the rules of English about the way words go together to create meaning. They are obviously wrong. But in other sentences the problem is more difficult to spot.

Is that it?

Yes. Basically, grammar means little more than getting the structure right – so that it creates clarity. Punctuation marks are tools which further help us to shape and organize what we are saying on the page, to help the reader understand our message.

Word Classes

The building blocks of grammar are the word classes. Look at this brief reminder of the different word classes and what their purposes are (a more detailed summary is given in the Glossary). Then look at how you can use them to develop your written English.

Nouns
the first parts of speech we ever learn to use; they allow us to name things:

> I ate *the pineapple.*
> *The cat* was sick on *John.*
> *Night* fell.

Verbs
these breathe life into sentences by telling us what someone, or something, is doing or being:

> I *ate* the pineapple.
> The cat *was* black.
> Night *fell.*

They also tell us about when something happens – past, present, or future (tense).

Adjectives

these enable us to describe nouns (things) more precisely:

> I ate the *stinking* pineapple.
> The *unhappy* cat was sick on *old* John.
> *Dark* night fell.

Adverbs

these enable us to describe verbs (the things people do) more precisely:

> I *hurriedly* ate the pineapple.
> The cat was *slightly* sick on John.
> Night fell *silently*.

Prepositions

these show us where events take place:

> I ate the pineapple *in* the garden.
> The cat was sick *on* John.
> Night fell *across* the world.

Conjunctions

these enable us to join sentences together:

> I ate the pineapple in the garden *and* watched the cat
> be sick on John *whilst* night fell across the world.

Pronouns

these enable us to avoid repeating the same noun:

> I saw the cat. I liked *the cat*.

This can be made much more readable by replacing the second reference to the cat by the pronoun *it*:

> I saw the cat. I liked *it*.

Other pronouns: I, me, you, he, him, she, her, we, us, they, them.

Activity

Now look at how knowing the different word classes allows Sam to revise her work experience report – adding greater precision to her verbs, changing their tense, using adjectives and adverbs to add detail where necessary. The changes she has made to the first few lines are highlighted. How successful is she in using grammatical knowledge to improve her assignment?

> For my *recent* work experience placement I *chose* Oscar's Wine Bar. *My* reason for choosing this was *that* I *think that I would like to pursue a career related to catering* when I *leave* school. *Because* I am not absolutely sure of my *future intentions, I thought that* this placement *might* help me to decide…

What kinds of changes do you notice in Sam's redrafted assignment? How would you develop it further? Take her next two paragraphs and experiment with redrafting them; or redraft an assignment of your own, paying attention to the way you can use word classes to vary the level of detail and precision in your writing.

Follow-up

- To develop greater sentence variety, see the next spread.
- To look at the way punctuation can add greater variety to your writing, see the various Punctuation spreads on pages 22–30.

Simple Sentences

Objectives:
- to define simple sentences
- to look at how they can be used to convey information in your written work

So Simple

There are three types of sentences:
- simple
- compound
- complex

In this spread, we look at the function of simple sentences.

Simple sentences give one main piece of information centred around one main verb which says what happened (the main verb in each example is highlighted):

> I *had to start* work at 9.30.
> It *was* cold.
> For my work experience placement I *chose* Oscar's Wine Bar.

Sentence features
- start with a capital letter; end with a full stop, question mark, or exclamation mark
- can be any length:

> It is dark. Are you ready? = 2 simple sentences

Advice points
- useful for giving information clearly and directly
- use too many at a time and they become repetitive and irritating:

> I *enjoyed* work experience. It *was* interesting. I *learnt* a lot. I *had to get up* early each morning. I *wasn't used* to this. It probably *did* me good.

Comment to Sam
You start with a simple sentence:

> 'For my work experience placement I *chose* Oscar's Wine Bar.'

This makes for a clear, direct start. Later, your writing becomes tangled and unclear in places because you link so many sentences with *as, but, so*. This can make it seem to ramble a bit...

> 'But I thought that if I got there and a bus had just gone by I would be late so I got there at 8.45 and caught the bus straight away.'
> 'He was on a youth training scheme but he had to start work at 9.00 as he helped to clear up.'

If you were to break your ideas down into smaller units, using some simple sentences as well as longer ones, you would help the reader to follow your work. You would also add rhythm to your writing – like this:

> 'But I thought about what might happen if I got there and a bus had just gone by. *I would be late.* I got there instead at 8.45 and caught the bus straight away.'

Activity   You can make simple sentences work harder by adding descriptive details using adjectives, adverbs, and phrases. These will add information about Who? How? When? and Where?

> I enjoyed work experience.
> + adverb
> I *thoroughly* enjoyed work experience. (says how)
> + phrase
> I thoroughly enjoyed work experience *last week*. (says when) or:
> I thoroughly enjoyed work experience *at Oscar's Wine Bar*. (says where)

Take the following simple sentences and experiment with ways of adding details without letting them become overloaded with information:

> I had an interview.
> I felt nervous.
> I answered many questions.
> The interviewer was aggressive.
> I was disappointed.

Remember that many simple sentences have their most powerful effect when they are at their most direct. Do not load every simple sentence with masses of adjectives, adverbs, and phrases.

Working on   Look at the opening of this short story by American writer Raymond Carver. Look how clear his style is, how he uses straightforward vocabulary, different lengths of sentences, and dialogue to give the text variety...

> My mother is packed and ready to move. But Sunday afternoon, at the last minute, she calls and says for us to come eat with her. 'My ice-box is defrosting,' she tells me. 'I have to fry up this chicken before it rots.' She says we should bring our own plates and some knives and forks. She's packed most of the kitchen things. 'Come and eat with me one last time,' she says. 'You and Jill.'
> I hang up the phone and stand at the window for a minute longer, wishing I could figure this out. But I can't...
>
> *Raymond Carver, 'Boxes'*
> from *Elephant and Other Stories*

- How can you tell the extract is set in America?
- Raymond Carver uses almost no descriptive words. How does he make us feel that the people and places in the extract are real?
- Try rewriting the extract, adding lots of detail (for example, instead of 'My mother' you might say 'My elderly mother'). Then look at what the effect is of adding in too much description.

Follow-up
- For ways of adding variety to your written style, see 'Compound Sentences' on page 14 and 'Complex Sentences' on page 16.
- To examine how punctuation can help give clarity to your writing, see 'Basic Punctuation' on page 22 and 'Advanced Punctuation' on page 25.

Compound Sentences

Simply Connect

Objectives:

- to look at one way of developing more variety in your sentence structure
- to examine the strengths and weaknesses of compound sentences

Compound sentences are the easiest way of adding more information to sentences. As children, we learn to create compound sentences very early – simply by adding basic sentence connectives like *and, but, or*...

> We went to the zoo and I saw lots of animals and there were giraffes and camels and an elephant and I had an ice cream but Mummy wouldn't let me have any chips and we saw the monkeys and then I fell over and hurt my knee but it was all right and I...

In other words, compound sentences simply join together simple sentences using basic connectives. They can therefore express two or more ideas, like this:

2 simple sentences:

> The money was spent on cheesecake.
> Everyone was happy.

1 compound sentence:

> The money was spent on cheesecake *and* everyone was happy.

✓ Allows you to group ideas together into one longer sentence.

✗ Can become very repetitive and confusing if too many simple sentences are joined together in this way.

Activity

To get a feel for the way compound sentences can work, look at the paragraph below and notice how the sentence structure assists the reader's understanding:

> Tomatoes contain chloroplasts. No one is sure what chloroplasts actually do, but it seems to be the case that they give tomatoes their red colour. Carrots also contain chloroplasts and this explains their orangey colour. It has been suggested that the colour is a way of attracting pollinating insects but that wouldn't explain why the part of the carrot which grows underground should be orange. Perhaps we will never know the answer.

Although it contains some difficult ideas, this paragraph is fairly easy to read because of its sentence structure. The opening simple sentence gives the main subject (and is called a topic sentence). Compound sentences add detail. The final simple sentence rounds the topic off with a straightforward statement.

Now you try the same technique. Choose one of the lists of facts on page 15 and write a readable paragraph which combines simple and compound sentences.

Humphrey Bogart

- Oscar-winning film star of the 1940s and 1950s.
- Born the son of a doctor.
- Childhood in New York.
- Served in the Navy in World War I.
- Started his career as manager of a touring acting company.
- Began acting himself in 1922.
- First film in late 1930s was *The Petrified Forest*.
- Became well-known for playing heroic gangsters.
- Best known films = *The Maltese Falcon* [1941] and *Casablanca* [1942].
- He won an Oscar for *The African Queen* [1952].
- In this, he played opposite Katherine Hepburn. He was an alcoholic trader on a flimsy boat, travelling through Africa.
- He died in 1957.

Ella Fitzgerald

- Black US singer and composer.
- Born in 1918 in Newport News, Virginia.
- Singing career began when she won a talent contest in Harlem, New York.
- Joined Tiny Bradshaw's band and then Chick Webb's.
- First big hit was 'A-tisket, A-tasket' in 1938.
- Webb died and she led the band for two years.
- Between 1940 and 1948 she had five hit records.
- Three of them were with the vocal group The Ink Spots.
- She began to tour the world.
- She appeared with famous names like Count Basie, Duke Ellington, and Oscar Peterson.
- She appeared on television and in films in the late 1950s.
- She is particularly well-known for her haunting singing of ballads by Cole Porter, Irving Berlin, and Rogers and Hart.

Follow-up
- To add greater variety to your sentences, see 'Complex Sentences' on page 16.
- To learn about how punctuation can give more meaning to your writing, see 'Advanced Punctuation' on page 25.

Complex Sentences

Complex Types

Objectives:
- to examine the way complex sentences can add variety and clarity to your writing
- to practise using different types of complex sentences

Complex sentences add variety to your written style. They allow you to express more than one idea in each sentence, adding complexity and interest. But they need careful handling.

Three ways of creating complex sentences:

1 Using advanced connectives

Connectives like *however, although, because, despite*, used at the **start** of a two-part sentence, can have a powerful effect:

> *Although* I like cheese, I prefer chips.
> *Despite* his best efforts, the man still wept.
> *Because* she enjoyed wind surfing, she chose a seaside holiday.
> *Despite* receiving several warnings, the boy still bit the dog.

2 Using relative clauses

A relative clause is a way of adding detail to a main sentence. It is easy to recognize because it begins with the words *which, who, that, where, when*.

> The dog, *which was up to its knees in water*, began to howl.
> My grandfather, *whose bald head glistened in the morning light*, stared at me.

Notice that the main sentence carries the main information:

> The dog began to howl.
> My grandfather stared at me.

The relative clause simply adds more detail, creating an island of words within the main sentence. Use commas to indicate the relative clause.

3 Using '-ing' clauses

These are also called present participle clauses. They are another way of creating two-part sentences which carry more information and have more variety than simple sentences. The first part of the sentence uses an '-ing' verb; the second part continues the idea like this:

> *Starting* at four am, Susan had finished her paper round by nine.
> *Eating* a diet of fried lobster entrails, I have found that my skin has become rather crusty.

✓ Another way of adding variety to your writing.
✗ Can easily backfire if you don't make the '-ing' verb agree with the subject of the sentence. Look at this sentence and note that it does not make sense:

> Walking down the street, it was very foggy.
> (Who is doing the walking?)

It should be written as:

> Walking down the street, I noticed that it was very foggy.

Activity   Saira, in Year 10, has written a coursework assignment about J. B. Priestley's play, *An Inspector Calls*. It suffers from too many simple sentences, lacking variety and interest. Rewrite the extract, experimenting with different sentence types, with the aim of giving it a more interesting style:

> The Birling family are enjoying their celebration. Sheila and Gerald are to get married. Then the doorbell rings. Edna announces a visitor. He is waiting in the hallway. His name is Inspector Goole. He is a mysterious and sometimes menacing man. Mrs Birling describes him as 'quite rude'. Only Sheila and Eric really listen to him. He warns the family about Eva Smith. He says they have to listen or there will be 'fire and blood and anguish'. No one is sure what that means. Sheila remembers the words at the end of the play. The attitude of her parents and Gerald frightens her. She wants to leave. The words of the Inspector echo through her mind.

There are a number of problems with this assignment:
- it retells the plot too much
- it jumps too quickly between ideas, without looking in depth at any single character
- chiefly it feels lifeless and dull because the use of simple sentences becomes repetitive ('He is waiting in the hallway. His name is Inspector Goole. He is a mysterious and sometimes menacing man.')

Your mission is to breathe new life into the essay, mainly by aiming to add variety to the sentence styles. You might also make some of the vocabulary more ambitious. Use the extract to experiment with introducing some complex sentences, using the techniques outlined in this spread. Also use some simple and compound sentences.

Your starting-point might be a complex sentence like this:

> Quietly enjoying their celebration of Sheila and Gerald's engagement, the Birling family are surprised when Edna announces a late-night visitor...

Follow-up
- To examine the way in which punctuation can help give your written style clarity and vitality, see 'Advanced Punctuation' on page 25.
- To learn more about improving your creative writing, see 'Creative Writing' on page 110.

Standard English

What is Standard English?

Try this quick quiz and see what you understand by the phrase:

Standard English is...

- proper English
- posh English
- an accent used by educated people
- the dialect used in education, law, business, and most books

The first three definitions are misleading; the last is correct.
To fully understand what Standard English is, we have to know a number of other language terms.

Some definitions

Dialect
a variety of English which has some of its own vocabulary and grammar features.

Accent
the way we pronounce words.

It is important to realize that there are different varieties of English – such as Yorkshire English, Scottish English, Norfolk English, American English, and so on. Different dialects, for example, may contain some of the following vocabulary:

Standard English	Yorkshire Dialect	Newcastle Dialect
alleyway	ginnel (Leeds) snickleway (York)	
bread roll	bap	stotty

Different dialects may also contain different grammatical features:

Standard English	Yorkshire Dialect	Cockney Dialect
I like to go out most evenings	I like going out on a night	
She didn't come back		She never come back

Why do we need Standard English?

Standard English became essential when the printing press arrived in Britain. Since texts were now going to be printed for a wide audience, a decision had to be made about which of the many regional dialects should be used. Because the first presses were established in London, the dialect of the London area became standard in books. It became established as the standard dialect in schools and universities, in courts and government, and so became the most widely-known of all dialects.

Without it, communication would be less efficient. Someone writing a book with the title *Bats about Bogles* might be understood in Suffolk (it means 'crazy about scarecrows'), but readers with other dialect words for scarecrows would be confused. Standard English, in other words, gives speakers of English a large common core of words and grammar with shared meanings.

A Map of Old English

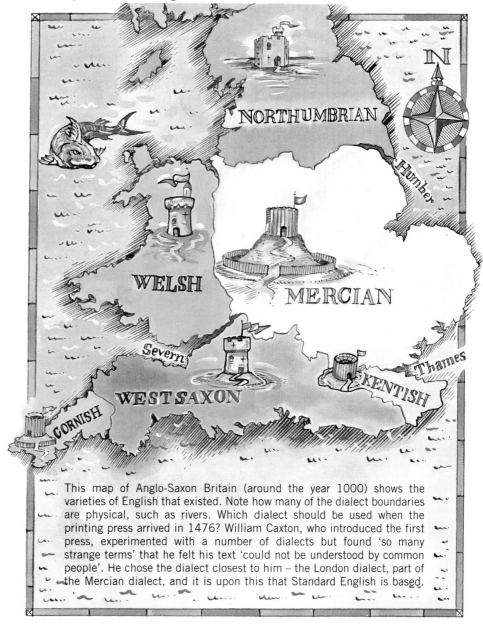

This map of Anglo-Saxon Britain (around the year 1000) shows the varieties of English that existed. Note how many of the dialect boundaries are physical, such as rivers. Which dialect should be used when the printing press arrived in 1476? William Caxton, who introduced the first press, experimented with a number of dialects but found 'so many strange terms' that he felt his text 'could not be understood by common people'. He chose the dialect closest to him – the London dialect, part of the Mercian dialect, and it is upon this that Standard English is based.

Varieties of Standard English

It is important to realize that Standard English can itself vary...
... in style
... in vocabulary
... in grammar
... through time

In style

Even when we use Standard English, we are likely to vary the way we use it according to the situation. In formal situations we might say:

> I cannot believe it.

and in informal situations we might say:

> I can't believe it.

Both are Standard English expressions. One is simply less formal.

In vocabulary

Standard American English contains words which we use in different contexts.

Standard English	Standard American English
lift	elevator
jacket	vest
petrol	gas

In grammar

Look at the way grammatical structures vary between different versions of Standard English.

Standard English	Standard Scottish English	Standard American English
Your hair needs washing.	Your hair needs washed.	
I had just got into the car.		I had just gotten into the car.

Through time

Standard English in the late 20th Century is more direct than it was in the late 19th Century. Look at the example on page 21 from the opening of Thomas Hardy's novel, *Tess of the d'Urbervilles*:

Tess of the d'Urbervilles

On an evening in the latter part of May a middle-aged man was walking homeward from Shaston to the village of Marlott, in the adjoining Vale of Blakemore or Blakemoor. The pair of legs that carried him were rickety, and there was a bias in his gait which inclined him somewhat to the left of a straight line. He occasionally gave a smart nod, as if in confirmation of some opinion, though he was not thinking of anything in particular. An empty egg-basket was slung upon his arm, the nap of his hat was ruffled, a patch being quite worn away at its brim where his thumb came in taking it off. Presently he was met by an elderly parson astride on a gray mare, who, as he rode, hummed a wandering tune.

'Good night t'ee,' said the man with the basket.

'Good night, Sir John,' said the parson.

The pedestrian, after another pace or two, halted, and turned round.

Thomas Hardy

Activity

1 Write a modern Standard English version of these paragraphs of Thomas Hardy's book, and then list the *vocabulary* changes you have made and the *grammatical* changes. How does your revised version feel different? What has it gained and what has it lost?

2 Write a dictionary of dialect words for a dialect you know, or which your parents or grandparents use.

3 Find out some further examples of vocabulary differences between Standard English and Standard American or Standard Scottish English.

Follow-up

- To look at the way language varies in different situations, see 'Formal v Informal Speech' on page 56.
- To examine accents in more detail, see 'Attitudes to Accents' on page 61.

Basic Punctuation

Quick Quiz

Which of these statements do you agree with?

- Full stops stop sentences getting too long.
- Commas tell the reader when she should breathe.
- Commas can also join sentences together.

All of these statements are inaccurate. Follow their advice and you could end up more confused than when you started. Ignore everything you think you know about punctuation and start again with these statements:

1 Punctuation is a way of making our meanings clearer. It helps us to divide thoughts up neatly. It has nothing to do (in most writing) with reading aloud, nothing to do with breathing, and nothing to do with stopping sentences getting too long. So what is it?

2 Punctuation is a way of signalling to the reader what we mean. For example look at two versions of this statement. Notice just how vital punctuation is:

> I hate idiots like you. I find them terrible.
> I hate idiots. Like you, I find them terrible.

A missing full stop can create a baffling sentence:

> King Charles the first prayed for half an hour after he was beheaded.

You won't be able to get punctuation right until you think and write in sentences (see the spreads on sentences). Once you see punctuation as a tool for creating clear meanings, you won't go far wrong.

Full stops

The most important and powerful punctuation mark, it marks the end of one idea ready for the next. When in doubt about which punctuation mark to use, use a full stop.

> The cat looked hungrily at the bird. She licked her lips. She prepared to pounce. Then the door opened. She sloped off again into the corner of the room.

Commas

Often used wrongly when full stops should be used. For example:

> The man walked into the room. He looked old.

Students are sometimes tempted to write this as:

> The man walked into the room, he looked old.

Although both sentences are about the man, they are two different ideas. One describes what he did; the other what he looked like. With commas: when in doubt, leave them out.

Commas have three important functions:

1 to separate items in a list:

> The house was cold, damp, dark and very unpleasant.
> The sun rose, bright, fresh, and welcoming.
> I saw a thin, red trickle of blood.

2 to add clarity by creating an island of words within a longer sentence:

> The woman, who I had seen earlier in the day, reappeared from the station.
> The dog, looking mean and badly-treated, moved towards me.
> Deciding to follow the woman, who looked as if she was about to burgle the caravan, I slipped on my trainers and crept down the path.

In these sentences, the main sentence could stand alone:

> The woman reappeared from the station.
> The dog moved towards me.
> I slipped on my trainers and crept down the path.

The commas allow the writer to give more detail, separate from the main sentence.

3 to address someone directly:

> Did you buy this, John?
> Hello, Sam.

Question marks

Question marks are used in direct questions:

> What time is it, please?
> Where am I?
> What the heck is that?

But not in indirect or reported questions:

> I asked what time it was.
> I wondered where I was.
> I wondered what the heck it was.

Exclamation marks

Exclamation marks are overused – especially in informal letters and some newspapers. Some people seem to think that they add drama to what they write! They even use two or three at a time!!!

Advice: use exclamation marks for dialogue, to show moments of high emotion:

> 'Help!' she cried. 'Get me out of here!'
> 'Hey, Nigel! Come back!'
> 'Don't do that!' he commanded.

Never use more than one at a time and, where possible, avoid using them at all.

Working on Practise using the basics of punctuation by reworking this Year 10 pupil's draft of an imaginative assignment based on the title, 'A World of Your Own'. Use full stops, commas, question marks, and exclamation marks to make the piece communicate more clearly:

I settled down into my seat preparing myself for another boring history lesson. Mr Crick stood at the front of the room he looked nervous. He wore a dark suit, I noticed it didn't quite fit. I wondered what today's fascinating topic would be? I looked around the room, all my classmates were there. I noticed Helen Ruth Inyaat and Paul all looking as blank as I felt. 'Here we go!' said Ruth.

Mr Crick started the lesson. 'Jim turn round, I'm waiting to start.' The whole class paused in anticipation, Mr Crick was well known for his bad temper and anything could get him going. What this time?

'So you know all about the peace treaties of World War One do you Jim?!' shouted Mr Crick. Jim hadn't heard, he was locked in a world of his own. The class all now watching Mr Crick grew tense as he walked towards Jim's desk. Still Jim hadn't realized what was going on, he just sat there, his eyes glazed over. Mr Crick's ruler smashed across the desk! Jim looked up with a look of panic...

Michelle (Year 10)

- How many changes have you made? What were the key changes the essay needed?
- What general comments about the assignment would you have? How could the story have been improved?

Follow-up • To learn about advanced punctuation, see the next spread.
• To find out how apostrophes should be used, see 'Apostrophes' on page 28.

Advanced Punctuation

Objectives:

- to learn about punctuation marks which can give more subtle shades of meaning to your writing
- to practise using them

Beyond Basics

The basics of punctuation – full stop, comma, question mark, and exclamation mark – are easily the most useful. In fact, for many pieces of writing you could get by with the full stop alone to indicate the end of each idea.

But the best writing often deals with complex issues and shades of meaning; it adds detail to ideas; it explains, clarifies, and questions. For writing of a more sophisticated nature, you need punctuation which can serve a more sensitive purpose. This is not something that can be easily learnt: it comes from looking at the way writers write and experimenting in your own writing.

Look at this example of a piece of text which deals with a complex subject, and notice how the writer uses punctuation to help the reader follow her ideas.

The Wheelchair Tennis Match

They are picking blackberries. At the end of the garden, beyond the sycamores and the laurels and a dispirited green-stained fence, lay a piece of waste ground. Poll doesn't know who owned it. It was sandwiched between their garden and the next but no one knew who owned it. To nobody, they thought. To them. It was used as a lavatory by all the children in the road although to the casual passer-by it must have looked impenetrable because of the bramble bushes. They were enormous: tall, wide, dense, circular. White and sweet-smelling in May; dull and green in July; murderous in September when defending their fruit from raiders. In September, the children's legs and arms bore witness to the frenzy of repeated attack: in embedded thorns, in loud weals, in untidy tears and rusty smears, in precise razor cuts beaded with blood.

They were not deterred. They – Poll and her younger sister Annie and their whole gang of six-year-olds (Julie, Nicko, Peter, Jen, Rosemary, Rachel) – ate all day. They ate anything, everything. Stealing from garden to garden – their parents' gardens; the gardens of deaf, blind and infirm neighbours – they descended on vegetable patches and orchards and laid waste. The earth-clogged, the worm-holed, the mouth-drying, the throat-burning, the colicky-unripe, the fizzily-fermenting, the gone-to-seed and -to-flower, everything.

But on this particular afternoon, the one Poll remembers, their gang is elsewhere…

Georgina Hammick

A first reading

This opening of a short story is not easy to read. It is full of complex description and detail. A first-impression of the style of this story might observe:

- complex, precise vocabulary (such as *deterred, colicky-unripe, weals*)
- use of lists to add detail (eg, *tall, wide, dense, circular*)
- lots of hyphenated words to make description more specific *(worm-holed, gone-to-seed)*
- islands of words within main sentences (At the end of the garden, *beyond the sycamores and the laurels and a dispirited green-stained fence,* lay a piece of waste ground.)
- semi-colons used to separate related ideas (White and sweet-smelling in May; dull and green in July; murderous in September)
- the piece is lively to read because the vocabulary and expression is unexpected.

Colons

Colons work like headlights in the dark – pointing to something that's ahead:

> There was a good reason for his failure: he was too upset to win.
> The detective opened the door and surveyed the scene: brightly-lit table lamp, cigarette smouldering in the ashtray and a half-open window.

Because they lead up to something, colons are frequently used in front of lists:

> Remember to bring the following: packed-lunch, raincoat, and money for the telephone box.

Semi-colons

A semi-colon is a pause somewhere in strength between a full stop and a comma. It has two main functions:

1 It can join two or more related sentences which would feel disjointed if separated by a full stop. For example:

> If you like cheese, have some more; if you don't, give it a miss.
> I noticed the cat at the side of the grass; I looked at it; I walked quickly past.

2 It can separate longer items in a list, following a colon:

> The journey consisted of: an early start from home; a long and tedious journey by car; an action-packed ferry crossing; and a brilliant drive through the blazing heat of northern France.

Hyphens and dashes

Hyphens are used to join up words that would be hard to read if written as single words. For example:

> door-to-door; ex-boyfriend; twenty-three

If in doubt, leave them out.

Dashes are occasionally useful for inserting islands of words into sentences:

> Mrs Peters ducked beneath the table – she was a quick mover –
> as the walls of the house began to shake.

This could have been achieved with brackets, but dashes make the sentence more informal and, perhaps, more dramatic. In general, dashes give writing an informal feel – keep them for note-making rather than finished assignments.

Activity

Look back to Sam's work experience report (on page 9), and see whether you can redraft it using more ambitious punctuation, to add greater variety and shades of meaning.

Working on

Look at this extract from Elizabeth Bowen's novel *The Death of the Heart*. Notice how she describes a complex impression of two people on a bridge. Look at how she organizes her text, making it easier for the reader to follow, by using a variety of punctuation marks to clarify ideas...

The Death of the Heart

On a footbridge between an island and the mainland a man and woman stood talking, leaning on the rail. In the intense cold, which made everyone hurry, they had chosen to make this long summerlike pause. Their oblivious stillness made them look like lovers – actually, their elbows were some inches apart; they were riveted not to each other but to what she said. Their thick coats made their figures sexless and stiff as chessmen: they were well-to-do, inside bulwarks of fur and cloth their bodies generated a steady warmth; they could only see the cold – or, if they felt it, they only felt it at their extremities. Now and then he stamped on the bridge, or she brought her muff up to her face. Ice pushed down the channel under the bridge, so that while they talked their reflections were constantly broken up.

Elizabeth Bowen

1 Look at how the text reads if we reduce it to simple sentences controlled only by full stops:

> A man and a woman stood talking. They were on a footbridge between an island and the mainland. They were leaning on the rail. The intense cold made everyone hurry. They had chosen this for their long summerlike pause...

What is the effect? How does the rhythm of the text feel different? How is the meaning changed?

2 Now look back to Sam's work experience report (on page 9). She is also trying to capture a variety of impressions – fear of being late, first impressions of the workplace, meeting people, starting work. See whether you can redraft it using more ambitious punctuation and vocabulary, to add greater variety and shades of meaning.

Follow-up
- To examine ways of organizing ideas, see 'Note-making' on page 124.
- To revise use of apostrophes, see the next spread.

Apostrophes

Apostrophe Confusion

Objectives:
- to clarify the two uses of apostrophes
- to give you some practice in using both types

Apostrophes cause problems. Many people – not just at GCSE – simply are not clear about their purpose. This leads them to put apostrophes in words where they are not needed and to leave them out where they are. This is not a new problem. At the start of this century the playwright George Bernard Shaw was arguing that it might be better if some types of apostrophes were abandoned altogether.

What do you understand of the uses of apostrophes? Try this quick self-test.

> **Which of these sentences contains a correct usage of the apostrophe?:**
>
> **1** I canno't eat any more.
> **2** She likes going to disco's.
> **3** He is a man who likes his potato's.
> **4** The cat was washing it's paws.
> **5** Outside I can see that its still raining.

You will have found some of those easy – especially number one. But did you spot the fact that *every* use of the apostrophe is wrong? If not, then you may find this refresher course useful.

Apostrophe Refresher Course

There are two uses of the apostrophe:
1 For elision (two words being squeezed into one)
2 For possession (to show that something belongs to someone)
You need to be able to get these two uses clear in your own mind… then the whole process will seem much simpler. You might even just read half of this spread and return to part two at a different time.

1 For elision
In spoken English we frequently elide two words into one:

> do + not = don't
> does + not = doesn't
> could + not = couldn't

With very few exceptions, the rule is always the same: the apostrophe is used here to show that a letter has been dropped out when the two words have joined.

Problem cases
There are very few problems – but here's the chief one:

> It + is = it's

But there is another word, with a completely different meaning which is spelt *its*. You will come across that word in the next section.

To test whether you mean it's or its, simply read the sentence through using *it is*:

✓ It's clear that the car won't start = It is clear that the car will not start.

But:

✗ The dog had eaten it's dinner = the dog had eaten it is dinner.

Another slightly awkward customer:

shall not = shan't

Hint: generally, elided words suggest informality. For example, 'I can't see you later' is more informal than 'I cannot see you later'. Use elided words (can't, don't, mustn't) for dialogue in stories and for informal writing. Use formal forms (cannot, do not, must not) for formal assignments, analysis, and writing about literature.

2 For possession

Apostrophes also show who something belongs to (though we can usually tell without the apostrophe) – which is why George Bernard Shaw argued against the use of apostrophes for possession:

The fish's bowl = the bowl belongs to the fish
The dog's bad smell = the bad smell belongs to the dog

The apostrophe, in other words, shows who or what the object belongs to. Apostrophes do work as a useful form of shorthand here. Look at this phrase without apostrophes:

The girls trousers

It is impossible to tell whether the trousers belong to one girl or several. To make it clear without using apostrophes you would have to write:

The trousers belonged to the girls.

But a carefully-placed apostrophe can tell the sharp-eyed reader how many people the objects belong to:

The girl's trousers = the trousers of the girl
The girls' trousers = the trousers of the girls

In other words, look at exactly where the apostrophe is positioned. If it is after the singular form (girl + *'s*) then the objects belong to one; if it is after the plural form (girls + *'*) then the objects belong to more than one person.

For each of these examples, say whether the object belongs to one or more than one person/animal:

1 the cat's litter-tray
2 the cats' litter-tray
3 the writers' meeting
4 the teacher's strange habits
5 the lightbulbs' bright beams

Just to make sure you have the hang of it, add the apostrophes to these phrases, using the guidance about the number of subjects to help you:

6 the boys bad temper (1 boy)
7 the farmers bad language (more than 1 farmer)

8 the rocking chairs unreliable legs (1 rocking chair)
9 the cooks revolting soup (more than 1 cook)
10 the potters peculiar sculptures (1 potter)

Awkward customers

There is one real problem word, which you will already have encountered beneath 'apostrophes for elision':

its = belonging to it

'The cat was washing its paws' is correct. The best way to tell is because if you said 'The cat was washing it is paws', then the sentence wouldn't make sense.

Every time you use its/it's, apply that test and you won't go wrong.

One last small problem – people's names.
If the name ends with '*s*' and you can hear an extra *s*, add it:

The shoes that belong to Gus = Gus's shoes
The bad jokes of James = James's bad jokes

As a final test, decide whether these sentences contain apostrophes of elision (E) or possession (P), and punctuate them correctly. Beware: there are some trick questions here…

11 I saw that we werent going to arrive on time.
12 The turtle raised its head above the waterline.
13 Both computers memory chips failed.
14 I couldnt believe my eyes when I saw the price of the potatoes.
15 I have decided that its now or never.
16 I hope that Jessicas mother is okay.
17 I hate discos.
18 Franciss friends seem like a nice bunch to me.
19 When shall we eat those tomatoes?
20 Theres too much to do here.

You will find the answers on the 'Feedback' pages at the end of this book.

Follow-up   • For advice on the punctuation of dialogue, see 'Writing Dialogue' on page 114.
• For a quick checklist on apostrophes, see 'Glossary' on page 218.

Spelling Matters I

Objectives:
- to look at ways of correcting spellings
- to discuss how much teachers should correct work

Dealing with Spelling

In Barry Hines' novel, the main character Billy Casper has little interest in school. When he produces any written work at all for his English teacher, it contains dozens of errors.

A Kestel for a Knave

A tall story
One day I wolke up and my muther said to me heer Billy theres your brecfast in bed for you there was backen and egg and bred and butter and a big pot of tea when I had my brekfast the sun was shining out side and I got drest and whent down stairs we lived in a big hous up moor edge and we add carpits on the stairs and in the all and sentrall eeting. When I got down I said wers are Jud his goind the army my muther saide and hees not coming back. but your dades coming back in sted. there was a big fire in the room and my dad came in caring his cas that he tulke a way with him I havent seen him for a long time but he was just the same as he went away I was glad hed come back and are Jud had gon away when I got to school all the teacherr were good to me they said allow Billy awo you gowing on and they all pated me on the head and smiled and we did interesting things all day. when I got home my muther saide I not gowing to work eny more and we all had chps beans for awur tea then we got redy and we all went to the pictures we went up stairs and had Ice cream at the intervells and then we all went home and had fish and chips for awur super and then we went to bed.

Barry Hines

How should a teacher respond to a piece of work like this?
Here is the dilemma:
- If you correct every mistake you might simply demoralize the student, so that he never feels he will be able to achieve success.
- But if you don't show him what he is doing wrong, how will he ever improve his spelling?

What do you think?

Activity If you were Billy Casper's English teacher, which spelling mistakes would you correct? Which are the most important ones for him to correct, and why? What comment would you give? What mark?

Follow-up
- To look at common spelling mistakes at GCSE, see 'Spelling Matters II' on next spread.
- To look at what examiners look for when marking written work, see 'Examiner's Question & Answer' on page 196.

Spelling Matters II

Objectives:

- to consider some ways of improving your spelling
- to look closely at word origins as a way of improving spelling

ONE IN TEN IS A DUNCE AT SPELLING

One in ten adults who took a simple spelling test for a survey failed to provide a single correct answer. Only one in six scored full marks.

One thousand people were asked to spell necessary, accommodation, sincerely, business, separate and height. Women performed better than men, with more than 40 per cent scoring at least five compared with 30 per cent of men. Only 27 per cent of those tested could spell accommodation.

The Times, 12 November 1992

Rules and Advice

Notice the suggestion in this headline – that spelling is linked with intelligence, making a bad speller a 'dunce'. If it makes you feel better, few people are perfect spellers, even some of our most famous writers: Shakespeare spelt many words incorrectly; Jane Austen could not spell *friend*; and Charles Dickens spelt *suspense* as *suspence*, *chimney* as *chimnie*, and *stationery* (meaning 'papers') as *stationary* (meaning 'stopped').

Making a spelling mistake does not mean that you are dim or illiterate. It can have many causes – a moment's forgetfulness, working under pressure, a faulty memory, or basic laziness. It is also a fact that English spelling is made difficult by the number of exceptions to spelling rules. Playwright George Bernard Shaw showed how unpredictable English spelling could be with this word:

ghoti

Activity

Can you work out which everyday word Shaw is spelling? He is using the sounds these sets of letters make in other words. Look at the different sounds and see if you can decide what the well-known word is:

gh + o + ti

Think creatively and you might just work it out. The answer is on the 'Feedback' pages at the end of this book.

What can you do to improve your spelling at GCSE?

Three Pieces of Spelling Advice

1 Learn from your mistakes

Have a notebook with each page devoted to a separate letter of the alphabet. When you receive a corrected piece of work (in any subject), note the correct version of words in your booklet. In this way, during your course, you will build up a personal spelling dictionary. Look at this list of tricky spellings that one Year 11 class came up with:

beginning	lose/loose
necessary	been/being
separate	its / it's
believes	could have (not could of)
tries (not trys)	all sort (not alsorts)
carries (not carrys)	all right (not alright)
you're / your	as well (not aswell)
there/their/they're	a lot (not alot)

2 Actively learn spellings

You won't learn to spell words correctly without devoting time to it. Look for patterns in words:

be**lie**ve contains a **lie**

or think of memory devices:

station**e**ry has the 'e' for envelope
station**a**ry has the 'a' for automobile (think of a parked car)

or make up rhymes, however silly:

necessary = never eat chips: eat salmon sandwiches and raspberry yoghurt.

3 Learn spelling rules, where they exist

- To form the plural of words ending in 'y', drop the 'y' and add *ies*:
  try ⇨ tries
  cry ⇨ cries
  hobby ⇨ hobbies
  hippy ⇨ hippies

- To form the plural of words ending in 'ey', simply add *s*:
  valley ⇨ valleys
  volley ⇨ volleys
  monkey ⇨ monkeys

- 'i' before 'e' except after 'c':
  believe (i before e)
  thief (i before e)
  receive (after c)
  deceive (after c)
  Beware: there are a few exceptions: *neighbour, weird, science*

- When adding *ing* or *ed* to a word, short vowel sounds gain an extra consonant and long vowel sounds do not:

short vowel sounds	**long vowel sounds**
h*o*p + ing = hopping	h*o*pe + ing = hoping
c*a*n + ing = canning	c*a*ne + ing = caning
sh*a*m + ed = shammed	sh*a*me + ed = shamed

Note how the 'e' on the end of these words (can*e*, hop*e*) makes the vowel sound long.

- Drop the silent 'e' when adding endings that begin with a vowel (such as *ance, able, ed, er, ing, ible, or, ous*):

  love + able = lovable

  hope + ing = hoping

  sense + ible = sensible

- Keep the silent 'e' when adding endings that begin with a consonant (such as *ful, less, ly, ment, ness*):

  love + ly = lovely

  care + ful = careful

  like + ness = likeness

  But remember the exceptions:

  true + ly = truly

  argue + ment = argument

  whole + ly = wholly

- Keep the silent 'e' when adding *able* and *ous* to words that end in *ce* or *ge*:

  notice + able = noticeable

  advantage + ous = advantageous

- Words ending in 'l' keep the 'l' when adding *ly*:

  cool + ly = coolly

  local + ly = locally

  disgraceful + ly = disgracefully

- Words ending in 'c' gain a 'k' when adding *ed, ing*, or *y*:

  panic + y = panicky

  mimic + ed = mimicked

- Words ending in 'n' keep the 'n' when gaining *ness*:

  thin + ness = thinness

  sudden + ness = suddenness

- Words ending in double consonants, keep them when gaining a suffix:

  purr + ing = purring

- All words ending in *ful* (except *full*) have only one 'l':

  beautiful

  thoughtful

  sinful

- Words ending in *ee* or *oo* remain unchanged when adding a suffix:

  see + ing = seeing

  glee + ful = gleeful

  coo + ing = cooing

- Some words change their spelling according to whether they are verbs or nouns:

Verbs (doing words)	**Nouns (objects or things)**
*a*ffect (fear affects Macbeth)	*e*ffect (fear is the main effect)
practi*s*e (you need to practise)	practi*c*e (it takes practice)

Activity Look at this first draft of a Year 10 work experience assignment in which the spelling has been put into 'error overdrive'! Work out which spelling errors could be avoided by knowing the rules listed in this spread. What advice would you give this student about how to improve his spelling?

Work Experience Report (First draft)

When I was chosing my work experience placement I put fenwicks as my last choice because I couldn't fine another office job. I didn't think I would get it but unfortunatly I did. Really I would have preffered an office job to working in a shop. When I was interviewd I was told that I would be working on clothes or toys but I didn't no exactly what I would be doing. I hopped that it would be intresting and generaly it was.

On my first day the manager said I shouldnt be nervous. She told me I just had to practice speaking politly to people and find out what they required. She said I should be carefull to listen and to avoid any arguements. I tryed hard to do this and really hopped that I would be sucessfull. I was pleased when work experiance was over. It wasn't really a very exiting job, but I quiet enjoyed it.

- How many spelling mistakes did you spot?
- Which are the most serious ones?
- Which rules should be the priority for this student to learn?

Follow-up
- For examples of common errors, see 'Spelling Matters I' on page 31.
- For advice on redrafting work, see 'Drafting Skills' on page 122.

Self-assessment

Objectives:

- to learn about the spoken English requirements at GCSE
- to identify your own strengths and weaknesses in speaking and listening

Attitude Matters

Which of these comments best describes your attitude to spoken English activities?

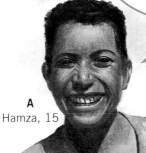

A Hamza, 15

I really enjoy discussion lessons because I feel that I can get involved with whatever topic we are discussing. It's a chance to say what I think.

B Liz, 15

I feel much more confident about my written work. Spoken lessons make me feel uncomfortable – you never know when you might get picked on

C Michael, 14

I'm fine when we're working in small groups, but when I'm asked to speak in front of the class I get stuck for words and feel really stupid.

D Kelly, 15

Everyone else in my class seems so confident – they just say what they think. I'm too embarrassed to say anything in case I show myself up.

You would be surprised at how many people feel nervous about spoken English work. Yet it is a vital part of studying English at 14 to 16.

The National Curriculum for English says:

'Pupils should be given opportunities to talk for a range of purposes, including: explanation, description and narration; exploration and hypothesis; consideration of ideas, literature and the media; argument, debate and persuasion; the development of thinking; analysis'

'Pupils should be given opportunities to talk in a range of contexts, including those that are more formal...'

'Pupils should be encouraged to listen attentively, both in situations where they remain mostly silent and where they have the opportunity to respond immediately...'

'Pupils should be given opportunities to participate in a wide range of drama activities... and be encouraged to develop both their communication skills and their ability to evaluate language use...'

To emphasize the importance of speaking and listening, all examination boards are required to give a certain percentage of marks in GCSE English for spoken activities:

The Structure of GCSE English Language

Continuous Assessment = 40%

Final Examination = 60%

Continuous Assessment breaks down into:
Reading 10%
Writing 10%
Speaking and listening 20%

Activity Use this questionnaire to examine your strengths and weaknesses. Make a note of your answers and then follow them up in the Self-help Panel that comes after it.

Are You Speaking Confidently?

1 When I have to give a formal talk, I...
a usually speak confidently, covering all the points I have prepared.
b hesitate at first but improve as I go along.
c suffer badly from nerves and express myself badly.

2 In class question-and-answer sessions, I...
a like to get involved, saying what I think and justifying my opinions.
b usually wait until asked what I think.
c avoid eye-contact with the teacher and prefer not to get involved if possible.

3 Working in a small group, I...
a enjoy working with others and usually get the discussion going.
b prefer to listen, but will contribute when I have something to say.
c usually don't get involved and sometimes find the others overpowering.

4 When asked to role-play a character from a book, I...
a get into character, using accents and improvisations.
b base my ideas firmly on what I have read and find it hard to improvise.
c hate it! If I have to take a part, I make sure it's the smallest one possible.

5 When a teacher asks an unexpected question, I...
a say something – and it's usually relevant.
b can get slightly muddled, but try to say something.
c freeze up and can't think of what to say.

Self-help Panel

Look at your answers.

If you mostly answered **a**
You are a confident speaker in most situations. But are you also a tactful chairperson? Look at 'Chairing Meetings' on page 45.

If you mostly answered **b**
You enjoy some activities – probably in smaller groups – but find the formal situations more difficult. See 'Writing a Speech' on page 52.

If you answered mostly **c**
You lack confidence in speaking, though you may be an excellent listener. You're probably better at speaking than you think you are. To think more about the patterns of your own speech, see 'Rules of Conversation' on page 42.

Storytelling

Tales to Tell

Before the printing press made books widely available, people relied almost completely upon the spoken word for their entertainment and information. One of the most important oral traditions was storytelling, and people up to the 16th Century would make their living as professional storytellers, wandering between communities telling tales...

Urban myths

In the past few years there has been a spate of 'urban myths' – modern-day spoken legends which are passed between people. The tellers usually claim that 'This happened to a friend of a friend...' but no one seems truly sure where they originated. One other ingredient: they are frequently grisly in their subject matter.

Here is one such urban myth. Use it to look at some of the main techniques of storytelling.

The Baby-sitter

There was this baby-sitter that was in Montreal baby-sitting for three children in a big house. She was watching TV when suddenly the phone rang. The children were all in bed. She picked up the phone and heard this guy on the other end laughing hysterically. She asked him what it was that he wanted, but he wouldn't answer and then hung up. She worried about it for a while, but then thought nothing more of it and went back to watching the movies.

Everything was fine until about fifteen minutes later when the phone rang again. She picked it up and heard the same voice laughing hysterically at her and then hung up. At this point she became really worried and phoned the operator to tell her what had been happening. The operator told her to calm down and that if he called again to try to keep him on the line as long as possible and she would try to trace the call.

Again, about fifteen minutes later, the guy called back and laughed hysterically at her. She asked him why he was doing this, but he just kept laughing at her. He hung up and about five seconds later the operator called. She told the girl to get out of the house at once because the person who was calling was calling from the upstairs extension. She slammed down the phone and just as she was turning to leave she saw the man coming down the stairs laughing hysterically with a bloody butcher's knife in his hand and meaning to kill her. She ran out onto the street but he didn't follow. She called the police and they came and caught the man, and discovered that he had murdered all the children.

Activity

1 How can you tell that this is a spoken rather than written story? Which words and sentences tell you?

2 How successfully does it work as a story – is it frightening?

Here is what one group of Year 10 pupils said about improving the story:

> *The ending is too obvious – you could see what was going to happen.*

> *It doesn't really build up the suspense well enough.*

> *It isn't very believable because we don't really know who the babysitter is or what the house is like.*

3 Are there other points you would add?

Storytelling Checklist

Based on these comments, a checklist of ingredients for successful storytelling might include:

- give detail about people and places – just enough to catch our interest
- add false clues into the story – so that it builds the suspense by tricking us
- cut the story early enough to leave some things to the listener's imagination
- move the location from Montreal closer to home – it becomes more realistic and frightening
- perform it with good intonation, a straight face, and careful pacing – slow at the start, faster at the end
- make it sound as if it is being told, not read
- pause occasionally to build tension

Here is how a Year 10 pupil retold the story based on the checklist. The numbers shown refer to information given in the 'Feedback' pages at the end of the book – informing us how the speaker uses some typical techniques of storytellers.

This friend of my sister's heard about someone who went baby-sitting once. It was her first time – she needed the extra money – and some people in a big house near Acton Tressell asked at short notice if she could help them out. **(1)**
She arrived at the house dead on time and walked up the drive. She was quite surprised how isolated the house was as she went up to the front door. She rang the bell and waited. It took ages for anyone to answer. She had to simply wait out there in the cold and she pulled her coat tight round her as the wind seemed to grow stronger. **(2)**
   This girl started to wish she'd asked her mum to wait for her after she'd dropped her off. Here she was stuck at a house she didn't know in the middle of nowhere. **(3)** Just as she was beginning to get herself all worked up, she heard footsteps and the front door opened. She walked into the house and the couple told her that the children were already safely in bed. It should be easy. All she had to do was sit downstairs, watch TV, and hope that they didn't have nightmares. **(4)**
   Well, the couple were in a hurry and quickly left. The baby-sitter sat on the sofa and watched TV. There wasn't

much on and she ended up sitting through some stupid game show. She was just about to get herself a drink when the phone rang. She sat where she was. Should she be answering a telephone in someone else's house? Of course she should - anyway it could be the people she was baby-sitting for. Perhaps they'd forgotten something or had a message for her. Or perhaps it was one of her friends. **(5)**

She picked up the phone and - (mad laugh here) - someone on the other end simply laughed at the top of his voice. It sounded awful, like a madman. She didn't try to speak, just held the phone away from her ear and then slammed it down. Her heart was racing. Who was that? And why had they chosen this house to call?... **(6)**

Activity

You can tell that this is a spoken story from the beginning of the first sentence: 'This friend of my sister's...'. A written version would be more likely to have a more formal opening. There are other clues that this is a spoken story – in the vocabulary (filler words like 'well' and informal phrasing like 'it took ages') and the structure (look at how the speaker keeps us in suspense). Study more closely the language of this spoken version:

1 What do you like or dislike about this version of the story? Is the pace too fast, too slow, or about right? How do you rate the amount of detail? How does the speaker make the language more informal than in the earlier version of the story?

2 Continue the story, using the kinds of techniques the storyteller has already introduced. Work out a storyline in your mind, and then try telling it to a friend, or recording it on tape. With practice you will become confident at pacing the story, giving the right amount of detail, judging the listener's response. Avoid anything bloodthirsty. The secret is to build suspense rather than create easy horror.

Follow-up

- To examine the way writers build tension in novels, see 'Building Tension' on page 158.
- To look at the differences between spoken and written English see, 'Speech v Writing' on page 66.

Rules of Conversation

Objectives:

- to learn about the rules of conversation
- to reflect upon your own performance in conversation

Language Rules!

All language has rules. Without them, it could not work. For example, look at these two descriptions:

> The table on the floor is
> Happily eating the broken carrot wept Harold

- Can you say what is wrong with these two statements – why exactly they don't make sense? How precise can you be in saying what is wrong with them as sentences in English?

Even our most informal spoken language is governed by certain rules. If we break them or ignore them, we can have problems in communicating successfully.

- If you were describing to a Martian the essential ingredients of conversation, what would these be? Don't be afraid to include really obvious elements. Start like this: to have a successful conversation you need...

Now read through the conversation rules which follow and, working with a partner, read the examples aloud. All are taken from Harold Pinter's play, *The Lover*. Then try the experiments. They should help you to think about the way you normally perform in conversations.

1 Turn-taking

Rule

'One person speaks and then gives the other person a turn. We signal that it is the other person's go by looking at them and, usually, by dropping our voice at the end of a sentence – except when asking questions, when our intonation rises'.

Sarah: How could I forget you?
Richard: Quite easily I think.

Comment: Sarah's question invites Richard to take part. Her intonation rises at the end of her sentence and she would make eye-contact with Richard to indicate that it is now his turn.

Experiment:

Try breaking this rule.

Speaker A talks and doesn't allow Speaker B a chance to get involved.

Speaker B: try your best to get involved in the conversation. What techniques do you use? How successful are they?

2 Relevance

Rule

'Both speakers refer to the same topic, otherwise something seems to have gone wrong'.

Sarah: Aren't you hungry?
Richard: I had a heavy lunch.
Sarah: How heavy?
He stands at the window
Richard: What a beautiful sunset.
Sarah: Weren't you?

Comment

Sarah's last reply doesn't seem relevant to Richard's comment. The rule of relevance has been ignored. It makes us try to find a reason – perhaps she hasn't been listening, or has something on her mind, or is referring back to an earlier topic.

> **Experiment:**
>
> Try holding a conversation in which neither of you refers to the same topic as the other speaker. What problems do you encounter? How does it feel?

3 New topic markers

Rule

'To change to a new topic we usually indicate what we are doing by using phrases like 'by the way, actually, that reminds me...'

Sarah: It's a cold supper. Do you mind?
Richard: Not in the least.
Sarah: I didn't seem to have time to cook anything today.
Richard: Oh, by the way... I rather wanted to ask you something.
Sarah: What?

Comment

Richard signals a new, more important topic by using a new topic marker, 'Oh, by the way.' His use of the word 'Oh' suggests that he may just have remembered the topic – or may be pretending just to have remembered it!

> **Experiment:**
>
> Try holding a conversation which moves from one topic to the next *without* using new topic markers:
>
> A TV programme you saw last night
> School
> Holidays
>
> What is the effect of changing topics *without* signalling it?

4 Positive feedback

Rule

'We usually use familiar phrases ('really, I know'), non-verbal signs ('Uh-huh, Mmm') and body language (nodding, smiles, frowns) to show that we are listening and responding to what the other person is saying'.

Sarah: He's terribly sweet.
Richard: Mmm-hmmm.
Sarah: Has his moods, of course.

Comment

Sarah is giving her opinion. Richard uses a non-verbal sign to show that he's listening and agreeing, but without interrupting the flow of Sarah's thoughts.

Experiment:

Speaker A: talk on a topic for one minute (e.g. holiday plans).

Speaker B: give positive feedback of the three types listed above. How much positive feedback is too much? When does it actually begin to irritate the main speaker?

Activity

1 Look at a two-page extract from a play – for example, Harold Pinter's *The Caretaker*, J B Priestley's *An Inspector Calls*, Samuel Beckett's *Waiting for Godot* – and write an analysis of the different rules of conversation you can spot in use. Also notice any rules which are being broken. Organize your assignment under the four headings used in this spread.

2 Take part in some conversations with friends or relatives who have not read this spread. Break various rules of conversation – for example, avoid using eye-contact to signal their turn to speak. Write an account of your experiment, showing what you did and how they reacted.

Follow-up

- To examine the differences between written and spoken English, see 'Speech v Writing' on page 66.
- To look at some features of formal spoken English, look at 'The Language of Speeches' on page 48.

Chairing Meetings

Objectives:

- to examine a transcript of a meeting and to consider how well it was run by the chairperson
- to think of techniques for chairing meetings effectively

Charity Committee

A group of Year 11 pupils are on a school Charity Committee and it is their brief to produce activities for Children-in-Need day. There are seven people on the committee and Lisa has been nominated as chairperson. At the end of the meeting she says:

Activity   Read through this transcript of part of the meeting and make a list of the points you think Lisa gets right or wrong in her handling of the group.

Transcript

Lisa: Now we really need to get some good ideas for Children-in-Need day...

A: When is it?

Lisa: Eh?

A: What date is it? Do we know yet?

Lisa: Yes, it's on November 4th and we really need to get some good ideas.

B: So that's a Friday, isn't it?

C: How about a non-uniform day? Get pupils to pay not to wear school uniform.

A: Yeah, good idea.

Lisa: Just hang on a sec, we need to just decide on a few things.

D: They had a non-uniform day at my sister's place and they raised about £700.

Lisa: Okay, let's discuss the idea of a non-uniform day.

A: Why not make it fancy dress – you know, people dressing up in weird outfits and stuff?

Lisa: Who thinks fancy dress is a good idea?
lots of voices – unclear

E: You should dress as one of the Beatles, Rob, with that haircut.

B Very funny!

F: The trouble is that non-uniform days are always the same. Can't we think of something more – you know – more unusual?

E: You could get the sixth form to wear uniform that day – charge them to.

F: What about some kind of concert or something? Charge people to come and see a band play.

C: Which band?

E: Rob, you could do a Beatles number couldn't you?

Lisa: Wait a minute – let's just stick to the non-uniform idea. Are there any other comments?

E: That band Desperate Remedies are pretty good, and they're probably cheap.

C: Are they any good though?

Lisa: Wait – we're still discussing non-uniform day.

E: My brother knows one of them – he could ask if you want...

Working on

1 Look again at the transcript and use these prompts to decide how it could have been better run.
 • How did Lisa start the meeting off? How could she have got things off to a better start? Where does she need to be stronger? How should she have dealt with interruptions?
 • What roles do the other speakers play? Who is most helpful? Who is least? What should Lisa have said to each of them?
 • How could organization – of the room, of paperwork, of seating – perhaps have helped to make the meeting run better?

2 What would your three main points of advice to Lisa be about running a future meeting?

Activity Look at this list of hints for running effective meetings. Then either produce a role play with friends in which you show how the Charity Committee meeting could be better run, or write down a scripted version of events showing how things ran differently.

Chairing Meetings: Some Advice

1 Planning

If you simply get a group of people together to discuss an item without any further preparation, you cannot expect it to be a success. Start by deciding:
- what are you aiming to achieve at the meeting?
- what decisions need to be made?
- what is the best time and where is the best place to hold the meeting?
- what do people need to know in advance?

2 Have a clear plan

Formal meetings have an agenda – a list of topics which will be raised. The best agendas show whether the items are for information or discussion, and show how much time has been allocated to them. This may be too formal for some of the meetings you chair – but it does give a sense of purpose to the discussion and allows you, as chairperson, to remind people of the need to stick to the agenda.

3 Arrange the room

Least formal is a circle of chairs; then sitting around a table; most formal is a traditional classroom layout. Place yourself somewhere where you can be seen by everyone.

4 Adopt the right style
- be business-like
- keep an eye on the time and hurry people along if necessary
- work out where you stand on each subject in advance, so that you can give your opinion without having to think for too long
- don't let any one person dominate – invite people who haven't yet said anything to express their opinion
- if someone talks for too long, be prepared to interrupt them politely
- keep summarizing progress – show what has been decided so far
- stay calm

Follow-up
- To examine transcripts of speech in more detail, see 'Speech v Writing' on page 66.
- To look at how to prepare and deliver a speech, see 'Writing a Speech' on page 52.

The Language of Speeches

Objectives:

- to spot some of the techniques used by successful speech-makers
- to recognize the way audience and purpose affect the way speeches are made

Almost Speechless?

Some people say that the art of making speeches is dying out. Who needs to address a large crowd in person when you can use television? Then why develop a complex argument when viewers can instantly change channel? In an age of electronic communication, what place is there for old-fashioned speech-making?

Yet speeches remain an important part of the way countries are governed, people are informed, and ideas are debated. If you want to get your message across to friends or enemies, you tell them what you think. Speech has a power and an immediacy which writing can lack.

Look at this example of a political speech. It was made by the former leader of the Labour Party, Neil Kinnock, who used his own experience of family and education to criticize the then Prime Minister's values. Read the speech (aloud, if possible), and then use the prompts which follow to look at the techniques he uses.

The First Kinnock...

Why am I the first Kinnock in a thousand generations to be able to get to university? Why is Glenys the first woman in her family in a thousand generations to be able to get to university?

Was it because all our predecessors were 'thick'? Did they lack talent – those people who could sing, and play, and recite and write poetry; those people who could make wonderful, beautiful things with their hands; those people who could dream dreams, see visions; those people who had such a sense of perception as to know in times so brutal, so oppressive, that they could win their way out of that by coming together?

Were those people not university material? Couldn't they have knocked off all their A-levels in an afternoon?

But why didn't they get it?

Was it because they were weak? – those people who could work eight hours underground and then come up and play football?

Weak? Those women who could survive eleven childbearings, were they weak? Those people who could stand with their backs and their legs straight and face the people who had control over their lives, the ones who owned their workplaces and tried to own them, and tell them, 'No. I won't take your orders.' Were they weak?

Does anybody really think that they didn't get what we had because they didn't have the talent, or the strength, or the endurance, or the commitment?

Of course not. It was because there was no platform upon which they could stand; no arrangement for their neighbours to subscribe to their welfare; no method by which the communities could translate their desires for those individuals into provision for those individuals.

And now, Mrs Thatcher, by dint of privatization, and means test, and deprivation, and division, wants to nudge us back into the situation where everybody can either stand on their own feet, or live on their knees.

That's what this election is about as she parades her vision and values, and we choose to contest them as people with roots in this country, with a future only in this country, with pride in this country. People who know that if we are to have and sustain real individual liberty in this country it requires the collective effort of the whole community.

Of course you hear the Tories talking about freedom. We'll be hearing a great deal of that over the next month from the same people who have spent the last eight years crushing individual freedoms under the weight of unemployment and poverty, squeezing individual rights with cuts and means tests and charges.

I think of the youngsters I meet. Three, four, five years out of school. Never had a job. And they say to me, 'Do you think we'll ever work?

They live in a free country, but they do not feel free.

I think of the fifty-five-year-old woman I met who is waiting to go into hospital, her whole existence clouded by pain.

She lives in a free country, but she does not feel free.

I think of the young couple, two years married, living in Mam and Dad's front room because they can't get a home. They ask, 'Will we *ever* get a home of our own?'

They live in a free country, but they do not feel free.

And I think of the old couple who spend months of the winter afraid to turn up the heating, who stay at home because they are afraid to go out after dark, whose lives are turned into a crisis by the need to buy a new pair of shoes.

They live in a free country – indeed, they're of the generation that fought for a free country – but they do not feel free.

How can they – and millions like them – have their individual freedom if there is no collective provision?

How can they have strength if they do not have care?

Now they cannot have either because they are locked out of being able to discharge responsibilities just as surely as they are locked out of being able to exercise rights.

They want to be able to use both.

They do not want feather-bedding, they want a foothold.

They do not want cotton-woolling, they want a chance to contribute.

That is the freedom they want.

That is the freedom we want them to have.

Neil Kinnock

Activity

1 What do you like or dislike about Neil Kinnock's speech? Which part of it is most or least effective? How would you summarize its overall message?

2 Pick out 5 examples of repetition, either of words or sentences, which you find especially powerful.

3 How does Neil Kinnock use references to his own background to make points about the present and future?

4 Use the points below to make comments about his purpose, audience and tone:

Purpose

What is he trying to achieve through this speech? How can you tell?

Audience

Is his audience sympathetic, hostile, or neutral? How can you tell?

Tone

Is his tone aggressive, neutral, angry, mocking, personal, emotional, gentle, warm, public...? How can you tell?

5 If you were giving advice to Neil Kinnock about how he could improve his speech, what specific suggestions would you make?

Speaking out

Now compare Neil Kinnock's modern speech with one written more than a century ago. Sojourner Truth was sold at the age of nine to a slave auction. She later escaped slavery to become a campaigner against discrimination, fighting in particular for the equal rights of women. Read the speech aloud and compare it with Neil Kinnock's, using the prompts below to focus your ideas.

Ain't I a Woman?

That man over there say
a woman needs to be helped into carriages
and lifted over ditches
and to have the best place everywhere.
Nobody ever helped me into carriages
or over mud puddles
or gives me a best place...
Ain't I a woman?
Look at me
Look at my arm!
I have ploughed and planted
and gathered into barns
and no man could head me...
And ain't I a woman?
I could work as much
and eats as much as a man –
when I could get to it –
and bear the lash as well
and ain't I a woman?
I have born thirteen children
and seen most all sold into slavery
and when I cried out a mother's grief
none but Jesus heard me...

and ain't I a woman?
That little man in black there say
a woman can't have as much rights as a man
cause Christ wasn't a woman.
Where did your Christ come from?
From God and a woman!
Man had nothing to do with him!
If the first woman God ever made
was strong enough to turn the world
upside down, all alone
together women ought to be able to turn it
rightside up again.

Sojourner Truth

Working on Compare the speeches. Find evidence from the text to support your ideas.
Which speech...

- uses more repetition?
- uses more abstract nouns (words like *truth*, *justice*, *freedom*) – ideas rather than things?
- is more personal?
- is more aggressive?
- uses simpler language?
- is more emotional?
- do you prefer, and why?

Follow-up
- To look at ways of writing your own speech, see 'Writing a Speech' on page 52.
- To investigate more well-known speeches, see Brain MacArthur (ed.), *The Penguin Book of Twentieth Century Speeches* (Penguin) and David Cannadine (ed.), *The Speeches of Winston Churchill* (Faber).

Writing a Speech

Step-by-step

During your GCSE course you will probably be asked to participate in a class debate, or to make a speech on a topical or controversial issue. The idea of this might fill you with terror. But there are techniques that will make it easier. Try this step-by-step plan for speech-writing.

1 Choose your subject carefully

If you have a choice of the subject, select an issue which interests you – you are more likely to make a good job of it if you feel involved. A class of Year 10 students recently made speeches on the following issues:

- smoking
- racism
- sexism
- drug abuse
- leisure facilities for teenagers
- politics
- abortion
- hunting
- vivisection (tests on animals)
- whaling
- healthy eating

2 Marshal your facts

Spend some time doing your research, gathering as much information about the subject as possible. Your sources of information might include:

- reference books (library/home)
- leaflets (hospitals, supermarkets, shops, Citizens' Advice Bureau, charities, pressure groups)
- newspapers (national and local)
- magazines (special interest)

At this stage, do not try to write your speech; simply get as many facts down on paper as you can. Here are the notes on 'Smoking' which one Year 10 student, Daniel, made:

- *people need air to live*
- *smoking can harm people around the smoker – passive smoking*
- *cigarettes have 4 ingredients: nicotine, tar, carbon monoxide, ammonia*
  - *nicotine = poison – affects the heart, blood vessels, etc. – highly addictive*
  - *tar = sticky brown fluid – causes lung cancer*
  - *carbon monoxide = deadly gas found in car fumes*
  - *ammonia = strong substance used in toilet cleaners*

3 Think about audience, purpose, and tone

Before planning the details of a speech you need to be clear upon the following:

Audience: who are you addressing?
- how many?
- what age group?
- what do they already know about the subject you will be talking about?
- do they have opinions which are generally sympathetic or opposed to yours?

Purpose: what are you trying to achieve?
You should be able to finish this sentence: 'This speech is intended to persuade people that...'
For example:
...that smoking is harmful and should be banned in all public places
...that testing cosmetics on animals is wrong
...that all bloodsports – fox-hunting, hare-coursing, badger-baiting, even fishing – are cruel

Tone: should you be serious, humorous, low-key, aggressive, calming... a combination of these?
Of course, it will depend partly upon your audience and partly upon your purpose.

4 Plan the outline of the speech

With the above three points in mind, make a list of the main details you wish to cover and place them in a clear order. Your main ideas will be drawn from your research notes. When you have prepared this outline, you may find that certain points need further research before you can write your first draft.

5 Use the techniques of professional speech-making

If your speech is to be effective, it needs to be different from an essay in several ways. It needs to persuade, irritate, amuse, entertain as well as inform your audience (see 'The Language of Speeches' on page 48).
Here are some techniques to try out:
- use emotional words (e.g. trust, faith, pain, suffering, danger)
- repeat key words frequently
- repeat important phrases ('People say fishing doesn't hurt fish. People say fish have no nerves in their mouths. People say a lot of things they cannot prove...')
- use rhetorical questions – questions designed to make the audience think about a question which *you* then answer ('Is it fair to use animals like this? Of course it's not...')
- address your audience directly ('When was the last time you thought about the products you buy and how they were tested?')
- aim to get a balance of facts and opinion
- use your final paragraph to summarize your argument, using emotional language and repetition

To Smoke or Not to Smoke

Year 10 student, Daniel, chose to write a speech on the dangers of smoking. It was aimed at a teenage audience.

Smoking Speech

You probably know that fresh clean air is hard to come by because of all the cars and power stations pumping fumes and smoke into the air. You need fresh clean air to stay alive, so why make it harder for yourself by smoking?

Smoking doesn't just harm you. It harms the people around you and it also pollutes the air around us. We owe it to ourselves and our environment to kick this filthy habit.

What do you actually know about cigarettes? Perhaps if everyone knew the facts no one would ever smoke. There are four different ingredients to a cigarette:

NICOTINE
Nicotine is one of the worst poisons. It is a main killer to man, it affects the heart, the blood vessels, and the nervous system. Nicotine is also a very addictive drug which can kill you.

TAR
Tar is a sticky brown substance which collects in your lungs. It is a very slow killer and it is a cause of lung cancer.

CARBON MONOXIDE
Carbon monoxide is a deadly gas which is in the smoke of a cigarette.

If you keep smoking, you will get more carbon monoxide in your blood, and that makes less room in your blood for oxygen. This gas is also found in car fumes, which also pollute the air.

When smokers run, they become short of breath quicker than a non-smoker does, this is because there is not as much oxygen in the blood as a non-smoker.

AMMONIA
Ammonia is a strong, smelly substance which is used in small amounts. It is also found in oven and toilet cleaners. But it isn't just the smokers themselves who suffer; the people around you do as well, but it is now known that the people around you suffer even more.

Smoking harms people, but it also damages societies. For example, many countries grow tobacco, and most of these countries have starving people. Why don't they stop growing tobacco and start growing food crops for all the hungry people?

So as I round up my speech, I just say to all the people who smoke and make other people suffer as well, you need good clean air to stay alive and there isn't much of it around. There will be even less if smokers don't wake up to the damage they're doing.

Activity

1 Read through his first draft and decide what advice you would give Daniel on redrafting it...
Make your hints as precise as possible, using these headings:
- Sense of Audience, Purpose, Tone
- Content and Structure
- Rhetorical Techniques

2 Think about how Daniel should deliver his speech to the audience. What advice would you give him in response if he asked you these questions?:

How should I use notes – written out in full on paper, written onto different cards for different sections, just key words, or should I try to memorize the whole lot?

Sometimes in assemblies I notice speakers moving around as they talk, instead of just standing on the spot. I fancy trying this – it might give more life to my speech. But will it distract the audience?

Should I use any props? I've got some fairly unpleasant photos of damaged lungs and things. Would this add to my speech or just distract the audience again? If I use props, should I hand them round as I'm talking?

3 Following the step-by-step plan, prepare, draft, and redraft your own speech. Choose a subject from the list at the start of this section or any other topic which particularly interests you. Try to make your speech about 3-4 minutes in length.

Follow-up
- To think about the differences between spoken and written English, see 'Speech v Writing' on page 66.
- To look at ways of writing about controversial issues, see 'Discursive Assignments' on page 118.
- To examine techniques used by other speech makers, see 'The Language of Speeches' on page 48.

Formal v Informal Speech

Varying Speech

We don't speak in any fixed way. Our speech will vary according to:
- the *audience* we are speaking to
- what the *topic* is
- what our *purpose* is

Usually we won't need to stop and think about how we need to speak: we'll simply adjust our speech according to the audience, topic, and purpose, moving our language along a scale of *formal* to *informal* expression.

Put this to the test: what goes wrong in the following speech situations?

Activity   1   You are on interview for a part-time post at a local hotel. The Manager asks you why you are interested in the job...

James Bury
HOTEL MANAGER

Hmmmm, I dunno really. I s'pose I've always fancied working at a fairly posh place like this since I was a kid. I thought you'd probably pay more than the B&Bs round the corner, you know, and I knew the tips would be okay. I'd already tried to get a job at the Merry Shopkeeper but they didn't have no vacancies, so I thought I'd give it a whirl in this place, so here I am.

Of course, *what* you have said has probably destroyed your chances of getting the job, but there's also a problem with the *style* of your language. Using the headings below, pick out examples of casual English and think of how you would express them more formally:

	Informal Usage	Formal Replacement
Vocabulary	*e.g. fancied*	
Abbreviations	*e.g. dunno*	
Grammar	*e.g. didn't have no*	

2 There is a scale of formal to informal words which we use or avoid according to the context in which we are speaking.

Draw out the formal to informal scale. Then for each of the words below, plot where you think they should be placed on the scale:

> toilets
> bathroom
> john
> washhouse
> loo
> WC
> water closet
> little boy's room
> bog
> latrine
> khazi
> powder room
> spend a penny

Which of these audiences would you use these words with? Which would you never use?

- parents
- parents' friends
- teacher
- close friend

3 Take another topic – such as death or words meaning 'good' – and plot a similar scale of formal to informal usage. Words for death can range from very formal words, like 'deceased', to slang expressions like 'kicked the bucket'. Words meaning 'good' often vary according to people's ages. A few years ago teenagers in Leeds would describe something they thought of as good as 'fash' or 'mega'. Their parents might say 'brilliant' or 'great'. Grandparents might say 'grand' or 'super'. What different words can you think of? Again, organize them on a formal to informal scale.

4 Now think of a situation where very formal language would be inappropriate – for example, trying to buy an ice-cream or asking a friend if they're busy tonight. Write a brief script, like the interview example above, and then write a commentary explaining what is wrong with the speaker's formal style.

Follow-up
- To look at the appropriate usage of English in letter writing, see 'Conventions of Letters' on page 108.
- To compare spoken and written English, see 'Speech v Writing' on page 66.

Dialects

Objectives:

- to investigate what a dialect is
- to explore some of the dialect features of your own region

The English Language

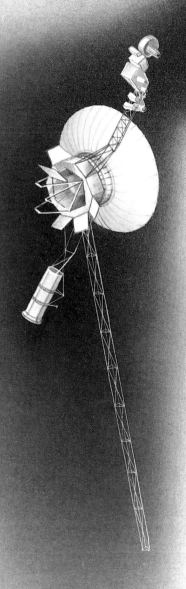

The Story of English

On 5 September 1977, the American spacecraft Voyager One blasted-off on its historic mission to Jupiter and beyond. On board, the scientists, who knew that Voyager would one day spin through distant star systems, had installed a recorded greeting from the people of the planet Earth. Preceding a brief message in fifty-five different languages for the people of outer space, the gold-plated disc plays a statement, from the Secretary-General of the United Nations, an Austrian named Kurt Waldheim, speaking on behalf of 147 member states – in English. The rise of English is a remarkable success story. When Julius Caesar landed in Britain nearly two thousand years ago, English did not exist. Five hundred years later, *Englisc*, incomprehensible to modern ears, was probably spoken by about as few people as currently speak Cherokee – and with about as little influence. Nearly a thousand years later, at the end of the sixteenth century, when William Shakespeare was in his prime, English was the native speech of between five and seven million Englishmen and it was, in the words of a contemporary, 'of small reatch, it stretcheth no further than this island of ours, naie not their over all'.

Four hundred years later, the contrast is extraordinary. Between 1600 and the present, in armies, navies, companies and expeditions, the speakers of English – including Scots, Irish, Welsh, American and many more – travelled into every corner of the globe, carrying their language and culture with them. Today, English is used by at least 750 million people, and barely half of those speak it as a mother tongue. Some estimates have put that figure closer to one billion. Whatever the total, English at the end of the twentieth century is more widely scattered, more widely spoken and written than any other language has ever been. It has become the language of the planet, the first truly global language.

Robert McCrum, William Cran, Robert MacNeil.

Varieties of English

Based on how much the English language is used around the world, it would be easy to imagine that there is a single standard form called 'English'. But in fact there are lots of different varieties or dialects of English.

An old Hindu proverb suggests that 'language changes every 18 or 20 miles'. In an age of television this is probably less true than it was, but different regions still hold onto their own forms. For example, in the Lake District all of these words mean the same thing. Can you guess what it is from the sound or shape of the words, or simply by a wild guess?

> *deg frap heft joggle nope scaitch whang*

To find out if you were right, see the 'Feedback' pages at the end of the book. Until the early 19th Century use of local words like these would have been much more widespread. If you travelled from Norfolk to the Lake District, language around you would be changing all the time – not only people's accents, but their words and grammar (dialect).

Take a word like *scarecrow*. Different regions have their own words:

> *bogle flay-crow mawpin mawkin bird-scarer moggy*
> *shay guy bogeyman shuft rook-scarer...*

And different regions might also have their own grammatical forms. All of these are possible in different areas of Britain:

> He's a man who likes his beer.
> He's a man that likes his beer.
> He's a man at likes his beer.
> He's a man as likes his beer.
> He's a man what likes his beer.
> He's a man he likes his beer.
> He's a man likes his beer.

The Standard English version is the one given first of all.

Activity

1 What are the advantages and disadvantages of having so many different varieties of English? Look at this list and see which you most and least agree with:

   a a variety of words and grammars makes the language more interesting
   b it allows different regions to keep their own identities
   c all of those sentences communicate clearly – there is no need for a standard way of saying them
   d it might lead to confusion if there were never a standard form of English
   e printing would be difficult because who would decide which version to use?

2 Why did regional varieties of English come under pressure in the early 19th Century? Think about the effect that these events might have on language:

   • people moved from rural to industrial areas in search of work
   • roads, canals, and railways were built, enabling easier travel
   • levels of literacy (reading and writing) were improved due to greater provision of education

3 Think about the dialect words you use in informal situations. Dialect words are frequently used to describe:
- food and drink (bread rolls, mid-morning snack)
- the weather
- the personal characteristics of people

Generally, regional dialects are used in informal spoken situations and in casual letters to people we know. More formal communication is usually in Standard English. Compile a list of words which occur in your dialect.

Standard English	Regional dialect	Your dialect
bad-tempered	narky, crusty	
to pester	mither	
an idiot	wazzock, thickhead	
child	nipper	
good	bazzin', cracking	
bad	hanging	

4 Compile a dictionary of dialect words used in your area to describe different subjects. Give Standard English definitions of the words. You might also refer to dialect words used by certain age-groups – like this list produced by a Year 11 pupil from York:

Ding   n. very poor

Fed   n. policeman

Gadgee   n. an average man

Geezer   n. a distinguished, well-respected member of the community

Ginga   n. a person with ginger hair

Gitty/ goaty   n. small area of facial hair worn below the mouth which as an option can be worn below the chin and shaped into a point

Gype   adj. very poor

Follow-up
- For more about the dominant dialect of English, see 'Standard English' on page 18.
- To look at social attitudes to accent, see 'Attitudes to Accents' on page 61.

Attitudes to Accents

Voice Box

It is impossible for an Englishman to open his mouth without making some other Englishman despise him.

G.B. Shaw

Accent is the pronunciation of language, the way we speak it.

What do you already know about accents? Test your current knowledge:

> **True or false...?**
>
> **1** Some people speak without an accent.
> **2** Accents reveal a person's intelligence.
> **3** Some accents sound better than others.
> **4** BBC accents are the top accents.
> **5** Someone speaking with a strong accent is less likely to get a job than a person with a neutral accent.

Once you have thought about your answers, refer to the answer panel on page 62. Then consider some of the attitudes to accent sometimes seen in our society.

Regional accents

1 Look at the list of accents below. Of the ones you know which do you **most** like and which do you **least** like? Try to say why.

Scots (Glasgow)	Scots (Edinburgh)
Cockney	Southern
Yorkshire	Somerset
Birmingham	Welsh
*RP (– 'posh' or 'proper' English)	Irish (Southern)
Liverpool	Irish (Northern)
Geordie	

(*RP means Received Pronunciation. It is the most formal accent in English, frequently used by newsreaders, some politicians, and lawyers. Turn to page 64 to find out more about it.)

2 Which accents would you most expect the following people to use:

a lawyer	a Conservative politician
a newsreader	a newspaper journalist (*The Times*)
a stand-up comedian	a newspaper photographer (*The Sun*)
a Labour politician	

Accents and Prejudice

If you were able to label *any* of those jobs with accents, you should ask yourself why. Why should a lawyer be expected to speak differently from, say, a newspaper photographer? Why shouldn't we expect BBC newsreaders to read the news in a Liverpool accent? Accents, in other words, are often used to label or stereotype people.

Look at this survey of attitudes to accent:

Key

Birmingham

N. Wales

Lancashire

Received Pronunciation

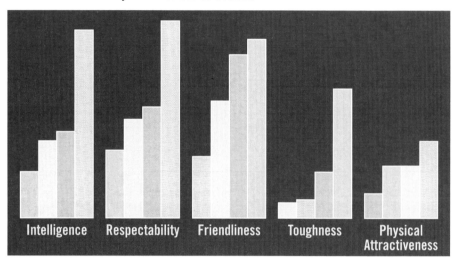

Intelligence   Respectability   Friendliness   Toughness   Physical Attractiveness

Twenty university students were asked to rate 4 speakers according to their intelligence, respectability, toughness, and physical attractiveness. They were played a tape recording of each speaker reading the same text: the speakers' accents were Birmingham, N. Wales, Lancashire, and Received Pronunciation.

Activity Discuss these talking points:
- What do the results show about the way different accents are perceived?
- What do you notice about the difference in attitude towards rural and urban accents?
- Would the results have been the same if *you* had been answering the questions?

Answer panel

1 False – everyone speaks with some kind of accent.
2 False – accents relate to where you were brought up and how you were educated. They do not reveal anything of your intelligence.
3 False – It depends what you mean by 'better'. Some people might *like* some accents more than others, but that simply means one accent is different from another or more attractive, not better than it.
4 False – again, 'top' is too vague to mean anything. BBC accents are influential in education and the media, but they are not in any way better than other accents.
5 *Possibly* true – but it all depends on what the job is and what the attitude of the employer is. If your strong accent allows you to do the job effectively, there is no reason why you should stand less chance than someone with a more standard way of speaking.

Working on

It should be clear from this spread that accents are a sensitive issue, used by people to make judgements about the speaker. Read through these different opinions and decide which one you most agree with:

Of course accents matter. They show people something about who we are. We can't escape them. If we don't like the way we speak, we should change it.

Accents shouldn't matter at all. We should be pleased that people speak in a variety of ways. In fact we should encourage it by getting more regional accents in the media, by encouraging politicians to use their own accents instead of RP, and by being more open-minded towards the way people speak.

Accents shouldn't matter and usually they don't. So long as you can be clearly understood, then you should be proud of your accent. However, not everyone is so tolerant. If you feel your strong regional accent might count against you, you should be prepared to standardize it, to increase your chances.

Activity

1 Produce a language autobiography which traces the history of your own accent. Look at the influence of where your parents and grandparents were brought up, whether the family has moved, and any new influences this has had on your pronunciation. Are there certain words which you pronounce in a different way from your friends? Are there any influences in your accent which you can trace to other sources – TV, music, friends – rather than your family? Write, in as much detail as you can, about your own accent.

2 Do a study of the way accents are used in television commercials. Compare the voices used for certain products – such as bread, soap powders, chocolate, and beer. Which commercials use regional accents and which use RP? Why do you think this is? Write up your results in the form of a survey.

Follow-up

- To look at the concept of regional dialects, see 'Dialects' on page 58.
- To look at the way spoken English is assessed in class, see 'Assessing Speech' on page 68.
- To learn more about RP, see 'Received Pronunciation' on page 64, and refer to the Glossary.

Received Pronunciation

What is RP?

Most accents tell us something about a speaker's geographical background – the area of the country where they have lived. RP (Received Pronunciation) doesn't belong to any region. You can hear people use it in Scotland or in Cornwall. It is an accent which we associate with people of the highest social class – that's why it is sometimes called 'posh' or 'proper' English or 'BBC English'.

RP is an accent used by around 3% of English speakers. If so few people use it, why is it so influential?

A Brief History...

In 1870 the Education Act led to a boom in preparatory schools, with the children of the middle classes (lawyers, doctors, clergymen, army officers) attending schools which were frequently situated in isolated market towns, like Uppingham, Oakham, Sherborne, and Worksop.

Before the 1870s regional accents were taken for granted. Some of Britain's most respected politicians spoke with strong accents: Sir Robert Peel (Midlands); Lord Stanley (Lancashire); Lord Gladstone (Liverpool). By the 1890s all this was changing and boys in school would be laughed at if they held on to their regional accent. Non-standard accents were seen as a sign of being uneducated. Pressure was on to learn RP.

RP was associated with the higher army ranks, civil servants, scholars – in other words, people with authority and power. This bred imitation, as people tried to achieve similar levels of social success.

The early days of the BBC were presided over by Lord Reith, who believed that there was a 'right way' to speak English, so BBC newsreaders, wearing dinner jackets on the radio, spoke in RP accents .. and generally still do.

Activity   1 Look at the international phonetic alphabet, which lists vowel and consonant sounds which are difficult to write down using the normal alphabet (like the 'uh' sound in *the*).

/iː/	as in s<u>ea</u>, fee, me field	/ɜː/	as in b<u>i</u>rd, her, turn
/ɪ/	as in h<u>i</u>m, village, women	/ə/	as in butt<u>er</u>, sof<u>a</u>, <u>a</u>bout
/e/	as in g<u>e</u>t, head, Thames	/eɪ/	as in <u>a</u>pe, waist, they
/æ/	as in s<u>a</u>t, hand, plait	/aɪ/	as in t<u>i</u>me, cry, die, high
/ʌ/	as in s<u>u</u>n, son, blood, does	/ɔɪ/	as in b<u>oy</u>, noise, voice
/ɑː/	as in f<u>a</u>ther, car, calm	/əʊ/	as in s<u>o</u>, road, toe, know
/ɒ/	as in d<u>o</u>g, swan, cough	/aʊ/	as in <u>ou</u>t, how, house
/ɔː/	as in c<u>or</u>d, saw, all, more	/ɪə/	as in d<u>eer</u>, here, fierce
/ʊ/	as in p<u>u</u>t, wolf, good	/ɛə/	as in c<u>are</u>, air, bear
/uː/	as in s<u>oo</u>n, do, soup, shoe	/ʊə/	as in p<u>oor</u>, sure, four

/p/	as in <u>p</u>ie	/s/	as in <u>s</u>o
/b/	as in <u>b</u>y	/z/	as in <u>z</u>oo
/t/	as in <u>t</u>ie	/ʃ/	as in <u>sh</u>oe
/d/	as in <u>d</u>ie	/ʒ/	as in bei<u>g</u>e
/k/	as in <u>c</u>oo	/h/	as in <u>h</u>i
/g/	as in <u>g</u>o	/m/	as in <u>m</u>y
/tʃ/	as in <u>ch</u>ew	/n/	as in <u>n</u>o
/dʒ/	as in <u>j</u>aw	/ŋ/	as in si<u>ng</u>
/f/	as in <u>f</u>ee	/l/	as in <u>l</u>ie
/v/	as in <u>v</u>iew	/r/	as in <u>r</u>ow
/θ/	as in <u>th</u>in	/w/	as in <u>w</u>ay
/ð/	as in <u>th</u>e	/j/	as in <u>y</u>ou

Compare RP pronunciation with a northern accent. Look at how the symbols allow us to show more precisely the difference in pronunciation between two accents:

Word	RP pronunciation	Northern
bath	/bɑːθ/	/bæθ/
cup	/kʌp/	/kʊp/

Notice how we use the punctuation mark / to mark the beginning and end of a phonetic transcription.

2 Read the History of RP section on page 64 in an RP accent, using the phonetic alphabet to guide you. Then write a paragraph comparing the RP accent with the one you normally use. Which words in particular would an RP speaker pronounce differently to you?

Follow-up
• For discussion of regional accents, see 'Attitudes to Accents' on page 61.
• To look at the rise of Standard English, see 'Standard English' on page 18.

Speech v Writing

Objectives:

- to explore the differences between spoken and written English
- to consider when each mode of communication might be more appropriate

Telling Tales

Here are two pieces of text. They are both personal accounts of events that have happened to the authors. But one is a transcript (exact copy) of a spoken story and the other is a written story. Spot which is the *spoken* account and which is the *written*. Then make a list of the clues that helped you to decide. You will find the answer in the 'Feedback' section at the end of the book.

A: Hamza

One night I was sitting in the living room eating popcorn. It was then I thought I heard footsteps in the garden at the front. I slowly turned the volume down on the TV, stepped over to the window, lifted the curtain very slowly and... there wasn't anything there.

It was nearly 12pm when I decided to go to bed. I couldn't sleep well, so I was listening to some music on my personal stereo. I was just about to fall asleep when I heard some tools rattling. I thought to myself, 'Tools? At this time of night?'. I quickly got out of bed and looked out of the landing window. I saw a transit van parked on the drive. It was backed up onto the drive. I also noticed that one of the rear van doors was open. I knew they were burglars when I saw the van.

I was looking out the window when I saw a movement in the house next door. She looked out of the window and was looking at the van. She saw me and was trying to say something to me. I couldn't really understand her. Moments later there was a smash downstairs in the kitchen. There were some things falling on the floor. Suddenly there were some cars braking very hard outside the house. It was the police. The men downstairs must have panicked and tried to do a runner. Luckily the police came just in time. I didn't call the police. It must have been my neighbours...

B: Lindsay

Right when I was little we always used to go and stay with my grandma and my sister and they used to have this cat right and it was white except it was always dirty and it was really fat and every time we went me and my sister used to ask how old it was and er my grandma always used to say twelve right and this went on for about six years. She used to just keep on saying twelve and then one year we asked how old it was and she said eighteen and so anyway right and so the next year it died and so my grandma said it did well to live till ten and she was just really dizzy all the time and that's it.

Activity

1 You can probably tell quite easily which is the spoken and which is the written account. But *how* can you tell? Use these prompts to find clues in each text:
   - the way the ideas are structured
   - the way ideas are linked – words like *and, so, but,* and *then*
   - use of verb tense (past and present)
   - beginnings and endings
   - use of dialect words and dialect forms
   - use of punctuation to clarify and order ideas
   - amount of detail

2 Rewrite Lindsay's account using standard written English – by changing words, inserting punctuation, removing repetitions, and editing out words that are associated with spoken rather than written English. Then write a paragraph explaining in detail the changes you have made.

Follow-up
- To clarify the difference between Standard English and dialect forms, see 'Standard English' on page 18.
- For more on autobiography, see 'Non-fiction: Autobiography' on page 70.
- For more on punctuation, see 'Basic Punctuation' on page 22.

Assessing Speech

Spoken English

People are sometimes surprised that spoken English can be assessed at all. It's fairly easy to mark someone's written work, they might say, and you can set a comprehension test to find out about their reading... but how can you assess their spoken English?

Activity   What problems are involved in assessing spoken English? Look at this list and place them in order of biggest to smallest problem:
- it is based on gut reaction – not scientific enough
- people are nervous when being assessed and unlikely to perform at their best level
- it is hard to assess someone's work in a group, because it would be artificial to sit and watch them without joining in
- what might be good spoken English to one person may seem boring to another
- speakers with strong accents might be at a disadvantage
- shy people suffer

Some of these are real problems in assessing spoken English; others simply do not matter. Perhaps surprisingly, when a group of teachers sit and assess students speaking, their assessments are very similar. Probably if you were asked to assess a teacher giving an assembly, your group's assessments would be similar.

What do you look for in a good public speaker? What do you look for in someone who can communicate well in a smaller group?

Look at this list of criteria and decide how important it is for a formal, e.g. speaking in front of class, and informal situation, e.g. participating in small-group discussion.

A good public speaker...
- makes eye-contact with audience
- keeps still when talking
- listens well
- speaks loudly enough
- varies the pace
- seems interested in the subject
- uses vocabulary which is interesting but understandable
- does not twitch or fidget when speaking

Are there any other features you look for in a good speaker?

GCSE Criteria

Below is a summary of the kind of criteria used by your English teacher to assess students. It is similar to the lists issued by all of the examination boards. To see how it works, you might use it in class to assess each other's English, during formal and informal spoken activities. That will help you to feel at ease with the idea of being assessed, and show you how the criteria change at different grade boundaries.

Grade G

The student...

- can listen with concentration
- can vary tone, pace, and intonation when speaking to a known audience
- is more confident with concrete rather than abstract subject-matter

Grade F

The student...

- can give structured accounts of familiar subjects
- responds to questions and opinions in a range of situations
- joins in a range of group tasks
- uses some features of Standard English grammar and vocabulary

Grade E

The student...

- can give an organized, longer account of events or experiences
- can convey effectively information or points of view
- listens to others and can respond in some detail to what they have said
- can vary what they say according to situation and audience

Grade D

The student...

- reacts to others in a variety of ways
- understands and discusses quite complex information
- presents information systematically
- participates constructively in discussions and debates
- uses intonation and pace effectively to hold listeners' attention

Grade C

The student...

- can convey information effectively and clearly, even when it is unfamiliar subject-matter
- is able to spot and respond appropriately to assumptions and bias in the speech of others
- makes active decisions about style and delivery
- matches language to purpose, topic, and audience
- shows confident use of Standard English when appropriate

Grade B

The student...

- makes use of more subtle vocabulary and grammatical structures
- participates supportively in group activities
- uses a variety of sources in evaluating information, ideas, or feelings

Grade A

The student...

- argues persuasively
- empathizes with real or imagined experience
- uses tone and gesture to show irony
- shows assured use of Standard English
- sensitively uses speech in a variety of situations, matching it to audience, topic, and situation

Grade A*

The student...

- listens attentively and responds persuasively in both familiar and unfamiliar situations
- establishes and maintains an appropriate atmosphere
- uses mature vocabulary, phraseology, tone, intonation, and pace
- has a sensitive impact on the listeners
- is consistently effective and interesting in communicating to a wide range of audiences – some of them known, some of them unknown

Follow-up
- Look at 'Assessing Writing' on page 127.
- For more information on speeches, see 'Writing a Speech' on page 52.
- If you have any questions concerning spoken English, refer to 'Examiner's Question & Answer' on page 196.

Non-fiction: Autobiography

Objectives:

- to examine the language of autobiographical writing
- to compare literary with non-literary autobiographies

Defining Autobiography

Even if you had never heard of or read any autobiographies, you could probably guess what the word means by looking closely at it:

auto + bio + graphy
auto = Greek for 'self'
bio = Greek for 'life'
graphy = Greek for 'writing'

So autobiography is a written account of one's own life (literally 'self-life-writing'). It is one of the most popular genres, written by politicians, celebrities, people caught briefly in the news, as well as by people who have no claim to fame at all. Why do they want to tell us about their lives? Why do we want to read about them? Here is what some writers have said:

Autobiography is now as common as adultery, and hardly less reprehensible (wicked).

John Grigg

Autobiography is an obituary in serial form with the last instalment missing.

Quentin Crisp

Only when one has lost all curiosity about the future has one reached the age to write an autobiography.

Evelyn Waugh

I have not much interest in anyone's personal history after the tenth year, not even my own. Whatever one was going to be was all prepared before that.

Katherine Anne Porter

These are quite negative views of autobiography. People write them for a variety of reasons, but probably the most rewarding autobiographies to read are those in which the writer has written in order to find out more about themselves – what one writer has called 'a search for innerstanding' (R. Pascal, *Design and Truth in Autobiography*).

Fiction versus non-fiction

Do autobiographies always tell the truth?

If you wrote about *your* life, how much would you reveal about your worries, hates, loves, desires, vices, or weaknesses? Of course, it depends who your audience might be. But if you knew that *anyone* was going to read what you had said, would there be some parts of your life that you would want to keep concealed?

In other words, when we consider autobiographies, it is important to bear in mind that they may not present the full picture and to remember the words of David Krause:

> Most fiction is autobiographical and most autobiography is fictional.

Activity

Look at the list of statements below. Which ones best apply to fictional autobiography (a life-story told by an invented character), and which to non-fiction autobiography (a life-story told by a real person)?

A The language will be more 'flowery' or poetic.
B The account will contain more facts – about people and places.
C There will be a greater emphasis on feelings.
D It will be structured like a story.
E Other people's opinions will be included.
F There will be lots of dialogue between different people.
G It will have a happy ending.
H It will have no proper ending.

Draw a chart like the one below and decide where to place each lettered statement – some might fit in both columns. Use the letter as a shorthand for each statement.

Fictional Autobiography	Non-Fictional Autobiography
A	B

Working on

Now put your theories to the test. The three extracts on pages 72–73 are from *Finding Courage*, a collection of stories – both fictional and autobiographical – celebrating everyday acts of courage by women all over the world. Can you tell from the language of the first few lines which are fictional and which are non-fiction? Use these prompts to help you decide.

- Look at the different narrators – who tells the story? What clues are there that they are 'real' people? Is it a first- or third-person narrator (i.e. told by 'I' or 'she' or 'he'). Does this make a difference?
- Is the language direct, factual, descriptive, polished...? What does this suggest?
- How much emphasis is there on description of people, places, and feelings? Does it feel real or imagined?
- Does the writer use dialogue? Does this add to your feeling that this is fictional writing, or does the conversation feel as if it really took place?

You will find the answers in the 'Feedback' pages at the end of the book.

Finding Courage

A: As We Are Now

I am not mad, only old. I make this statement to give me courage. To give you an idea what I mean by courage, suffice it to say that it has taken two weeks for me to obtain this notebook and a pen. I am in a concentration camp for the old, a place where people dump their parents or relatives exactly as though it were an ash can.

My brother, John, brought me here two weeks ago. Of course I knew from the beginning that living with him would never work. I had to close my own house after the heart attack (the stairs were too much for me). John is four years older than I am and married a much younger woman after Elizabeth, his first wife, died...

May Sarton

B: In a House of Wooden Monkeys

Summer rain sounded heavy on the new tin roof. Loud whispers ran up and down the rough wooden pews. Father MacIntyre was getting impatient. He knew Moses would not come and he could not perform the ceremony if Moses was not there.

'Yate, where is Moses? We have waited long enough,' the Father said.

'He soon come Father. He know we waiting for he.' The young woman answered, lowering her eyes to the fat brown baby she held close to her heart...

Shay Youngblood

C: Emei Shan

Finally I am away from the brown choking haze of the cities, from the clouds of cigarette smoke in restaurants, buses and trains throughout China. The air here is moist, clean, unaffected.

Steep, twisting mountain paths. Cobbled mosaics of rough-hewn boulders form a trail. Drifting houses of fog obscure views of lush fir and cedar landscapes. The light rain makes the already testy path even more treacherous. It is late April on Emei Shan in Szechuan Province, one of the five sacred Buddhist mountains in China...

Canyon Sam

Follow-up • To develop your sensitivity to different styles of autobiography, read some of the suggested titles in 'Wider Reading List' on page 216.

Non-fiction: Reportage

One Event: Two Versions

Compare these two accounts of the same event:

A
The old man spent some time getting the fire going again. When finally it caught, he muttered something to the youngster.

B
Old Jack raked the cinders together with a piece of cardboard and spread them judiciously over the whitening dome of coals. When the dome was thinly covered his face lapsed into darkness but, as he set himself to fan the fire again, his crouching shadow re-emerged into light. It was an old man's face, very bony and hairy. The moist blue eyes blinked at the fire and the moist mouth fell open at times, munching once or twice mechanically when it closed. When the cinders had caught he laid the piece of cardboard against the wall and said: 'That's better now, Mr Connor.'

Ivy Day in the Committee Room, James Joyce

Decide for yourself:
• Which extract do you prefer?
• How are they different – in style and tone?
• What do you think are their different purposes?
• What type of audience is each one aimed at?

Now look at the comments made by the authors of a book for would-be writers:

The first account is merely reportage; it tells what happened. But the second conjures the action; it has it happen here and now before our eyes. This is writing 'at first hand'. It is a knack. Some are born with it, but most young writers tend to reportage – and there are some, even quite good writers, who never acquire the knack. Usually the knack comes as with practice the writer's ear develops. Often it requires guidance.

The Way to Write, John Fairfax and John Moat

These authors clearly prefer the second version. Perhaps you do too. But the important point is that each version is *appropriate for different purposes*. If you used the style of Text B to tell the police about a crime you had seen, you might be in trouble for wasting valuable time. Or if you wrote GCSE creative writing assignments in the style of Text A, you would receive comments from your teacher asking for greater detail.

In other words, the way we write depends on our *purpose* and *audience*. This applies to reportage as much as to any other form of writing. It is easy to assume that the language of reporting is always factual. In fact, it can be simply another form of storytelling.

Reportage or Fiction?

Writer Tom Wolfe records his own realization that journalism or 'reportage' could feel more like fiction...

The New Journalism

... in the fall of 1962 I happened to pick up a copy of *Esquire* and read a story called 'Joe Louis: the King as a Middle-aged Man'. The piece didn't open like an ordinary magazine article at all. It opened with the tone and mood of a short story, with a rather intimate scene; or intimate by the standards of magazine journalism in 1962, in any case:

'Hi, sweetheart!' Joe Louis called to his wife, spotting her waiting for him at the Los Angeles airport.

She smiled, walked toward him, and was about to stretch up on her toes to kiss him – but suddenly stopped.

'Joe,' she said, 'where's your tie?'

'Aw, Sweetie,' he said, shrugging, 'I stayed out all night in New York and didn't have time –'

'All night!' she cut in. 'When you're out here all you do is sleep, sleep, sleep.'

'Sweetie,' Joe Louis said, with a tired grin, 'I'm an ole man.'

'Yes,' she agreed, 'but when you go to New York you try to be young again.'

The story featured several scenes like that, showing the private life of a sports hero growing older, balder, sadder... What the hell is going on? With a little reworking the whole article could have read like a short story.

Tom Wolfe and E.W. Johnson

The recognition of a new way of writing leads Wolfe to suggest four techniques which give reportage a 'gripping' or 'absorbing' reality.

Techniques of New Journalism

1 Scene-by-scene construction, telling the story by moving from scene to scene and resorting as little as possible to sheer historical narrative.

2 Recording dialogue in full, like a novelist.

3 Using third-person point-of-view so that the events are presented to the reader through the eyes of a particular character rather than through the journalist's own eyes.

4 Recording everyday gestures, habits, manners, styles of furniture, clothing, and so on – all in order to show something about the people who are being described.

Activity Reportage in action

Here are two different accounts of war: the first is a newspaper report; the second employs the bolder fictional techniques of 'New Journalism' as described above by Tom Wolfe. Both give an account of war. Use the prompts which follow to compare the style and effect, and make notes.

A:

ATTACK BEGINS

British and French forces began an air and naval bombardment of military targets in Egypt at 4.30pm, yesterday, it was officially announced last night.

Early this morning the Admiralty announced that HMS Newfoundland, 8,800-ton cruiser, engaged on shipping-protection duties, had sunk an Egyptian frigate in the gulf of Suez, southern end of the Suez Canal.

The frigate, it was stated, failed to answer a challenge to stop. 'She was therefore sunk and survivors were taken aboard the Newfoundland,' said the Admiralty.

Egyptian survivors aboard HMS Newfoundland.

Daily Mirror, 1 November 1956

Even if the name of the newspaper were not included here, you would know that this was a newspaper report. But how do you know? What clues can you find in...
- the layout?
- paragraph length?
- these phrases: *yesterday; it was officially announced last night; it was stated; said the Admiralty?*

Make a comment on each of these points.

Now compare it to this account of the Vietnam War by Michael Herr.

B:

During the bad maximum incoming days of the late Winter of 1968 there was a young marine at Khesanh whose Vietnam tour had run out. Nearly five of his thirteen months in-country had been spent there at the Khesanh Combat Base with the 26th Marines, who had been slowly building to full and then reinforced strength since the previous spring. He could remember a time, not long before, when the 26th considered themselves lucky to be there, when the guys talked of it as though it were a reward for whatever their particular outfits had been through. As far as this marine was concerned, the reward was for an ambush that autumn on the Cam Lo-Conthien road, when his unit had taken forty percent casualties, when he himself had taken shrapnel in the chest and arms...

Esquire magazine, September 1969

How can you tell that this is *not* the front page story of a newspaper? Find clues for:

- the way the text sometimes feels like a novel or short story – which words give it this effect?
- the narrator and central character – how do we see things from the point of view of the marine?
- the vocabulary – in what ways is it more informal and colloquial than in a newspaper report?
- layout, sentence, and paragraph length – how do these contrast with the newspaper front page?

Working on

1 Write up your notes comparing the two styles, drawing out the differences in the way the writers create their stories, and saying which style you prefer.

2 Choose a newspaper front page story from a recent newspaper and have a go at rewriting it using Tom Wolfe's four techniques of 'New Journalism'. Then write a paragraph commentary describing the process you went through.

Follow-up

- For hints on researching and structuring articles, see 'Writing Journalism' on page 116.
- To read more examples of 'New Journalism', see Tom Wolfe's anthology, *The New Journalism* (Picador).

Non-fiction: Diaries

Objectives:

- to examine the genre of diaries
- to identify some of their conventions and common language features

Diary Days

The writer Ronald Blythe has written about people's enthusiasm for diaries:

> All contain the magic of the frozen moment. Not even the arrival of the photograph album has been able to destroy the fascination of countless diary days.

Some diary-writers reveal their own attitudes to diaries:

> The period without the diary remains an ordeal. Every evening I want my diary as one wants opium.
>
> *Anaïs Nin, 1903–77*

> I have kept one now for thirty-four years. It is the history, in fact, of my mind... I hope that my journals, if ever they are thought worthy of publication, may give as much pleasure to others as other journals have given delight to me.
>
> *Benjamin Robert Haydon, 1786–1846*

> Having read my journal, I can hardly identify myself with the person it describes.
>
> *Richard Hurrell Froude, 1803–36*

> Only good girls keep diaries. Bad girls don't have the time.
>
> *Tallulah Bankhead, 1903–68*

What is the difference between a diary and a journal? Both words have similar origins:

> **Diary** = from the Latin *diarium* = 'daily'
> **Journal** = from the Latin *diurnalem* = 'daily'

Although there is often no difference these days between diaries and journals, there used to be a clearer distinction: diaries were private; journals were of greater public importance. The famous were more likely to write journals, with an eye to publishing them – celebrities and politicians still do this. Diaries are kept for other, more private reasons.

Why do you think people write diaries?
One important reason is to help us to sort the mass of impressions, senses, and experiences we encounter each day into some sort of shape or pattern. It is a way of making sense of and reflecting on our lives.

Activity　Look at the two diary extracts and use the following prompts to compare them.

Elizabeth Smith lived in Ireland for most of the 19th Century, and her diary records her strong opinions of people and places, as well as the effects of the terrible potato famine of the 1840s...

Queen Victoria was a compulsive diary-writer. In her lifetime she wrote millions of words, recording her response to public and private events...

Elizabeth Smith (1797–1885)

6 November 1846. Another blustering day after a stormy night, however as there is no rain it will dry the potatoes finely.

11 November. Mr Darker much afraid of this second potato field. The first had hardly a bad potato so that he was unprepared for this.

13 November. Half the potatoes in this new field are tainted, some very badly.

16 November. This had been a regular rainy day, the river all over the meadows. The papers still occupied with the potato disease though Lady Odela Villiers and her well managed elopement has been a God-send to them the last few days...

30 November. Mr Robinson came down yesterday to collect the rents, the Tennants paid well, were in good spirits, made no complaints, not even of their potatoes, were well dressed, so that altogether it was a most comfortable gale day (rent day). The potato failure has been much exaggerated, the disease is by no means so far spread as was supposed and the crop so over abundant that the partial failure will be less felt, particularly as the corn harvest was excellent. But people were much frightened and this caused a run on the Savings Bank which might have encreased the evil, that too is luckily over so that the prospects for the winter are brightening. John Robinson said nothing could more fully prove the encreasing prosperity of the country than the multitudes whom this panick proved to have been saving, the very poorest looking people drawing out their fortys, fiftys, hundreds. The crowds were so immense and so excited that horse and foot police were necessary to guard their lives.

16 January 1847. ...we called on Peggy Nary, who is going to turn her lodgers out of the house, having at last quarrelled with them. I don't on earth know what to do with her. She is going to white wash her kitchen! she says – herself – no one else would do it to please her. We then went on to Jem Doyle's. Most wretched it was, though very clean, he must go to the poor-house, he and his family. He had an ulcer on his leg, which will prevent his working for weeks and they will starve during this month, that there is no relief going. Widow Mulligan is also starving. So are the widow Quin and fifty more. They must be forced into the poor-house for they cannot otherwise be supported. They are the meanest feeling people ever were, they will accept of charity from anyone, live on it in idleness, but they won't go to the poor-house.

10 October. Sunday. Little in the papers but failures. Cattle dealers in Dublin have gone and caused immense distress, in fact paralysed the markets; not an offer for a beast of any sort at any of the late fairs. Banks, merchants, brokers, agents, all are bankrupt in all places. John Robinson has lost seven thousand pounds by bad debts, trusting people who have failed to pay; he must pay the millers who sent him the flour he so imprudently parted with out of his former profits, his capital, and learn wisdom by this shake. He hopes to recover about half this sum when the affairs of some of these firms are wound up...

17 October. Sunday again – the 17th – I hardly know how the week has gone – not a creature has entered the house but the Doctor. We have been as quiet as possible, indeed the country generally is very dull; people are oppressed by this frightful amount of bankruptcies, almost everyone either themselves or their friends affected by some of these numerous failures. Then the winter prospects look very gloomy. The destitution is expected to be wider spread than last year for the very poor will be nearly as ill off while the classes above which then relieved them are all this year in serious difficulties. No money anywhere; the little hoards of cash and goods all spent and nothing to replace wither. The ministry says the land must support the people on it. Half the country having been left untilled for want of means to crop it while a million of money was squandered in destroying the roads, much of it finding its way into pockets full enough before. The Queen has ordered the begging box to go round all the English churches for us!

Queen Victoria (1819–1901)

Thursday, 21 October 1875. Much grieved at its being a worse day than ever for the funeral of Brown's father, which sad ceremony was to take place to-day. The rain is hopeless – the ninth day! Quite unheard of! I saw good Brown a moment before breakfast; he was low and sad, and then going off to Micras. At twenty minutes to twelve drove with Beatrice and Janie Ely to Micras. As we drove up (unfortunately raining much) we met Dr Robertson, and all along near the house were numbers of people – Brown told me afterwards he thought above a hundred...

The sons, and a few whom Brown sent out of the kitchen, were in the other small room, where was the coffin. A small passage always divides the kitchen and the sitting-room in this old sort of farmhouse, in front of which is the door – the only door. Mr Campbell, the minister of Crathie, stood in the passage at the door, every one else standing close outside. As soon as he began his prayer, poor dear old Mrs Brown got up and came and stood near me – able to hear, though, alas! not to see – and leant on a chair during the very impressive prayers, which Mr Campbell gave admirably. When it was over, Brown came and begged her to go and sit down while they took the coffin away, the brothers bearing it. Every one went out and followed, and we also hurried out and just saw them place the coffin in the hearse, and then we moved on to a hillock, whence we saw the sad procession wending its way sadly down. The sons were there, whom I distinguished easily from their being near good Brown, who wore his kilt walking near the hearse. All walked, except our gentlemen, who drove. It fortunately ceased raining just then. I went back to the house, and tried to soothe and comfort dear old Mrs Brown, and gave her a mourning brooch with a little bit of her husband's hair which had been cut off yesterday, and I shall give a locket to each of the sons.

When the coffin was being taken away, she sobbed bitterly.

We took some whisky and water and cheese, according to the universal Highland custom, and then left, begging the dear old lady to bear up. I told her the parting was but for a time. We drove quickly on, and saw them go into the kirkyard, and through my glasses I could see them carry the coffin in. I was grieved I could not be in the kirkyard.

Saw my good Brown at a little before two. He said all had gone off well, but he seemed very sad; he had to go back to Micras to meet all the family at tea. All this was terribly trying for the poor dear old widow, but could not be avoided. Already, yesterday morning, she had several of the wives and neighbours to tea. Every one was very kind and full of sympathy, and Brown was greatly gratified by the respect shown to him and his family to-day...

Diaries Compared

- Which is the most/least private? How can you tell?
- Which contains more emotion? How can you tell?
- Which is most concerned with recording everyday events, however trivial they may seem?
- What clues can you detect about the period in which each diary was written?
- How do the personalities of the writers differ? Write down some key words to describe your impression of each writer.
- Which would you most like to read more of? Why?

Follow-up
- To look at the language of autobiographies, see 'Non-fiction: Autobiography' on page 70.
- To read more diaries, see 'Wider Reading List' on page 216.

Non-fiction: Travel Writing

Going Places

Almost all works of fiction involve descriptions of places. Without them, novels, short stories, and plays would seem flat, unrealistic, and unbelievable. How do novelists use places to bring the worlds of their novels to life? Look at this extract from Charlotte Brontë's novel *Villette,* in which she describes her character's view from the deck of a ship.

Villette

I was not sick till long after we had passed Margate, and deep was the pleasure I drank in with the sea breeze; divine the delight I drew from the heaving channel waves, from the seabirds on their ridges, from the white sails in their dark distance, from the quiet yet beclouded sky, overhanging all. In my reverie, methought I saw the continent of Europe, like a wide dreamland, far away. Sunshine lay on it, making the long coast one line of gold; tiniest tracery of clustered town and snow-gleaming tower, of woods deep massed, of heights serrated, of smooth pasturage and veiny stream, embossed the metal-bright prospect. For background, spread a sky, solemn and dark blue, and – grand with imperial promise, soft with tints of enchantment – strode from north to south a God-bent bow, an arch of hope.

Charlotte Brontë

This is a *fictional* account of a journey, though we know from Charlotte Brontë's life that it was based on the writer's own experience. How does she attempt to make places come to life?

Here are some of her techniques. For each one, find one or more examples from the text. The first is done for you:

Technique	Example
visual adjectives 1 – colours	white, gold
visual adjectives 2 – light + darkness	
adjectives of size	
simile (comparison using as/like)	
emphasis on the variety of what she sees	

The language, in other words, works hard to make the reader see a landscape. How successful do you think the extract is in conveying a strong sense of place?

Non-fiction Travel

If fiction frequently uses places as a backdrop to the action, the genre of travel writing has a different focus. We read travel writing because we want to read of real people in real places. Places (and how we get between them) are the central interest.

But travel writing has to be more than a merely factual account, otherwise it would read like a travel guide... Confused? Read on...

Compare a travel guide with some travel writing, and consider the differences.

Italy: The Rough Guide

L'Aquila's centre is relatively compact and best seen on foot. Of its sights, only two are outside the central core – the 99-spouted fountain, a short walk from the railway station, and the church of Santa Maria di Collemaggio, which is a stroll away from the Porto Bazzano below the main piazza... L'Aquila's restaurants and trattorias are reasonably-priced and numerous, with good hearty traditional Abruzzese fare on offer at Trattoria del Giaguaro...

You would immediately know that this text was taken from a guidebook. But how can you tell?

Compare the language of *The Rough Guide* with Charlotte Brontë's fictional account.

Guide book	Fiction
Highly specific references e.g. L'Aquila, Trattoria del Giaguaro	*Some specific references* e.g. Margate, Europe
Facts and figures e.g. 99-spouted fountain	*Unexpected phrasing – sometimes poetic* e.g. beclouded sky, overhanging all an arch of hope
Familiar phrases of tourism e.g. 'best seen on foot', 'a stroll away', 'good traditional fare'	*Emphasis on emotions of the narrator* e.g. deep was the pleasure I drank in
Writer does not intrude e.g. no use of *I* or *me*	*Focus is character and story – not place*
Focus is detailed sense of place	*Purpose:* to entertain
Purpose: to inform	

Travel writing combines features of various genres – part guide book, part autobiography, often with the written style of a novel. It usually aims to communicate a strong sense of place and of the experience of travel, but also to reveal something about the writer's attitude and feelings.

Read this example of travel writing by Jonathan Raban. In it he has moved into the deep South of the USA and notices in his cabin an invasion of ants...

Hunting Mr Heartbreak

It took me a while to notice the ants. Unpacking my sponge bag in the bathroom, I thought I saw the brown shagpile carpet ripple like a cornfield in a wind. Looking closer, I saw a colony of ants the size of wasps out on some kind of jungle-exercise in the woolly undergrowth. When I flushed the cistern, a hundred or so ant-marines tumbled into the toilet bowl from their positions under the rim.

I drove the Spirit back into town, a mile away, and consulted my new friend William, the pharmacist.

'They black ants? Or are they a kind of reddy-brown?'

'Black – I think.'

'I *hope* it's black ants you got out there. If they're a *brown* ant, it could be you got *fire ants* on your place. Then you got problems.' He was searching around among his poisons. 'Friend of mine, he had fire ants once... he just went out into his back yard one morning... end of the day, his daughter came home, found him laying there *dayud*. Fire ants. Yes – he was killed by the fire ants,' he said with the same soft twinkle that he'd used to speak of tornados. 'That was a misfortunate man.'

As he spoke, my ants started changing colour rapidly from black to brown.

'But if they're inside your house, they'll most likely be black ants. I hope so, anyway; I wouldn't like to think of you with fire ants in your house. How big you say they are?'

I found it had to control the trembling of my forefinger and thumb.

William nodded and smiled; he looked significantly pleased by what I'd shown him.

'Oh, yes, we do get them real big around here–'

Before I left the drugstore with two bottles of sweet antbane, he asked me if I knew about brown recluse spiders. They were worse than fire ants; far worse. There was probably a brown recluse somewhere out at my place, most people had them, without knowing. They were inconspicuously small – no bigger than William's thumbnail. They didn't spin giveaway webs. They just hid, and waited to get you. If you left a pair of boots in a closet, a brown recluse might well take up residence in a toe. If there was some rotten wood in your porch, or up in the rafters... The brown recluse was the duke of the dark corners of Alabama. William knew a lot of people who'd died, or been permanently paralysed, after being bitten by a brown recluse.

'Why, the Reverend Billy Graham – *he* was bitten by a brown recluse. He got treatment, but that's why he still walks so stiff. That was a brown recluse spider.'

Back at the cabin, I moved as cautiously as if I was burgling it, examining each patch of carpet before I dared to plant a foot there.

But there was no question: my ants were coal-black; not deadly, just a nuisance to be got rid of. Following the instructions on the bottle, I booby-trapped the house with half-inch rectangles of white card, then shook out on each card a couple of drops of the poisonous clear syrup. Within a quarter of an hour, the ants were assembled round the cards like so many guests at an all-male black-tie dinner. I watched over them with an odd hostly feeling of benevolence. Poisoners, I remembered, tend to have milk-and-water manners – like Dr Crippen, described by the sea captain who was responsible for his arrest as 'the acme of politeness".

As they rose from their banquet to return to headquarters, the ants blundered away from table, limped, staggered, fell to their knees. Their legs kept on waving feebly long after their thoraxes had hit the deck. Quietly cheered by the slaughter, I poured myself a finger of Scotch and went out to sit in my rocker on the porch and admire the scenery...

...Whisky in hand, I walked down to my boathouse. As my foot touched the pier, it triggered off a series of bellyflop splashes, making me spill my drink. A fallen beech tree, its bark stripped bare, lay out along the water, and turtles were tumbling in from their perches on its trunk. They came in all sizes, from babies the size of silver dollars to grown-ups as big as soup tureens. They crashed into the lake like a row of falling bricks. I was glad they were shy: a snapping turtle could amputate whole hands of fingers with a bite, or take a clean half-moon of flesh from your calf, if you were caught at close quarters with it.

Jonathan Raban

Activity

1 Look closely at the different styles of Raban's account. For each of the statements listed below, find an example from the text.

Guidebook	Autobiography	Style of fiction
Specific references to people and places	Writer is clearly present in the text	Unexpected, lively phrasing
	Emotions/attitudes are revealed	Use of dialogue
		Use of similes to bring the descriptions alive

2 Write your own travel piece, based either on a journey or visit abroad you have had, or using the techniques of travel writers and applying them to a familiar, regular journey – such as your daily route to school. Aim to make the description of people/places vivid.

Follow-up
- For more on adding detail to your own writing, see 'Creative Writing' on page 110.
- To read more travel writing, see the 'Wider Reading List' on page 216.
- For more on Similes, see 'Imagery' on page 144.

Reading for Meaning I

Introduction to Comprehension Tasks

One of the key elements of English at GCSE is reading for meaning – sometimes called 'comprehension'. The National Curriculum for English requires students to be taught to:

- extract meaning beyond the literal, explaining how choice of language and style affects implied and explicit meanings
- analyse and discuss alternative interpretations, unfamiliar vocabulary, ambiguity, and hidden meanings
- analyse and engage with the ideas, themes, and language in fiction, non-fiction, drama, and poetry
- select information
- compare and synthesize information drawn from different texts
- make effective use of information in their own work
- evaluate how information is presented
- sift the relevant from the irrelevant, and to distinguish between fact and fiction, bias and objectivity

If that sounds terrifyingly complicated, the required skills can be summarized like this:

You will already be able to do many of these, probably without realizing it. Some of the skills will simply need practice. Later spreads focus on the different reading skills involved.

Types of Comprehension

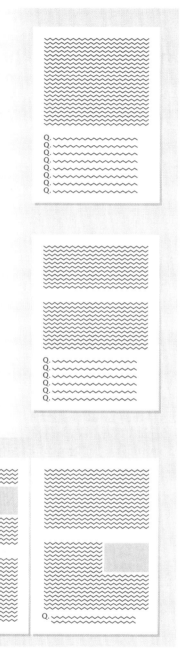

A Reading and Response
- questions (usually between 1 and 10)
- first questions often fact-spotting (understanding surface meanings)
- later questions are opinion/reading between the lines
- last question often involves extended writing, perhaps asking for your personal response to the text

B Comparisons
- questions (usually between 1 and 10)
- first questions may focus on *individual texts* (surface meaning)
- later questions may ask for comparison of writers' attitudes, themes, language (meanings beneath the surface/fact v opinion/selecting information)
- final questions will be more open-ended, asking for personal response (e.g. write a letter) or extended task (e.g. continue the story)

C Active Comprehensions
- several texts (usually between 2 and 5)
- possibly some early fact-spotting questions
- often just one open-ended task and no questions
- task requires you to sift information, re-present it in a different form for a different audience (e.g. a leaflet for teenagers; script for radio documentary)
- these often include response to diagrams and statistics

Activity
1 What do you like and dislike about each of the comprehension formats?
2 What are your own strengths and weaknesses in doing comprehensions? Take the reading skills listed in the spider diagram on page 86 and place them in order of easiest to most difficult.

Follow-up
- See the following spreads to develop key areas of your reading skills.
- For a sample question paper, see 'Eating Meat' on page 99.

Reading for Meaning II

- to learn about the types of comprehension questions which you will encounter
- to practise spotting these different types of questions

Identifying Comprehension Questions

Within any of the three formats described in the previous spread, you could find a number of different types of questions. There are three main areas of understanding which teachers and examiners require you to demonstrate:

A
- whether you have understood the text/s as a whole
- whether you can spot key details
- whether you can summarize parts of the text
  These are all **spotting** questions.

B
- whether you can read between the lines
- whether you can express an opinion based upon evidence within the text
  These are all **interpretative** questions.

C
- whether you can take the main arguments/ideas of a text and present them in a different way, or express your own views at greater length
  These are **open-ended** questions.

With a little practice, these three types of questions are easy to identify:

A: Spotting questions

These questions ask you to spot facts and details. They usually require short, one-sentence answers. Just occasionally they require single-word answers. They might even ask you to quote a word or sentence from the text.

Early questions may focus on details in the text; later questions may be more general, or vice versa – there are no standard formats here. But the secret to answering these questions is to spot the relevant information for the answer in the text, and then to express yourself clearly and directly.

Examples:

1 How may people were in the train when the disaster happened?
2 What was the narrator doing at the time of the crash?
3 Name three thoughts which passed through her head.
4 In your own words explain what the word 'triumphant' means.
5 Choose one sentence which sums up the author's attitude to hunting

- Notice how the questions are asking you to respond with precise, relevant information.

B: Interpretative questions

These questions ask you to do more than spot facts. They require you to express an opinion or make a judgement about details in a text. Often they focus particularly on the writer's use of language. Interpretative questions will often require more detailed answers than spotting questions because they will ask you first to make a point, and then to support it with evidence from the text.

Examples:

1 What do you think the writer means when she says 'we stepped out of the house like Arctic explorers'?
2 How can you tell that the writer wants us to feel sorry for the animals he describes? Give three examples to support your opinions.
3 How does the writer use language to make the product seem exciting and different?

- Notice how these questions require you to interpret the text and to make a judgement about the writer's choice of words or meaning.

C: Open-ended questions

These questions are usually placed last, so that you have more time to develop your response. Questions are usually more general, asking you for your point of view on the text or issues as a whole. Sometimes they ask you to rewrite the extract from a different character's point of view; or to write about it as if you were addressing a different audience.

> **Examples:**
>
> 1 Do you agree with the author that hunting is 'only a sport and not at all cruel'? Write about your opinion on the issue.
> 2 Imagine you are Kingshaw at the end of the extract. What do you do next? Write a continuation of the story.
> 3 The author has presented strong views against tobacco advertising. Imagine you work for a large tobacco manufacturer. Write a letter to a national newspaper explaining why you think cigarette advertising should be allowed.

- Notice how much more of a personal response these questions require from you – but don't feel that you can therefore ignore all the information in the text. Base your answer firmly in what you have read.
- Note also that question types B and C are becoming much more frequent in GCSE examination papers.

Activity

1 Look at the list of questions below and work out what 'type' of questions they are. Label them A, B, or C.
- Pick out a sentence which shows that the narrator was in a bad mood.
- What two reasons are given for eating more vegetables?
- Why does Danny decide to stay at home?
- How has the extract changed your opinion about whaling?
- With close reference to the extract, how can you tell that the weather is turning colder?
- Which character did you most admire and why?
- What does the writer mean by using the phrase 'feet firmly in the clouds'?
- What advice would you give to Samantha?
- What does the weather suggest about Ray's mood?
- Which type of camera gets the best results?

2 Choose an extract from the first chapter of a novel, or a leaflet, or one of the extracts used in other sections of this book. Develop your skill in identifying different types of comprehension questions by setting up your own questions based on the extract.

Aim to include 3 'spotting' questions; 3 'interpretation' questions; and 1 or 2 'open-ended' questions. This will prove good practice in developing your ability to read texts closely.

Follow-up
- To practise your close reading skills, see 'Advanced Reading Skills' on page 91.
- To develop your ability to use quotations, see 'Writing about Literature' on page 170.
- To check your answers to Question 1 in Activity above, see 'Feedback' on page 223.

Advice Column

Students sometimes complain that they seem to get plenty of practice at reading and responding to texts in exam conditions... but not enough hints on what to do. This page simply lists some techniques which may help you to be more systematic in your reading of texts and your response to them.

Active Reading

- Read the text through carefully, making it as active as possible. What does the title suggest that it will be about? What do you predict? As you read, use a pencil to underline key words and phrases.

- Look for key words, connections, patterns, changes in pace, direction or mood, similarities and contrasts.

- Look at the setting and atmosphere – how much detail is there?

- Look at the way the characters are presented. Do we see them from the inside or outside? How can you tell? Who do we sympathize with and why? What do we learn of characters' appearance, behaviour, feelings, attitudes, motives?

Active Answers

- Now read the questions through. What types of questions are there? What are you being required to find in the text?

- Reread the extract, using the pencil to identify links between ideas; making points about characters and themes; unusual or important wording.

- Begin your answers. Check to see whether the number of marks per question is given. If it is, vary the length of your answer according to the marks available. For one mark, as a general rule, aim to make one point. For two or three marks a short paragraph is probably required.

- Always answer in full sentences unless the question specifically asks for a word or phrase. Don't therefore start an answer with 'Because...'. A question which asks 'Why was the boy upset?' should begin, 'The boy was upset because...' or 'He was upset because...'

- If the final question is open-ended, leave yourself plenty of time to do it justice. Write a brief paragraph plan before you start, just to make sure that you cover all the required points. Make sure that you:
  (a) structure your ideas into paragraphs
  (b) give examples from the text.

- Don't be afraid of giving your own opinions of the text: just make sure you support them with evidence.

Advanced Reading Skills

The Reading Process

When we begin learning to read, we start by gradually recognizing different words – sometimes by recognizing the shape of the word, sometimes by working out what the letters spell, sometimes by making an informed guess according to the context. Our early reading is largely a matter of **decoding** text.

Advanced reading skills sound impressive, and perhaps wrongly difficult, but they will help you to become more confident in dealing with all kinds of texts. Advanced reading skills involve making judgements about texts, spotting clues, moving quickly through them.

Four Techniques

These are the four techniques of advanced reading which, with practice, might help you to read texts more effectively.

Activity   1 **Skimming**

Skimming a text means getting the gist of it – the general feel of what it is about, what its purpose is, and perhaps what its tone might be. It means **not** reading in detail.

Look at this piece of text. Give yourself 10 seconds to decide:
- what kind of text it is
- what it is about
- what its purpose is

If you're fascinated by BBC wildlife programmes, then you'll be enthralled by *BBC Wildlife*: the monthly colour environmental magazine produced in co-operation with the BBC Natural History Unit.

Featuring the talents of the world's key wildlife and conservation experts, top photographers and well-known broadcasting personalities, the magazine will be enjoyed by the professional and enthusiast alike.

There's something for all the family.

As well as the monthly articles illustrated in full colour, there are regular features that include wildlife, questions, book reviews, exclusive monthly listings of programmes, competitions, and international news and discoveries sections.

Wildlife MAGAZINE **£2.30**

PLACE AN ORDER WITH YOUR NEWSAGENT AND EXPLORE THE WORLD OF NATURE FROM THE COMFORT OF YOUR ARMCHAIR.

2 Scanning

Scanning has a different purpose: we scan a text to find out some specific information. Once we have got what we need to know, we leave the text. So, like skimming, it is a quick-reading approach. But this time, instead of the gist, we look for detail.

Look at this text about Queen Elizabeth I and find out:

- where she was born
- who she had executed in 1587
- what she was known as

Queen Elizabeth I

Elizabeth I 1533–1603. Queen of England 1558–1603, the daughter of Henry VIII and Anne Boleyn. Through her Religious Settlement of 1559 she enforced the Protestant religion by law. She had Mary Queen of Scots executed 1587. Her conflict with Roman Catholic Spain led to the defeat of the Spanish Armada 1588. The Elizabethan age was expansionist in commerce and geographical exploration, and arts and literature flourished. The rulers of many European states made unsuccessful bids to marry Elizabeth, and she used these bids to strengthen her power. She was succeeded by James I.

Elizabeth was born at Greenwich, London, 7 Sept 1533. She was well educated in several languages. During her Roman Catholic half-sister Mary's reign, Elizabeth's Protestant sympathies brought her under suspicion, and she lived in seclusion at Hatfield, Herfordshire, until on Mary's death she became queen. Her first task was to bring about a broad religious settlement.

Many unsuccessful attempts were made by Parliament to persuade Elizabeth to marry or settle the succession. She found courtship a useful political weapon, and she maintained friendships with, among others, the courtiers Leicester, Sir Walter Raleigh, and Essex. She was known as the Virgin Queen.

Queen Elizabeth I, whose skin was so white that when she drank port, it could be seen flowing down her throat.

3 Previewing

Previewing a text is probably a technique you already use without thinking about it. It means using as much advance information about a text as possible to narrow down what it will be about – looking for clues like blurbs, illustrations, titles, headlines, contents, and the index. Using these clues, you can get a strong impression of the contents of a text, making the actual reading of it more straightforward.

You have been asked to read a book with the following title:

Sunrise with Sea Monsters

• what do you think it will be about?
• will it be fiction or non-fiction?

Now look at the table of contents. Do they confirm your thoughts? What do you now think the book will be about? Which clues are most helpful? See answers in the 'Feedback' section on page 223.

Contents

Introduction	*1*
The Edge of the Great Rift (1964)	7
Burning Grass (1964)	9
Winter in Africa (1965)	12
The Cerebral Snapshot (1965)	15
State of Emergency (1966)	18
Leper Colony (1966)	23
Tarzan is an Expatriate (1967)	31
Cowardice (1967)	40
Seven Burmese Days (1970)	48
The Novel is Dead, Allah Be Praised! (1971)	58
The Killing of Hastings Banda (1971)	63
Lord of the Ring (1971)	76
A Love-Scene After Work (1971)	83
V.S. Naipaul (1971 and 1982)	91
Kazantzakis' England (1972 and 1982)	101
Malaysia (1973)	106
Memories of Old Afghanistan (1974)	109
The Night Ferry to Paris (1975)	123
Stranger on a Train (1976)	126
An English Visitor (1976)	136
Discovering Dingle (1976)	140
The Exotic View (1977)	146
Homage to Mrs Robinson (1977)	152
My Extended Family (1977)	152
A Circuit of Corsica (1977)	166
Nixon's Neighborhood (1977)	171
Nixon's Memoirs (1978)	177
The Orient Express (1978)	182

4 Prediction

Prediction is similar to previewing except you use it once you have moved inside a text, rather than before you start reading. It means making informed guesses about where the text is going, so that you can move more rapidly through it.

Predicting what will happen next; where the text is going; what the conclusion might be – these are things active readers do all the time.

One other skill is useful for prediction – spotting **discourse markers**. Discourse markers are used by writers to organize their ideas. Often they tell us when a new idea is being introduced, or changed, or rejected. Discourse markers are words and phrases like:

first, next, then,
however, therefore, although

Look how these are used by a writer to organize the text, to move us from the present into the past, to give a clear sense of where each event takes place...

Use the title of the extract to preview the text. What type of writing will it be – factual, fiction, autobiographical, poetry, scientific?

A Saturday in August

Approaching the grassy area near the Venice Pavilion, Alicia Orozco immediately noticed that she stood out among the other women registering to march in the ERA Walkathon that bright August morning. First of all, she was the only Chicana in sight. Secondly, anticipating warm weather, she had worn a ruffled tube top to complement her trim white shorts and matching sandals. Everyone else was sportily attired in green ERA T-shirts, baggy shorts, and scruffy jogging shoes.

Self-consciously, Alicia moved into the milling crowd of registrants, searching for the table designated for "L through O" entrants. In line, she glanced around, searching for a familiar face, though not really expecting to find one.

The week before, she had read a Los Angeles Times article about the walkathon which would raise funds for the Equal Rights Amendment. Considering herself a feminist though she had never belonged to any organized group, she had decided, instead of lying on the beach reading, to make this weekend's moments in the sun worthwhile.

At work, she had timidly secured some sponsors for the event, knowing if she pledged herself to walk on their behalf she would not be able to talk herself out of attending.

Terri de la Peña

- Did you guess that the text would be either fiction – the start of a short story – or autobiography?
- What do you predict will happen to Alicia?
- Which discourse markers are used to organize the text?

Follow-up
- To practise these techniques, see the practice paper at the end of this section.
- To examine ways of distinguishing fact from fiction, see the next spread.
- For more on discourse markers, see 'Discursive Assignments' on page 118.

Fact v Opinion

Fact-finding

Look at this dictionary definition of a fact:

1 an event or thing known to have happened or existed
2 a truth verifiable from experience or observation

Now look at this list of statements about 'Goats' and decide which are facts and which are opinions? For each statement write down whether it is:

Fact (F); Opinion (O); Probably Fact (PF);
Probably Opinion (PO); or Not Sure (NS)

Goats

1 The plural forms of the word goat used to include the following: gete, geet, geete, geates, gait, gotes, and gayte.
2 Goats are sometimes used to lead unwilling cattle into the slaughterhouse.
3 Goats can separate the two toes on each foot, allowing them to grip and climb up near-vertical slopes.
4 Some Scots people believe that the wild goats of the Hebrides are descended from goats that survived a shipwreck in the 16th Century.
5 Deer dislike goats, probably because of their scent, which makes deer feel insecure.
6 Farmers claim that it improves the health of cattle to keep a goat with each herd.
7 Goats are also said to calm highly-strung horses and will stop a horse panicking in the case of fire.

facts adapted from
Almost Everything There is to Know, Tim Hunkin

Now look at those statements which you feel most sure about being factual. How can you tell? What clues in the phrasing of the other statements makes you less certain?

Activity Writers can be very skilful at concealing their own opinions, making you think that you are reading a factual report.

1 Read through the following newspaper article, and use the prompts which follow to untangle fact from opinion.

Dodging lessons at the Hi-de-hi school

UNDER the familiar and fatuous motto 'learning can be fun' 500 pupils from 14 state schools have been spending six days at Butlin's Somerwest World, a holiday camp at Brighton.

The children, all aged 14 and 15, are studying for the General Certificate of Secondary Education. They are being 'continually assessed', not examined, it goes without saying.

By playing snooker in the camp's snooker hall they are supposed to learn about angles of deflection. By playing darts they are supposed to teach themselves addition and subtraction.

Tomfoolery

Fruit machines, adapted to work without money, are supposed to teach them about the laws of probability governing the winning of a jackpot.

In the evenings they enjoy the attractions of Waterworld and the Somerwest recreational facilities – and all at just over half the peak season cost.

Rank Educational Services run the course, under the direction of Mr Alan Ridgway, who in the holiday season is the camp's director of entertainments.

Full marks to him and to Butlins for their private enterprise filling their camp in off-season times with six-day 'field courses' for children.

No marks at all for the local education authorities who waste public funds on such tomfoolery.

No marks for the teachers who go along with it, preferring to play snooker, darts and fruit machines instead of teaching geometry, arithmetic and probability the hard and proper way.

No marks to the parents who encourage their children to think that learning is a matter of fun and not a matter of work.

Daily Mail, 6 October 1987

a What definite facts are there in the article? Make a list.

b Can we tell who wrote the article?

c Now look at the writer's opinion. What can we tell of her/his attitude from:
* the wording of the headline
* the photograph
* the subheading ('Tomfoolery')

d What do the following sentences and phrases show about the writer's attitude:
* 'They are being "continually assessed", not examined, it goes without saying'
* '...they are supposed to...'
* 'waste'
* 'tomfoolery'
* 'No marks... '

e What evidence or quotations from other people does the writer use to support his article?

f If you were a parent, how would you react to the article? What would your attitude be to the school and the project?

g Note finally that a Butlin's spokesperson has said that there is no holiday camp at Brighton... How does this change your opinion of the article?

h Based on your examination of the article, make a list of 8 or more techniques the writer uses to give his opinion about the school camp.

2 Look at this brief factual entry from the *Hutchinson Encyclopaedia* about the use of animals in scientific experiments (vivisection). How successfully does it give a neutral presentation to a highly controversial issue. Are there any words which reflect the writer's opinion?

> **Vivisection:** literally, cutting into a living animal; used originally to mean experimental surgery or dissection practised on a live subject. Now often used by anti-vivisection campaigners to include any experiment on animals, surgical or otherwise.

Now write two versions of a newspaper article giving opinions – one as a supporter of vivisection; the other as an anti-vivisection campaigner. Make each piece around 150 words. In both, aim to persuade your reader subtly to support your view. Imagine that each text will appear in a newspaper – so you should use headlines, subheadings, and perhaps a caption to reinforce your message. Refer back to your list of points in question **h** to help you.

Then write a brief description of the decisions you made and how successfully you feel the articles have worked.

Follow-up
* To develop your ability to look beneath the surface level of texts, see 'Advanced Reading Skills' on page 91.
* To look at ways of writing newspaper articles, see 'Writing Journalism' on page 116.

Examining Data

- to look at ways of responding to data-handling comprehension questions
- to practise answering a sample question

Data Day

An increasingly frequent part of many GCSE English examinations is a question on a variety of non-literary sources which use statistics and other data, as well as text. These questions might include:
- leaflets
- tables
- lists of statistics
- grids
- fact-sheets
- quotations from experts

... and so on

With these questions, examiners will be testing your abilities to make sense of information from a variety of sources, and to draw conclusions from the data in front of you.

In this spread, look at the advice on answering such questions.

Advice

1 Do not be intimidated by data questions. They often contain lively, interesting materials and invite you to give your opinion.

2 On your initial reading, make a catalogue of the source material. That means listing what you notice: the type of text (leaflet, speech, etc), the main points, and anything you notice about the style and layout. A catalogue like this will help you find your way back through the data much more quickly.

3 Tune in to signs of opinion rather than fact. Candidates scoring highest marks are usually highly sceptical (questioning) of the source material. If a leaflet has been produced by a commercial company, you can be fairly sure that part of their purpose will be to recruit customers. Look at thow they do it.

4 In your answers, be as clear as possible. This might mean using headings, sub-headings, charts, and labels to convey what you have noticed. Find out in advance whether the exam requires essay-style answers or more of a report format.

5 Feel free to give your own opinion, but be sure to support it with evidence from the text, just as you would in a literature assignment.

Follow-up   • For advice on using quotations, see 'Writing about Literature' on page 170.
• Try the sample paper in the next spread; then see the sample answer with Examiner's comments.

Examiner's Comments: Reading Paper

Eating Meat

Read the two texts and complete the tasks which follow in one hour.

Text A

Meat - Britain's Favourite

We British really enjoy our meat. We always have. 98% of us sit down to meat meals regularly, and figures show that more of us will be eating meat in 1988 than ever before.

Why, because there's more to meat. More goodness. More convenience. More taste. More [i]n food have changed, so butchers and supermarkets have [k]ept pace, offering us leaner well trimmed and boneless cuts.

Meat tastes good. Even the smell of a good British roast, [si]zzling grilled steak, hearty casserole or trendy stirfry can [se]t those taste buds twitching.

Meat does you good. If you want to give your family [a] well balanced diet make sure they enjoy the nutritional [ben]efits of meat: protein for strong, healthy growth and [bod]y building; iron for healthy blood; zinc, vital for healing [pro]cesses; vitamin B12, which helps prevent anaemia; [thia]min, niacin and riboflavin for the conversion of [carb]ohydrates into energy.

[M]eat is so convenient. With many cuts available for [grilli]ng, stirfrying and microwaving, you can have a super [meal] on the table in minutes. Slower cooking casseroles and [pies] are wonderfully easy to prepare, especially when you [use] ready cubed or minced lamb, beef or pork. Whatever [you're] looking for, you'll find a meaty meal to suit your [taste] - and your pocket.

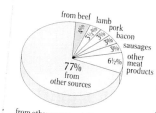

from beef lamb pork bacon sausages other meat products
4% 3½% 3% 3% 6½% 77% from other sources

Meat is great value for money. Even after inflation, meat and bacon still cost almost 20% less than in the early 1970s.

from other sources, which include eggs, fish & poultry

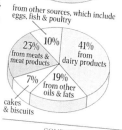

23% from meats & meat products
10%
41% from dairy products
7%
19% from other oils & fats
cakes & biscuits

SOURCES OF SATURATED FAT IN THE DOMESTIC PURCHASES (NFS, 1985)

Less fat needn't mean less meat. You and your family don't have to go without meat just because you're trying to cut down on fat in food. As you can see from the diagram, many other products contain fat too. What's more, there's always plenty of lean, well trimmed meat in the shops, and you can further reduce the fat content by grilling instead of frying. So give the family meat. It tastes good and it does them good.

Meat meals are packed with goodness – great for growing children.

THE PROTEIN CONTENT OF SOME ANIMAL & VEGETABLE FOODS

3% 12% 18% 30% 8% 24% 25% 6% 21% 2%

[E]GGS BAKED COD BRAISED BEEF WHITE BREAD ROASTED PEANUTS CHEDDAR CHEESE RICE DRY HARICOT BEANS RAW POTATOES

The protein in lamb, beef and pork compares very [fav]ourably with other foods. For a real meal – there's more to meat.

THERE'S

IRON FOR HEALTHY BLOOD PROTEIN FOR BUILDING MUSCLES VITAMINS FOR VITALITY CALORIES FOR ENERGY VITAMIN B12 ESSENTIAL FOR HEALTH NIACIN FOR GOOD SKIN MINERALS ESSENTIAL FOR HEALTH RIBOFLAVIN FOR GOOD SKIN AND EYES VITAMINS FOR METABOLISM

NOTHING COMPETES WITH MEAT

There's More to Meat, British Meat & Livestock Commission

Text B

Easy Ways to Eat More Fruit and Vegetables

- Get into the habit of eating two servings of vegetables, in addition to potatoes, with your main meal

- Add two servings of vegetables (plus potatoes or rice), when you serve a ready meal

- Make the most of seasonal produce as it is often the best buy

- Enjoy stir-fried vegetables (with a little added lean meat or fish, as liked) on a regular basis

- Step up your salad consumption. Both summer and winter salads can make satisfying meals

- Cook fruit in (unsweetened) fruit juice to sweeten instead of adding sugar

- Regularly include fruit in packed lunches and as snacks; take advantage of the different fruits in season

Sainsbury's Healthy Eating Symbol

To help you strike the right balance in what you eat Sainsbury's has introduced a new healthy eating symbol. It highlights some of the best choices of over 1,000 everyday foods. The symbol is used on a wide range of our products which are generally low in fat including; bread, potatoes, pasta, breakfast cereals, fruit, vegetables, some poultry, fish, lean meat, low fat dairy products and selected convenience foods such as sandwiches and ready meals. Many of these foods are also high in starch and fibre and don't contain much sugar or salt.

A new panel at the base of the nutrition label showing calories and grams of fat per serving is another innovation from Sainsbury's. Now you can easily see at a glance how much fat is in each food and keep a check on your daily fat intake, while still enjoying your favourite foods within healthy eating recommendations.

Recipe Cards

Look out in store for recipes using fruit and vegetables in the new series of Sainsbury's Healthy Eating Recipe Cards.

Please note: Some products featuring the healthy eating symbol in this leaflet may not as yet carry the symbol on pack in store.

J Sainsbury's plc
Stamford Street
London SE1 9LL

All items subject to availability. Some items available in larger stores only.
729/539

Text A

1 Pick out a sentence which you think is designed to *inform* the reader about meat. Then write a sentence to explain your choice. (2)

2 Pick out a sentence which you think is designed to *persuade* the reader to eat meat. Then write a sentence to explain your choice. (2)

3 Write a brief paragraph saying how you think the advertisement aims to encourage people to eat more meat. You might comment on:
  • layout
  • language
  • use of headings and slogans (6)

Text B

4 Pick out a sentence which you think is designed to *inform*. Then write a sentence to explain your choice. (2)

5 Pick out a sentence which you think is designed to *persuade*. Then write a sentence to explain your choice. (2)

6 Is this leaflet designed chiefly to inform readers about their diet or chiefly to persuade people to shop at Sainsbury's? How can you tell? Write a brief paragraph explaining your ideas, and supporting them with reference to the language and layout of the text. (6)

Comparing the texts

7 How do the two texts differ in their approach? Comment on the style of the layout, the use of facts and data, the tone of voice they adopt, who they might be aimed at. Write as much as you can on this question. (15)

Activity

1 If you have completed the test, look through your answers and try to spot any basic errors – information you missed out; clumsy phrasing; imprecise vocabulary; basic spellings; lack of punctuation.

2 If you are not going to complete the test in timed conditions, it would be useful to make some notes for what you would say in response to each question. You will then find the Examiners' comments on a student script more relevant.

3 How would you go about finding about how much a reader had picked up from reading a text? What questions would you ask about:
  • the content of the text
  • the written style
  • the use of layout?
Make a list of the types of questions you would ask and, in note form, the kinds of answers you would expect.

Follow-up
  • To learn more about reading texts for information, see 'Advanced Reading Skills' on pages 91–94.
  • For more on the format of information leaflets, see 'Writing to Inform' on page 104.

One Student's Response

Meat – Britain's Favourite / Easy Ways to Eat More Fruit and Vegetables

Always use quotation marks when you copy from a text and copy out the whole sentence.

1. I think that the sentence that I think is designed to inform people about meat is. ...protein for strong, healthy growth and body building, etc. I think this because it is telling people about what meat can do for them.

You need to say more about your choice.

2. I think that the sentence which is trying to persuade the reader to eat meat is. 'Whatever you're looking for, you'll find a meaty meal to suit your taste – and your pocket.' It does not give facts but tries to tempt us by taste and price.

Good answer.

3. I think that the layout of this sheet of paper is quite effective. I looked at it and it immediately caught my eye because of the mixture of information, illustrations and statistics. The headings were bold and there was a good slogan. The language was dramatic it sounded when you were reading it as if the person who was writing it was really excited about meat. I think that the company is doing all the advertising to get more money in. Yet loads of people are vegetarians.

It would be helpful to quote words and phrases from the passage to illustrate the points you make here.

4. I think the sentence that is trying to inform people about eating a more balanced diet is 'Get into the habit of eating two servings of vegetables in addition to potatoes, with your main meal.' I think this because Sainsbury's is actually telling people to eat a more balanced diet to keep up their health.

A good attempt to distinguish between 'inform' and 'persuade'.

5. I think that the sentence which tries to persuade people is 'Look out in store for recipes using fruit and vegetables in the new series of Sainsbury's healthy eating Recipe Cards.' I think this because they have designed this series of recipes to make people use more healthy foods for meals instead of just their usual things

6 I think that this Sainsbury's leaflet is designed to make

Always write comprehension answers in complete sentences.

You need to develop this by quoting more examples and saying something about layout.

more people shop at Sainsbury's because they are trying to make Sainsbury's look as if they care about the lifestyles of people. And their health. A sentence which backs my idea up is,

'Make the most of seasonal produce as it is often the best buy.'

Seasonal produce is also the dearer buy.

<u>Comparing the Texts</u>

7. The two texts differ in a lot of ways. I can see this by just looking at both of them and reading the first line. The Meat - Britain's Favourite leaflet I think is more effective because of the catchy language and slogans which are used. This gives more information about meat rather than where you can buy it and why because people know that when they read something like that like Sainsbury's did they immediately think that the shop is in no way interested in the shoppers' needs. Also the layout of the meat advertisement is much more catchy and confident than the healthy eating one which makes people also pay more attention to the meat advertisement. The pictures also make a better impression. There is no slogan on the vegetable leaflet and that makes it quite boring.

Unclear.

You need to say why it is so. Again it would be helpful to quote words and phrases.

You need to say more about Text B.

- You have made a good attempt to understand and compare and contrast the texts. Your vocabulary is not always precise enough.
- Some answers need more <u>details</u> (2, 6, & 7).
- Try to include words and phrases from the text to illustrate points you are making (3 & 7) even if you are <u>not</u> asked directly to do so as in 6.
- When you copy directly from a text always place the word(s) in quotations marks (2, 4, & 5).
- Always answer comprehension questions in <u>complete sentences</u> (6).

Language Grade D+ 17/36

Follow-up
- To learn more about reading texts for information, see 'Advanced Reading Skills' on pages 91–94.
- For more on the format of information leaflets, see 'Writing to Inform' on page 104.

Writing to Inform: Presenting Information

Objectives:

- to examine different ways of presenting factual information
- to examine an informative leaflet produced by a Year 11 student

Infomania!

We are surrounded by information – road signs, leaflets, posters, newspapers, television. All of these give us information in different ways at different times.

An increasingly popular GCSE task is to ask students to read some information and then to re-present it in another form for a different audience. To do this successfully you need to follow this process:

Read the information
- What are the main points?
- Who is it aimed at?

Look at the task
- Who is the audience (adult, child, teenager, person with particular interest, etc.)?
- What is the purpose (purely to inform/educate or also to entertain)?
- What is the required tone (serious, chatty, lively, solemn)?

Planning
- Which parts of the information will you need?
- What format should you use?

Drafting
- Quick sketch of layout

Writing
- Pay attention to audience, purpose, and style
- Use a variety of words and sentence types

Which format?

One of your key decisions will be which format or type of presentation to use. Usually you will be told to produce a leaflet, newspaper report, or formal letter. Each of these formats is featured in a spread in this section of the book, so that you can study their different requirements and conventions.

Activity

This task was set in a recent GCSE exam:

> 'Your school is taking part in a local Health Awareness campaign. Write a leaflet to be given out at the next Parents' Meeting. Your leaflet should be directed at one of the parents or guardians and should aim to persuade them to become fit. Give the readers reasons why they should become fit; ways of making time; sports or pastimes that would suit them specifically. Try to predict any arguments that they might have against exercise.'

How would you set about this activity?
- Who is the audience?
- What is the purpose?
- What tone would be appropriate?

Students were provided with the following information.

PRACTICAL WRITING

Fit for what?

People talk about 'being fit'... but fit for what? You don't have to be an athlete to be fit. Your fitness level should be in tune with your lifestyle. You should have plenty of energy to climb stairs or take a brisk walk, as well as performing other day to day activities without becoming tired or gasping for breath.

Being fit not only makes you look and feel better, it has many pay-offs for your health. It strengthens your heart and improves your circulation. It can also help lower your blood pressure and blood cholesterol levels, control your weight, and reduce your stress levels, all of which reduce your risk of suffering from serious illnesses such as heart disease.

How can I get fit?

All round fitness should include the three 's' factors. First, *stamina* which helps keep your heart and lungs healthy, muscular *strength* and *'stretchability'* to keep you supple and mobile. If you want to be collecting your old age pension in a tracksuit and training shoes, the time to start is today.

Exercise

All exercise is good for your body, but the best exercises for your heart are exercises which build your stamina. Stamina building exercise is any exercise where you exert yourself continuously over a period of time. This could be a brisk walk or jog, swimming or cycling at a good pace, or an aerobic workout.

A good session of any type of exercise releases pent-up tension. It can be difficult at the end of a long day – but instead of slumping in front of the telly, try a brisk walk, or a swim. You'll be surprised how recharged you feel, how much extra energy you've gained.

The golden rules of exercise are to start gently, to build gradually, and to do it regularly! To be effective, most experts recommend two to three sessions per week of at least 20 minutes each time. Varying your activity helps keep you motivated and makes exercise more fun; so why not look in at your local sports centre or fitness club? Staff there are trained to help you develop a fitness programme which will suit your ability.

Sport

'I'd love to try a new sport, but I don't have the time'

It's a common complaint and there's only one solution – make time. You should aim to make exercise an enjoyable 'habit' so that it becomes a regular part of your life – just like cleaning your teeth. You'll soon find yourself with new-found energy which will enable you to achieve things more quickly and efficiently – in effect making more time for yourself. Joining a class or taking up a sport with a friend means you can encourage each other and adds extra enjoyment.

Activities you may not have considered like golf, sailing, windsurfing, tennis, pony trekking, canoeing, bowls, and archery are available all over the country. The Sports Council (address overleaf) can give you more details about any new sport you would like to get involved with. Or if these sound too exotic perhaps you should think about activities, like walking, swimming, or cycling, in a new light.

There's something for all the family, whatever age, or stage of fitness.

Tips about exercise & a caution

1. Try to sneak some exercise into your daily routine. Why not get off the bus a few stops early and walk the rest? Use the stairs instead of the lift and for short trips leave the car in the garage and enjoy the stroll.

2. Remember to start slowly and build gradually.

3. Exercise until pleasantly tired, but don't push to exhaustion. The right level will leave you breathless but not speechless.

4. Always warm-up to prepare your muscles before exercising and include some gentle stretches.

5. 'Wind down' your exercise session, don't stop suddenly following vigorous exercise. Slow the pace of your activity to a comfortable level for a few minutes at the end of your session.

6. Leave an hour after heavy meals before starting exercise.

7. Don't ignore pain – it's your body saying 'stop!'

8. Easy, rhythmic movements are best – cycling, swimming, and walking are the best all round forms of exercise.

BUT: You can start exercising at any time of life, but if you've not taken any exercise for some time, are over 40, have recently been ill, or have any joint problems, check with your family doctor before doing anything too strenuous.

Working on   **1** Now read through one Year 11 student's finished version, written in one hour's examination conditions. As you read it, cover up the Examiner's margin notes, so that you can gather your own thoughts.

Make a list of the different ways that this student has chosen to present information through:

- particular words/phrases used
- aspects of layout used

2 Then read through what the GCSE Examiner says.

Informative writing (exam conditions)
"Fit for life"

FIT FOR LIFE
attractive heading

So why should I get fit?

1. Immediate sense of audience and purpose; picture effective in supporting 'fitness for life' approach.

Keeping fit is an essential ingredient for a happy and successful life: it reduces your chances of serious illness such as heart disease and can completely eradicate signs of stress - something we'd all be grateful for!

Picture of a parent and child jogging and enjoying it

2. Good use of vocabulary affecting audience.

Fitness is a natural rejuvenator and helps to reduce weight and blood pressure, so you can see that spending a few hours a week keeping fit is certainly worthwhile - you just keep on reaping the benefits!

TIPS FOR THE TOP

3. Use of bullet points good. Easy to follow and effectively varies style of presentation.

* Begin slowly and build up your exercise gradually
* Allow time to warm up your muscles before you begin - they're probably just as out-of-shape as you are!
* Don't push the exercise too far: pain and sheer exhaustion are your body's way of saying 'no'
* Even if you don't exercise very often to begin with, keep the sessions regular
* Don't exercise straight after meals

4. Developing a suitable tone; humour that does not patronize.

* After a session of vigorous exercising, allow your body time to wind down: after all it's your body that's done the work!

5. Neat juxtaposition of headings creates eye-catching question-and-answer style.

So what sport should I choose?

The most important factor in choosing an activity is to choose one you enjoy: motivation is the key to success, and you certainly won't be motivated if you drag yourself to the sports centre every week.

And don't worry about finding time – once you're fit you will do things so efficiently you'll have plenty of spare time!

Picture of people enjoying a swimming pool

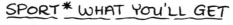

SPORT * WHAT YOU'LL GET

SWIMMING: Stamina, supple limbs

AEROBICS: Stamina, general fitness

WEIGHT TRAINING: Strength, stamina

6. Clear sense of layout. Concise, readable information allowing busy people to absorb it quickly and retain their interest.

YOGA: Supple limbs, flexibility

TENNIS/BADMINTON: Flexibility, stamina

JOGGING: Stamina, general fitness

CYCLING: Stamina, strong limbs

Each sport highlighted in a different colour

Oh, and of course with each sport you'll get fun and breathtaking excitement!

7. Accuracy is essential for a leaflet that is intended to persuade!

* NB To acheive noticeable results, experts recommend spending at least 20 mins per session, about two or three times a week.

HOW TO ACHIEVE ALL-ROUND FITNESS

* Every little bit helps: cycle or walk instead of using the car
* Try relaxing after a hard day by taking an evening stroll
* Encourage your family to keep fit too – if they're doing it too then they'll force you into it!
* Vary the sports you do for all-round benefits

8. Good 'balanced' layout.

Laura

Careful selection of material effectively communicates the importance of fitness for the intended audience. The clear but varied layout both captures and retains the reader's attention and the information is conveyed in a 'user-friendly' manner which is not patronizing, but adopts a pleasingly humorous tone at times.
Apart from the occasional spelling and grammatical error, the presentation is good.
Language grade A

Follow-up
• For more about reading beneath the surface of texts, see 'Advanced Reading Skills' on page 91.
• For more about newspapers/journalism, see 'Writing Journalism' on page 116.

Conventions of Letters

Is it a Letter?

Dear Rhoda

AT THAT AWKWARD AGE

Dear Rhoda, My teenage son has written to say that he's coming home from boarding school this summer and bringing two friends with him. If only he'd asked! We've our own friends straying and the only way we can put Luke's friends up (or rather down!) is in the cellar. It's warm and dry and we've plenty of camp beds etc. but it does smell musty – which worries me.

If I as much as mention it to Luke, he'll go 'boring, boring' and they'll all take off to Greece or somewhere. I'm only concerned because I care. What do you suggest?

I suggest you stop worrying... because the solution to your problem lies not in arguments with your son, but in your nearest good chemist or supermarket!

It's Neutradol Room Deodorizer. The most effective product of its kind on the market – so efficient, in fact, that it will absorb and destroy all stale smells in the cellar, all summer long.

One single Neutradol gel will keep on working for up to 90 days, keeping the air down there smelling fresh with all trace of mustiness gone. Your odour problem is over. Now all you've got to worry about is three strapping lads to feed on top of all the other guests!

Activity When is a letter not a letter...? Read this letter and its answer carefully. What do you make of it?

When you began to read this letter to Rhoda, you probably thought it was a letter to a magazine problem page. When did you realize that it was a fake? What clues made it seem like a genuine letter, and at which exact point could you tell that it was an advertisement?

Letters, in other words, are not always what they seem.

Conventions

Some GCSE students worry about being asked to write letters because they cannot remember the conventions or rules of layout. This unit gives you a checklist of conventions. But equally important is getting your style and tone right.

In writing a letter, your first decision has to be: who am I writing to? There are two general types of audience:

- formal: someone you do not know well
- personal: someone you do know well

Formal letters
Formal letters are likely to be used when...
- you are applying for a job
- you are asking for information
- you are writing to complain
- writing to a newspaper letters page

Example:

Write the date in full – e.g. January 1st, 1995 – not 1/1/95.

If you use punctuation in the addresses and date, be consistent – comma at the end of each line until the last one.

Sincerely and faithfully have small first letters when following Yours. Watch the spelling of sincerely.

your street name
your town
your postcode

today's date in full

the addressee's name
the addressee's title/position
the addressee's company
address – street
address – town
address – postcode

Dear Mr or Ms Surname
or Dear Sir/Madam   *(if the name is not known)*

Subject of letter
I am writing to you...
Your letter – formal style

Yours sincerely   *(if you know their name)*
Yours faithfully   *(if you wrote Dear Sir)*

Your name, legibly.

Personal letters
At GCSE a personal letter will be appropriate when...
- you are asked to imagine you are a character in a book
- writing to a friend
- you are asked to write to a friend asking advice/giving your opinion
- writing a letter of thanks to a relative

Example:

Some of these elements will vary according to who you are addressing. For some letters – probably very informal ones – you will just put the day rather than the date. You may not need to include your full address when writing to a close friend.

If in doubt, when working on a GCSE assignment, use the formal layout as shown here, keeping punctuation consistent.

your street name,
your town,
your postcode.

today's date.

Dear first name,
Your letter – informal style

Best wishes,
or All the best,

Your first name, legibly.

Follow-up
- For more information on formal and informal speech, see 'Formal v Informal Speech' on page 56.

Creative Writing

Objectives:

- to consider some ways of improving your creative writing
- to experiment with techniques of 'telling and showing'

Narrative Notes

Whichever syllabus you follow, English at GCSE requires some element of creative writing. This might be phrased as:

narrative writing   personal writing
descriptive writing   original writing

In narrative writing, the National Curriculum says students should:
- draw on their experience of good fiction
- develop their use of techniques
- use their knowledge of story structure, description of settings, organization of plot, and means of conveying characters and relationships

So how do you write a good story? Here is the advice of some successful writers:

> It's the writing that teaches you. It's the rotten stories that make it possible for you to write the good stories eventually.
> *Isaac Asimov*

> Nothing you write, if you hope to be any good, will ever come out as you first hoped.
> *Lillian Hellman*

> It helps to read the sentence aloud.
> *Harry Kemelman*

> When you catch an adjective, kill it.
> *Mark Twain*

> Get black on white.
> *Guy de Maupassant*

Activity

To write well, you have to be ruthless with your own work. The best writers are rarely satisfied with what they have written. Also, you need to practise: you will only write well by writing often.

As a way of developing your ideas about writing narratives, read this short extract from Year 10 student, Martin's opening to a detective story, which was written as a GCSE assignment. Then use the suggestions which follow to see how it could be improved.

> The yacht bobbed gently, the white-crested waves monotonously beating against the bow. The rudder sat idly, lichen encrusting itself upon it. A passing catfish swam close and then quickly scurried away into the depths below. From within the cabin came a faint ticking, all view of the yacht's interior obscured by rays of refracting light on the glass panes.

The arm hung loosely over the wooden rail. The fingers were of a bluish complexion and the nails which had become a foul yellow channelled the glistening liquid to their edges, from which after gathering into tiny droplets, it fell to an already stained floor in what seemed like an eternity.

***

The headlights barely distinguished the battered white posts which marked the entrance, through the cascading rain which had plagued the region for the past week. The driver's gloved hands methodically turned the steering wheel as chords of Chuck Berry passed by barely noticed...

Martin

The following five suggestions may help you improve the quality of your narratives.

1 Work hardest at your first paragraphs

> People say that I write quite simply, but they don't realize how much I rewrite. I rewrite a lot. I would rewrite the opening two or three pages maybe forty, fifty times until I had that sense that it was right. Then it's easy for me, because I set the tone by doing that.
>
> *Brian Moore*

Using a scale of 1 to 5 (top), how successful is Martin's narrative in:
* grabbing your attention?
* making you want to read on?
* conjuring up a real place with real people?

2 Make the reader work

We keep reading a story because we are interested in the characters, in what will happen next, because we want to find the answers to questions. In writing narratives, pose questions but hold back the answers. Notice how just when we realize that someone's arm is hanging over the boat's rail, the narrative shifts, leaving us wondering what is happening.

In Martin's narrative, what questions are posed? Complete this list of questions:

Whose yacht is this? Where are we? Whose arm is that?...

3 Aim for showing, not telling

Martin's narrative *shows* us objects very visually, but it avoids *telling* us the story at one go. If the narrative were rewritten with more telling than showing, it would read like this:

> A murder had been committed on the yacht which now bobbed gently in the harbour...

Notice how much of the suspense is removed from the story, how our key question is lost.

Look at this further example:

Showing

As she walked towards the house, the girl noticed that the door was opening. The forest was getting darker and the bright lights of the house looked inviting. She walked towards it, stopping behind a tree to see if she could hear voices. She couldn't. She moved closer.

Telling

Once upon a time a girl called Goldilocks was walking through a forest when she came across the brightly-lit house belonging to the Three Bears...

There are times when telling is more suitable than showing. What are the advantages and disadvantages of each style of storytelling?

4 Focus on detail

Detail is not mere 'padding': it can show us important information about characters. For example:

Bald version

Susan, who worked in a newspaper office, was very disorganized.

Detail

As she sat down at her desk, Susan heaped a pile of cuttings and memos onto the top of her in-tray. She hunted for a biro she thought she had seen earlier in the day.

The second version doesn't use fancy vocabulary; it doesn't try to be flashy. But it makes the reader work harder, *showing* us that Susan is disorganized rather than *telling* us. The result is that reading the narrative becomes more active and interesting.

Practise using detail to show character by writing a paragraph based on this bald sentence:

> The woman behind the counter was old and bad-tempered.

5 Do not overwrite

There is a danger in all creative writing to try too hard. Then the text becomes top-heavy with description, every noun accompanied by an adjective ('the pale sky') and every verb accompanied by an adverb ('she ate noisily'). Taken to extremes, writers rely on Thesauruses and come up with sentences like this (taken from a GCSE assignment):

> Then the prodigious obfuscate pervaded the empyrean
> and it began to rain.

This is someone suffering from a severe case of 'Thesauritis' – excessive use of the Thesaurus. The writer actually means:

> Then a large cloud filled the sky and it started to rain.

The foreboding crepuscular light of evening descended with splendiferous magnificence.

Look again at Martin's narrative. Would you agree that in places it is overwritten? What words would you remove to improve the narrative? Which sentences would you rephrase? Be ruthless in suggesting alterations to this first draft.

Working on

Now put these ideas into practice and write your own narrative. Here is a suggested starting point:

> As I closed the door behind me, I knew that life could
> never be the same again.

What will your story be about? What has just happened? Where is the door? Have you left someone? Argued? Broken up? Fought? Given bad news to them?

Spend some time thinking up ideas, and then write the opening of a narrative, paying attention to the five techniques listed in this spread.

Follow-up
- For an Examiner's comments on a piece of creative writing, see the end of this section.
- To look at other narrative techniques, see 'Writing Dialogue' on page 114.
- For more about creating tension, see the opening of Brian Moore's novel *Cold Heaven*, which is featured in 'Building Tension' on page 158.

Writing Dialogue

Talk, Talk, Talk

When you are writing a narrative assignment, or a report of a real experience, there are a number of different modes of writing open to you: **plot**, **description/detail** or **dialogue**.

Spend too much time on any of these and the assignment becomes unbalanced.

Too much plot...
We don't believe in the story because we haven't got to know the characters or setting; or it moves too quickly for us to feel any involvement.

Too much detail...
We get restless and want the storyline to pick up speed.

Too much dialogue...
We find characters saying things that simply don't add anything to the story or to our understanding of them as characters.

There is a danger that you see dialogue as an easy way of filling space. Here, for example, is what one Year 11 student wrote in the middle section of a work experience report:

> The door suddenly opened and in walked Mr Seaton.
> 'Hello, Gemma,' said Mr Seaton.
> 'Hello, Mr Seaton,' I replied nervously.
> 'How are you enjoying working with us?' he asked.
> 'Oh, I'm really enjoying it,' I said.
> 'That's good,' he said.
> 'Yes,' I said.
> 'Any problems at all?' he asked.
> I thought for a minute. 'No,' I said.
> 'Okay, then, but let me know if there are,' he said.
> 'Thanks very much, Mr Seaton,' I said, and he left the room.

Activity

1 What are the problems with this as an extract from an assignment? Comment upon:
   - interest level
   - use of words like *said* and *replied*
   - what the dialogue adds to our understanding of
     a storyline
     b characters
   - how you would suggest the writer improves it

Probably the best rule for dialogue is: when in doubt, leave it out. Only include extracts of dialogue when they will serve a purpose.

2 Use the prompts after the extract on page 115 to study how different writers use dialogue to vary the pace of their stories.

   In this extract, two boys think they are in a barn that is haunted.

The Levels

A pane of glass, loose in its frame, clinked in the room, the cold burning through our boots from the flags. I flicked my hood off, Dick did the same, we looked at each other.

'Colder in here than it is out,' he said, rubbing his hair and poking at a cupboard door.

'But it's not raining.'

I rubbed one of the windows, and peered at the rain, the sky, a huge shadow in itself.

'Dark soon,' I said.

'So what are we going to do?'

'What do you want to do?'

'Don't know.'

'We shouldn't be here.'

'Why not?'

'Well...'

Bang, the window in the room behind us banged shut, again.

'We should go,' I said.

'You're scared.'

'I'm not.'

'Then I'm looking around.'

'Oh.'

'You go back outside, if you want.'

I wasn't used to the planning taken from my control...

Peter Benson

- How does Peter Benson use dialogue to convey the boys' fear?
- How does the dialogue add to the tension?
- What does it show about the boys' characters and their relationship?

Notice that you do not need to label the speakers with *she said* or *he replied* all the time. Make the reader work harder at following who's speaking.

Notice also how effective it can be to start a narrative with unexpected dialogue:

> 'Everything is normal,' the doctor was saying. 'Just lie back and relax.' His voice was miles away in the distance and he seemed to be shouting at her. 'You have a son.'
> 'What?'
>
> *Genesis and Catastrophe, Roald Dahl*

The effect is to grab the reader's attention by throwing us straight into the middle of the action.

Working on Take the dialogue given at the start of this spread and rewrite in the form of an attention-grabbing narrative. Make sure that it contains the three elements: plot – description – dialogue. Imagine that Mr Seaton has walked into the room as Gemma is rifling through some papers in the filing cabinet, trying to find out more about the company's animal-testing programme...

Follow-up
- To look at the presentation of dialogue in drama texts, see 'Reading Drama' on page 154.
- To look at the way speech and writing differ, see 'Speech v Writing' on page 66.

Writing Journalism

Objectives:

- to examine the language of newspaper journalism
- to practise using journalistic techniques

Day by Day

The words *journalism* and *journalist* come from the Latin word *diurnalis* meaning 'daily'. Journalism, as its language roots suggest, is a form of writing written under pressure to meet deadlines. Frequently English examinations require you to produce a newspaper front page or article, and you will experience a similar sense of pressure to produce copy fast.

> Journalism is literature in a hurry.
> *Matthew Arnold*

Remember that there are two main types of newspapers in Britain – tabloids (popular papers) and broadsheets (the quality press).

Tabloids	Broadsheets
• smaller in size	• large format
• aimed at a mass audience	• aimed at educated readership
• mix news with entertainment, gossip, showbiz	• report news in greater depth and at greater length
• style is lively, snappy, full of puns (word-play)	• emphasis on analysis and comment by columnists
• examples: *The Sun, The Mirror, The Star, The Express, The Daily Mail, Today*	• examples: *The Times, The Guardian, The Independent, The Daily Telegraph*

crónica , diario popular   Lz Necion

Activity

1 What do you think a newspaper should contain? Use these prompts to sort out your ideas, listing the most to least important:

2 • business news
7 • cartoons
8 • celebrity profiles
6 • diary/gossip column
10 • horoscopes
1 • news
5 • opinion
4 • columns
3 • sport
9 • TV listings

2 What do you think should be the ratio of news to features? (50:50? 70:30?)

3 To give you a better feeling of the style of the two types of newspapers, read these extracts.

In November 1994, the National Lottery was launched in Britain. For a few weeks it seemed to dominate the media. But look how the emphasis of the tabloids and broadsheets differs, just as their language does. Compare the opening paragraphs of two Lottery stories published on the same day.

7 agresivo (handwritten)

viejo (handwritten)

colloquially = slang = idioma cultó (handwritten)

By JOHN ASKILL
and LENNY LOTTERY

OLD soldier Fred Baker rubbed his Lottery ticket on *The Sun's* Hand of Wad – and scooped £1.7million.
He stroked the entries for his old folk's syndicate across the palm of last week's winner Ken Pilton, printed on Saturday's Page One.
Then he watched stunned as **ALL SIX** numbers in one of the eight lines came up.
Fred, 64 – a *Sun* reader for 25 years – said yesterday: "I couldn't believe what I was doing as I stroked Ken's hand.
"I kept thinking, 'You are a silly b****r, – you must be mad.'
"But I did it, and I am convinced it brought me my luck.
"I've followed Lenny Lottery every day in *The Sun* – it's my paper.

When I saw the Hand of Wad, I thought, 'In for a penny, in for a pound.'

Fantastic

"I was smiling, but I thought 'Let's go for it.' There was nothing to lose."
Fred, a former state trumpeter in The Life Guards cavalry, shares the £1,760,966 jackpot with seven women neighbours.
All live in an old folk's flats complex in Newport Pagnell, Bucks. Each will collect £220,120.
Fred said: "Last week, we managed two winning numbers between the eight of us. This time seven of our entries had three numbers between them – except for the winning line. It's absolutely fantastic."

Wand = cacho de gusto (handwritten)

The HAND of good fortune reached out to embrace Camelot, the National Lottery's organizers at the weekend, with four pay-outs of £1.75 million. After the failure of the first week's draw to create a lottery millionaire, Camelot officials breathed a sigh of relief as the £7 million jackpot was shared between four winners. Camelot said claims for the four jackpot prizes of £1,760,966 would be verified today. A further 10 people are set to receive £216,734 each. A last-minute surge on Saturday brought sales for the second draw to £47.9 million, a drop of just £1 million on the first week. The prize pool of £21.5 million was £500,000 less.

Compare the two stories in terms of their...
• **purpose** (to entertain, persuade, inform? How can you tell?)
• **tone** (serious, comic, concerned, neutral?)
• **typical words** (pick out 3 from each paper)
• **layout** (how do they differ in use of text, subheadings, etc?)
• **labels for people** (use of occupations, characteristics, and age)
Then write your notes up as a brief comparison of the two stories.
4 Finally choose a newspaper story from a broadsheet newspaper and have a go at writing it in the style of a tabloid paper.

Follow-up
• To look more closely at the language of different reporting styles, see 'Non-fiction: Reportage' on page 74.
• To look at the way language changes in different contexts, see 'Formal v Informal Speech' on page 56.

Discursive Assignments

Objectives:
- to examine the requirements of discursive assignments at GCSE
- to look at ways of writing lively and persuasive assignments

For and Against

Many students at GCSE find discursive assignments the most difficult of all the written tasks they are set. Why?

A discursive assignment asks you to debate a particular question, giving evidence for and against. Some discursive assignments set in the past include:
- Consider the ways in which human beings use animals. Are all of these uses justified?
- 'The requirement that pupils should wear school uniform is both expensive and unnecessary'. Do you agree?
- 'Capital punishment is the only way in which crime in Britain will be brought under control'. Discuss.

All of these questions are expecting you to weigh up the arguments on both sides of the issue, and the result can be that assignments feel too much of a formula, as this skeleton plan suggests:

Consider the ways in which human beings use animals. Are all of these uses justified?

Intro: say which topics I will look at
say that I will give my personal opinion in the conclusion

1 bloodsports
arguments for
arguments against

2 factory farming
arguments for
arguments against

3 pets
arguments for
arguments against

4 animals serving humans – e.g. guide dogs, police horses, etc.
arguments for
arguments against

Conclusion:
my opinion
which uses are fair; which aren't, and say why

The advantage of an essay structure like this is that it is very clear. The danger is that it might feel rather mechanical when written. What can you do then to breathe life into discursive assignments?

Advice

1 Know your audience

Who is the assignment aimed at? If you are addressing an impersonal marker or teacher, then perhaps an impersonal, formal style is called for. But if you are given a specific audience – and you frequently are at GCSE – then you can alter your style accordingly.

For example, a discursive assignment which asks you to target a specific audience might say:

> 'Imagine you are required to persuade a group of factory farmers that their methods of production are inhumane. Write a speech to change their views.'

This is still not an 'easy' assignment, but you can probably feel that it would allow you to write more creatively. It also limits the number of topics you have to refer to – just factory farming, rather than several possible uses of animals by humans.

2 Balance facts and opinion

To write a successful discursive assignment, you really need to do some research. In examination conditions, you may be provided with information. If so, pick out the main evidence to support both sides of the argument. If you are producing a coursework assignment, try to get information from pressure groups (charities and political groups concerned with the issue you are writing about); refer to books; reference books like the *Hutchinson Gallup* annual books of facts, statistics, and trends can provide invaluable data.

3 Do not be afraid to be lively

Your examiner or teacher may have to mark dozens of discursive assignments on the same topic. Keep yours lively, with:
- a variety of sentence styles
- use of questions, statistics, quotations, and opinions to vary the tone
- use of humour if it is appropriate

4 Do not leave your point of view to the conclusion

It can be very artificial to read an assignment in which the real argument is left until the final paragraph. Include your opinion within each paragraph: state the facts for and against and then include your ideas. You do not need to say 'I think...' or 'I believe...' each time: simply stating 'This is not true' can feel much more powerful.

5 Question whether you need an introduction

In examination conditions particularly, introductions can simply waste time, especially if they read like this one:

> *Factory farming is a very controversial topic and people have strong views about it. In this assignment I am going to look in more detail at the arguments for factory farming and the arguments against. Then, at the end of my assignment, I will give my own opinion on the topic.*

This gets the assignment off to a very slow start. It could well be better to start with a topic sentence which leads into the main arguments for or against the issue, like this next one.

> *It sometimes seems as if everyone has a view on factory farming. The farmers themselves, of course, would argue that without it we simply could not feed our population. But what exactly is factory farming...?*

This has a much snappier start, and would continue by defining factory farming and giving both points of view, including the writer's.

6 Use discourse markers to hold your assignment together

A discursive assignment can feel very disjointed because of the way it ranges between different viewpoints. One way to make it feel more coherent is to use discourse markers like these:

- on the other hand
- however
- therefore
- even so
- it might also be argued
- then

Activity   Read this discursive essay, taken from *Hutchinson Gallup Info 92*. Then think about how successful it is by using the prompts which follow.

WHY CAN'T WE FEED THE WORLD?

Throughout the 1980s and 1990s, images of famine and starvation have flashed across our television screens in appeal after appeal for relief aid and money. At the same time, we hear of vast surpluses within the European Community, with butter and grain mountains, and wine and milk lakes. Surely something is going very wrong? Why can't we feed the world?

During the 1960s and 1970s, there was a rapid intensification of agriculture in many Third World countries, with the introduction of more productive crop strains, although these needed large inputs of artificial pesticides and fertilizers. This 'green revolution' led to increased productivity, but only for those farmers rich enough to buy the expensive new seeds and agrochemicals. Smaller farmers were doubly disadvantaged: unable to buy into the new agriculture, they also saw the price of their products fall as productivity increased elsewhere. Many were forced off the land, which was then concentrated into the hands of large landowners. The extra food was, in many cases, sold for export rather than circulating within the country.

This illustrates two major reasons for world hunger. In most Third World countries, almost all the productive land is owned by a tiny proportion of the population. And much of this land is used to produce luxury export crops, such as tea, coffee, cocoa, bananas, tobacco, and animal feeds, rather than producing the food needed within the country. In recent years, the drive to produce export crops has been given a new urgency by the enormous foreign debts that most Third World countries have accumulated, largely as a result of changes in international interest rates.

This is by no means the whole story, of course. In many countries there are still enormous problems in transporting food to areas where it is needed. Poor or non-existent roads meant that the famines in several East African countries continued despite there being a surplus elsewhere. Ethiopia continued to export grain throughout the worst of the famines in the 1980s.

There are wider environmental issues as well. Some agriculture innovations have done more harm than good, such as the poorly designed irrigation schemes that are causing soil to become contaminated with salt water in parts of Africa, and forcing farmers to abandon the land and move on. Deforestation is causing soil erosion, floods and local changes in weather patterns. Climate change on a larger scale, including global warming caused by air pollution, may be a factor in the rapid increase in desert land in some areas.

This means that simple food aid doesn't help in the long term, if at all. Sending free grain, for example, can simply depress the price of locally produced food, forcing farmers out of business and acting against the interest of permanent agricultural stability. Donated food has often been stolen and sold by corrupt officials. However, the real reasons for Third World hunger are far more difficult to tackle. Land reform movements have, as yet, had little success in many countries. Efforts to write off or defer repayments on huge national debts are blocked by the creditor countries. Building up an adequate infrastructure of roads and other transport systems is difficult, time consuming, and costly. Birth control is a sensitive issue both in many aid-donor countries and in poor countries. The large fluctuations in climate experienced over the last few years add a new uncertainty to the famine problem. But it is certain that something more than aid is going to be required.

- Look again at the opening paragraph. How well does the writer introduce the topic? What do you notice about the variety of sentences he uses?
- Pick out some of the discourse markers the writer uses to establish connections through the essay.
- How readable is the essay? How factual is it? Which parts are most/least interesting?

Working on

Now write your own discursive essay, practising some of the techniques presented in this unit. Choose your own topic, or use one of the starting-points given in 'Writing a Speech' on page 52. Use your essay to discuss and weigh up both sides of an article.

Remember to:

- research source materials (leaflets, articles, encyclopedias), so that you are using facts as well as your own ideas
- make a skeleton plan of the overall essay
- write a snappy, attention-grabbing first paragraph
- use quotations, facts, opinions, bullet-points to convey information
- give your own opinion without constantly stating 'I think' or 'I believe'

Follow-up

- To look at how to respond to data and statistics in examinations, see 'Examining Data' on page 98.
- For advice on spotting a writer's opinion, see 'Fact v Opinion' on page 95.
- To remind yourself of how varied sentence styles can improve your written work, refer to the units on sentences in Section 1: Language Skills.

Drafting Skills

Take Two

Sometimes GCSE students confuse redrafting with proof-reading. To proof-read a text means to look for printing errors – missing punctuation marks, spelling errors, gaps, and so on. Whilst that is an important part of improving an assignment overall, redrafting is a much more creative process because it involves reorganizing the whole shape of the text.

Here is how radical redrafting can improve your work. First look at this first draft of a section from a GCSE assignment written by James, a Year 11 student. Then look at the decisions he makes about what to change, cut, and develop. Then compare the second draft with the first.

First draft

Trace Macbeth's descent from victor to villain

At the beginning of the play Macbeth is respected by many people because of the good deeds he does. This is shown by 'O valiant cousin! Worthy gentleman' (Act 2, scene 2, line 24). Macbeth at the start of the play is bloodthirsty and brutal but in a good way. He is also known as being brave. This is shown by being heroic to his country - 'for brave Macbeth (well he deserves that name)' (Act1, scene 2, line 16). Also it is shown that when Macbeth does something good he is greatly rewarded for it. This is shown by 'What he hath lost, noble Macbeth hath won' (Act 1, scene 2, line 70).

James writes:

I wasn't at all happy with this. It didn't get the reader's attention - it felt boring. I discussed it with my English teacher who said she thought it jumped too quickly from one idea to the next and felt more like a set of notes than an essay. She also advised me to integrate quotations, so that the essay style felt less disjointed. I was also worried that the vocabulary seemed really obvious.

Second draft

Trace Macbeth's descent from victor to villain

At the beginning of the play Macbeth is respected by many people because of the heroic way in which he has fought, unseeming his enemies 'from the nave to the chops'. This blood-thirsty image gives us an early hint about why Macbeth is so highly regarded: he is prepared to be thoroughly ruthless in battle. We will see this quality again at the end of the play, when he has nothing left to fight for or defend and yet he rejects the idea of submitting. In this early part of the play, the respect of others is shown in their praise for Macbeth's actions, commenting 'O valiant cousin! Worthy gentleman' (Act 2, scene 2, line 24) and referring to him as 'brave Macbeth'. Also we see that when Macbeth does something honourable he is greatly rewarded for it: the title Thane of Cawdor moves from the shoulders of the executed traitor to Macbeth himself: 'What he hath lost, noble Macbeth hath won'.

Activity

1 Make a list of the ways James has changed his first draft – in terms of vocabulary, structure, and style. What has been improved? Has anything been lost? How could he further improve his essay style?

2 Look at this first draft of Susan's autobiographical assignment. What would you change in a second draft? Look at:
- amount of detail
- overall structure
- use of dialogue
- vocabulary
- sentence types

3 Write a redrafted version of this opening section – keeping the basic content the same, but injecting more life into the account.

It was around four o'clock on a chilly Friday afternoon and my mum was upstairs and my brother and me were playing pool in the garage. I heard the screech of brakes from outside. It was my dad coming home from work. "I have a surprise for you two," he said and he went into the kitchen and my mum was in there waiting. I thought he might have bought a new bike for me or something but it wasn't, it was some tickets for a holiday to Majorca for two weeks. At first I was quite surprised and I could not believe that we were going on holiday, so I said "When will we be going?" I couldn't believe it when he said two hours, I thought it would be four weeks. No wonder mum had been busy upstairs.

Follow-up
- To look at hints on writing literature coursework, see 'Planning Coursework' on page 189.
- To look at the way writers build tension in narratives, see 'Building Tension' on page 158.

Note-making

Objectives:

- to examine the skills involved in making successful notes
- to compare the notes made by two students

Take Note!

What is the difference between making notes and taking notes?

If you are asked to *make* notes, it usually means that you are given a text and asked to summarize its main points.

If you are asked to take notes, it usually means writing down a summary as something is read aloud or spoken.

All of us develop our own preferred way of noting information, but the important thing is to **organize** your ideas.

Activity Look at this extract of text about the writer John Steinbeck, author of *Of Mice and Men*. A GCSE class was asked to read the information and to make notes. What are the strengths and weaknesses of each set of notes on page 125?

Which notes:
a best capture the essential ingredients?
b are easiest to follow?
c use layout most successfully?

Steinbeck, John Ernst (1902–68) *US novelist whose work achieved*  *both popularity and critical acclaim. He was awarded a Pulitzer Prize (1940) and the Nobel Prize for Literature (1962).*
Steinbeck was born in Salinas, California, which provided the setting for many of his books. After studying marine biology at Stanford University, he attempted to earn a living as a journalist in New York, before returning to his native state. His first novel was *Cup of Gold* (1929), a romanticized adventure story, and neither it nor the two following books, *The Pastures of Heaven* (1932) and *To a God Unknown* (1933), attracted much attention. However, *Tortilla Flat* (1935), which described with affection and whimsy the lives of the California 'paisanos', became a best-seller; it established a successful formula that Steinbeck was to repeat in later years, as in *Cannery Row* (1945) and *Sweet Thursday* 1954). A change of tone was apparent in *In Dubious Battle* (1936) and in his best-known novels – *Of Mice and Men* (1937; filmed 1939) and *The Grapes of Wrath* (1939; filmed 1940). These novels combined an ease of style, to ensure a popular market, with serious social comment. Subsequent works include *Sea of Cortez* (1941), the non-fiction *Bombs Away* (1942) and *Once There Was a War* (1958), the short story *The Red Pony* (1945), *The Pearl* (1947), and the highly successful *East of Eden* (1952; filmed 1955).

A

Steinbeck, John Ernst

Life
(1902-68) Born in Salinas, California
Settings of his books

Studied Marine Biology – Stanford Uni got a Nobel
prize for Lit – + Pulitzer prize
Earnt living as Journalist in New York

Novels
1st book – Cup of Gold – (1929) not popular
2+3 – Pastures of Heaven, To a God Unknown, not pop.
Tortilla Flat – best seller

Good books
Tortilla flat (35)
Cannery row (45)
Sweet Thursday (54)
Dubious Battle (36)

Best known novel Of Mice and Men (37) filmed
The Grapes of Wrath (39)

"Sea of Cortez" (61)
"Bombs away" (42)
"Once there was a war (58)
Short story "The red pony" (45)
The pearl (47)
East of Eden (52) highly successful

B

JOHN ERNST STEINBECK

1902-68

PULITZER PRIZE (1940)
NOBEL PRIZE – LIT 1962

LIFE
NOVELIST USA
BORN CALIFORNIA
SETTING BOOK
MARINE BIOLOGY
STANFORD
NEW YORK – JOURNALIST

NOVELS	YEAR
CUP OF GOLD	1929 – romantic adventure
PASTURES OF HEAVEN	1932 ⎫ not much
TO A GOD UNKNOWN	1933 ⎬ attention
TORTILLA FLAT 'PAISANOS'	1935 – best seller
CANNERY ROW	1945
SWEET THURSDAY	1954
OF MICE AND MEN	⸱1937 ⎫ filmed
GRAPES OF WRATH	1939 ⎬ best sellers

Hints

What could you do to improve your note-making skills?
- Decide who the notes are for – you, friends, teachers, examiners?
- For yourself you might use more shorthand forms and pay less attention to overall presentation.
- Organize the information using headings: this helps you to sift what is essential and what is dispensable.
- Use bullet points rather than sentences to list key points: full sentences can waste time, especially when note-taking.
- If your notes will form the basis of an essay, number the paragraphs so that you have the order clear before you start writing the essay.
- Cross your notes through once if they feature at the start of an examination answer.

Listen to This

Taking notes when someone else is talking is a difficult business. Here's what two Year 10 students said about it:

> In History we have to take a lot of notes. The teacher talks about the subject and we have to get down the main points. The problem is, I'm never sure which points are the main ones.

> My problem is more basic than that – I find that as soon as I begin to write my notes I stop hearing what the teacher is saying – then I fall behind and get confused.

Taking notes from lectures and talks is one of the most frequent methods of learning – especially at university level. But it is a technique that has to be learnt.

Hints

It helps if you have a clear idea what the subject of the talk will be, what different topics it will cover, so that you can listen out for new information.

- Remember that you will not be able to copy down everything – it is not a dictation exercise – so just aim to get the important details down.
- It really helps if you see your notes as a first draft, and then go back through them later to sort them out, tidy them up, clarify points that didn't make sense.
- Do not leave it too long to do this – the original talk needs to be fresh in your mind.
- Use different techniques to organize your notes as you make them – underlining, heading boxes, bullet points, arrows to connect related ideas.
- Space notes out so that they are easy to look at when you refer back to them.

Activity Work with a friend to practise your note-taking skills. Ask them to choose an extract from a factual text (e.g. a history book or encyclopedia), and underline in pencil the six most important points. Then get them to read aloud while you practise taking notes. Then refer back to the text to see if you noted the really important points, and to look at how you might have organized your notes better using the hints above.

Follow-up
- For notes on revision, see 'Revision Advice' on page 191.
- For notes on revising your written work, see 'Drafting Skills' on page 122.

Assessing Writing

Grade Criteria

This is a summary of the kind of criteria used to assess your written English. It is a condensed version, but similar to the lists issued by all of the examination boards. Notice that it has two main features:

1 basic writing skills (writing legibly, redrafting, using punctuation, and spelling accurately)
2 style features (controlling plot, suiting language to audience, mixing personal belief with opinions from other sources)

To get the highest GCSE grades, you have to be able to show evidence of success in both areas.

Grade G
The candidate can...
- show signs of redrafting
- spell basic one-syllable words generally correctly

Grade F
The candidate can...
- write legibly for different purposes
- use generally accurate spelling and punctuation
- show some organization and imagination
- show knowledge of written Standard English

Grade E
The candidate can...
- produce independent writing in a variety of forms
- use effective language structures suited to different purposes and audiences
- use non-standard English forms only where appropriate

Grade D
The candidate can...
- show awareness of how a writer's choice of style affects the reader
- present subject-matter differently to suit the needs of specified audiences
- produce well-plotted narratives
- produce impersonal writing which is clearly organized

Grade C
The candidate can...
- show a sense of topic, purpose, and audience
- vary sentence-structure and vocabulary to engage and hold the reader's response
- spell generally accurately
- use punctuation to clarify meanings

Grade B
The candidate can...
- write powerful narrative and personal writing
- write persuasive or discursive pieces which combine personal opinions with beliefs from other sources
- choose forms of writing which are appropriate to purpose

Grade A
The candidate can...
- structure complex written material
- use a wide range of grammar and vocabulary
- use subtlety of tone

Grade A*
The candidate can...
- write with clear control and purpose, with a wide range of syntax, vocabulary, and styles

Examiner's Comments: Imaginative Writing

Being Followed

Here a Year 11 student was set a timed creative assignment: 'Imagine you are being followed'. It was written in 45 minutes, with the first 5 minutes devoted to planning. Examiner's comments have been added in the margins. Initially, cover these up with a sheet of paper, and read the assignment for yourself. What do you like or dislike about this piece? Then see what the Examiner says.

Plan
- *Setting: v cold*
  dark; occasional street lights
  ground covered in snow
  faint snow blizzard
- *been to friend's house*
- *dilemma – can't decide whether to take short cut or not*
- *keep remembering father's words "It's not you I don't trust, it's other people".*

Imagine you are being followed

The essay begins well immediately creating an atmosphere of intrigue.

Another two footsteps and I'd be back in the shadow again. I could scarcely see the next street light but I knew I had to reach it. I could feel the damp snow on the back of my neck as it turned into water and trickled down my back. The words came back as if to haunt

Early use of dialogue intensifies intrigue.

me – "it's not you I don't trust it's other people". My footsteps quickened. I knew I was being followed.
I couldn't hear the snow fall yet watched it glimmer in the light. It seemed to be working against me and I

Affective use of language.

felt each flake as a short stab stinging my face. I passed the familiar vicarage and yet it was no longer recognizable. The small gap in the wall was immediately transformed from my childhood safe haven to a threatening hole. I remembered the words

Develops a sense of threat by careful use of repetition.

"it's other people". I knew I was being followed.
The distant street lamp beckoned yet it became no closer.

Varied sentence structure and clever use of punctuation helps to create the developing feeling of panic.

Brief reference to earlier event increases reader's curiosity.

Good use of language by effective juxtaposition of physical and mental pain.

Repetition is again used well.

It needs a little more sense of place to make it solid.

I instinctly tried to quicken my pace but my feet refused to change from their mechanical stride. I could hear the faint sound of a radio accompanied by the hum of a car engine. It passed me; the driver completely oblivious to my panic. I could feel the dampness on my hands as I fumbled for the key inside my pocket. I already knew it was there but I had to check again. I daren't look back. I knew the footsteps were following me.

I tried to focus my mind on the party. It had been worth it, hadn't it? My head still pounded with the music but I could no longer make out the song I was thinking of. I tried to remember. I had to remember. I couldn't allow my mind to accept the reality of the situation.

The snow had turned to slush and I became aware of the tiny hole in my shoe. I could feel the damp rising through my sock. I had to do something. I turned quickly onto the narrow path through the woods and ran. The trees passed me in a blur: They scratched my face and tormented my mind. They seemed to stoop toward me. I thrust away the branches with my fists. I felt my knees ready to buckle yet I knew I had to make it. The panic surged in my head and drowned the thumping of the music. I remembered the words "it's not you I don't trust, it's other people".

The key fumbled in the lock and fell to the floor. I glanced round. I had been followed, I could see that. I remembered the words of my father. He was wrong, it wasn't only other people he couldn't trust. It was me.

Vicki, (Year 11)

An intriguing piece which conveys a convincing atmosphere of mystery, tension, and panic. Some effective use of language, punctuation, and syntax conveys a powerful sense of mental and physical suffering.
A little more information about your surroundings as you make the journey home would have made this a more well-rounded piece.
Language grade A -

Keeping a Reading Diary

Objectives:

- to look at ways of keeping an active record of your reading
- to develop your personal response to literature

An Active Diary

There is no doubt that being an active reader will help you with English at GCSE. You will be more familiar with following plots and characters, and you'll find it easier to predict events. You may also notice patterns and connections with other texts.

Keeping a diary of your wider reading will help you, but there is always the danger that it becomes a chore, that you feel you have to write notes after each chapter, and so on.

Here are some suggestions for ways of keeping your reading diary active:

1 *Limit the amount you write* – especially when summarizing the storyline. Ideally, try to summarize the storyline in brief bullet points.

2 *Use charts and tables to vary your response* – for example:
   - use a graph to show how characters' emotional development goes up or down
   - use a flow-chart to trace the plot
   - sketch descriptions of important settings, and label them

3 *Be sure to write about your personal response:* bits you like/dislike; parts that strike you as unexpected or predictable; characters you sympathize with or dislike – and say why.

4 *Make predictions as you read:* what will happen next? How will main characters develop?

5 *Spot words or phrases the writer keeps using* – especially if they are associated with a particular character. Keep these in a separate list.

6 *Make a note of the pages on which any key passages take place in the book* – e.g. good descriptions; insights into characters' behaviour; surprising events.

7 *Be creative in making leaps between ideas* – who does this character remind you of? What place does the setting make you think of?

8 *What key words would you use:* to describe main characters, plot, themes, and the writer's style.

9 *Pick out quotations* – choose those that are striking or memorable.

10 *Feel free to doodle and sketch* – your personal response to the text is vital, so express it however you want to.

Activity Look at this extract from a Year 11 student's reading diary. What features do you like or dislike about it?
- Is there enough/too much storytelling?
- Is the balance of personal response/analysis about right?
Use the 10 points listed above as the basis for your comments.

Spoilt by Georgina Hammick

I picked this up thinking it was a short novel and now realize it's a collection of short stories. First = Maeve Goes to Town. Middle-aged woman, bored by life and looking for adventure, accepts offer to go to fancy party 2-3 hours drive from home. Her kids can't understand her. She seems to need to go to prove that she's still independent. Terrible journey. Arrives. Terrible party - everyone ignores her. They are all snobs and snigger at the way she is dressed and behaves. Gets home and lies to her children, hinting that she met some wealthy man.

Not much to it really. Not sure what the moral is - be yourself, perhaps. Or is it 'don't be ambitious - accept your life is in a rut?!' Maeve's quite likeable but we learn very little about her earlier life, so I didn't feel massive sympathy for her. The party is well-described - it feels really awful. I got the ending wrong as I was reading: I predicted she would fall madly in love - in true Mills and Boon style. So, although it felt a bit flat at the time, the ending is probably quite a good one.

Philippa

Working on

Stories often have similar patterns, and it can be useful to describe them visually using a graph. Basing the plot-line on the main character's experiences,

comedies often look like this:

and tragedies often look like this:

Use a similar technique in your reading diary to compare the last three texts.

Follow-up

- For ways of studying character, plot, and style, see pages 174–178 in the 'Writing on Literature' section.
- For hints on making notes, see page 124.

Influential Texts I

Objectives:
- to learn more about the language history of the Bible
- to compare the Authorized version with a contemporary, spoken account

The National Curriculum requires students to:

'be introduced to texts whose language and ideas have been influential, *e.g. Greek Myths, the Authorized Version of the Bible, Arthurian legends*'

The Bible

No text has had more influence upon English Literature than the Bible. How much do you know about the World's best-selling book?

Bible Briefing

Did you know that:

- the name *Bible* comes from the Greek *ta biblia* meaning 'the books'?

- the Bible is made up of 39 books in the Old Testament and 27 books in the New Testament? How many can you name?

- the Old Testament contains such well-known stories as Adam and Eve, David and Goliath, Jonah and the Whale?

- the New Testament contains the Gospels (from the Old English *god spell* = good message) of Matthew, Mark, Luke, and John, telling of the life and teaching of Jesus Christ, plus letters, plus the Book of Revelations?

So what is the *Authorized* version of the Bible?

In 1534 Henry VIII defied the Pope and broke away from the Roman Catholic Church. It was a turning-point for language, as well as the history of Britain. Several English translations of the Bible began to appear – previously they had all been in Latin. Between 1535 and 1568 five major versions appeared, all of them instant best-sellers.

In 1604 the President of Corpus Christi College, Oxford, proposed that there should be one standard translation of the Bible available to all speakers of English and used in churches across the country. Six committees of translators were established and, six years later, they produced the final official, or 'authorized', version of the Bible. In honour of the King, it was also known as the King James Bible, and was published in 1611, as Shakespeare was beginning work on his final solo play, *The Tempest*.

The Language of the Bible

Compare these two versions of the David and Goliath story. One is from the Authorized version of the Bible (the first Book of Samuel, Chapter 17); the second is from Tony Robinson's television retelling of famous Bible stories, *Blood and Honey*.

The story so far... Saul's army has been threatened by the Philistines. The first king of Israel, Saul, is looking for a soldier to lead the fight against the Philistine warrior, Goliath...

Book of Samuel, Chapter 17

The Lord that delivered me out of the paw of the lion, and out of the paw of the bear, he will deliver me out of the hand of this Philistine. And Saul said unto David, Go, and the Lord be with thee.

38 And Saul armed David with his armour, and he put an helmet of brass upon his head; also he armed him with a coat of mail.

39 And David girded his sword upon his armour and he assayed to go; for he had not proved *it*. And David said unto Saul, I cannot go with these; for I have not proved *them*. And David put them off him.

40 And he took his staff in his hand, and chose him five smooth stones out of the brook, and put them in a shepherd's bag which he had, even in a scrip; and his sling *was* in his hand: and he drew near to the Philistine.

41 And the Philistine came on and drew near unto David; and the man that bare the shield *went* before him.

42 And when the Philistine looked about, and saw David, he disdained him: for he was but a youth, and ruddy, and of a fair countenance.

43 And the Philistine said unto David, *Am I a dog*, that thou comest to me with staves? And the Philistine cursed David by his gods.

44 And the Philistine said to David, Come to me, and I will give thy flesh unto the fowls of the air, and to the beasts of the field.

45 Then said David to the Philistine, Thou comest to me with a sword, and with a spear, and with a shield: but I come to thee in the name of the Lord of hosts, the God of the armies of Israel, whom thou hast defied.

46 This day will the Lord deliver thee into mine hand; and I will smite thee, and take thine head from thee; and I will give the carcasses of the host of the Philistines this day unto the fowls of the air, and to the wild beasts of the earth; that all the earth may know that there is a God in Israel.

47 And all this assembly shall know that the Lord saveth not with sword and spear: for the battle *is* the Lord's, and he will give you into our hands.

48 And it came to pass, when the Philistine arose, and came and drew nigh to meet David, that David hasted, and ran toward the army to meet the Philistine.

49 And David put his hand in his bag, and took thence a stone, and slang *it*, and smote the Philistine in his forehead, that the stone sunk into his forehead; and he fell upon his face to the earth.

50 So David prevailed over the Philistine with a sling and with a stone, and smote the Philistine, and slew him; but *there* was no sword in the hand of David.

51 Therefore David ran, and stood upon the Philistine, and took his sword, and drew it out of the sheath thereof, and slew him, and cut off his head therewith. And when the Philistines saw their champion was dead, they fled.

Blood and Honey

Towering over them was King Saul, and he was seriously angry.
   'I need one common soldier to challenge that irritating loudmouth.
   Which of you snivelling cowards is it going to be?'
   The brothers looked down at their feet.
   'Speak up!'
   No one did. Saul sneered with contempt and turned to go.
   'I will!'
   'Who said that?' Saul demanded.
   'Me sir – your harpist, sir.'
   'You? You couldn't knock the skin off a pickled herring.'
   'I'm a shepherd, sir. I fought a lion once.'
   'It was a dog, actually,' said Abinadab.
   'Don't waste my time, boy,' snapped Saul.
   'Why not give him a try?' piped up Jonathan. 'We've got nothing to lose.'

Ten minutes later David was dressed from head to toe in Saul's armour.

'Right, off you go,' ordered the King.

'I can't move,' answered David.

Saul gave him a push. CRASH! David went toppling to the ground.

'This is no good,' said David, crawling out of the armour, 'I'll go as I am.'

'You'll need a sword,' insisted Saul, and drew his own from its mighty scabbard.

'Thanks anyway,' replied David, 'but I can't even lift it.'

And as the whole Israelite army looked on in silence, the young David walked slowly towards the Philistines.

The two armies faced each other across the valley. Out of the Philistine ranks stepped Goliath, even sweatier and hairier than usual.

'Where's this so-called champion of yours?' he roared at the Israelites.

'Where's the poor misguided mutt who's just had his last breakfast?'

'I think he means me,' said David looking like someone who should have been revising for their GCSEs.

'Is this the best you can do, Saul?' guffawed Goliath. 'I'll chew his arms and legs off, and feed his kidneys to the foxes!'

David scrambled down the hillside towards him. When he came to a dried-up stream he stopped and poked round in the stones.

'Go home,' jeered Goliath. 'Go and get on with your homework.'

'I've got the God of the Israelites on my side,' yelled David. 'Him and me are going to chop your head off.'

'Oh yes, the famous God-in-a-Box!' chortled Goliath. 'Let's see how he likes this,' and he twirled his huge bronze javelin.

Nearer and nearer he came, his bronze fillings glinting in the sun. He was so close now David could smell the garlic on his stinking breath.

He pulled back his throwing arm and leered at the thought of the hole he was about to drill through his opponent's stomach.

David whipped out his catapult, loaded a stone and fired.

There wasn't a loud noise – just a soft thwop like an egg dropping into a bowl of porridge.

Goliath frowned and put his hand to his forehead. His fingers were covered in red. Then a trickle of blood dropped out of his nose and splattered onto his armour. He looked at David with a sad far-away look in his eyes, then toppled forward. CRASH! He lay at David's feet completely pole-axed.

David heaved the massive sword out of the giant's scabbard and brought it down hard. The Philistine army gasped, then David picked up Goliath's severed head and held it out to the Israelites.

There was a puzzled silence, then an excited muttering, then a blood-thirsty roar burst from the throats of the entire army. The Philistines could be beaten – a little kid like David could blow away their champion.

They raced down the slope with their swords drawn. What would the Philistines do? Turn and run, or stay and fight?

Whoosh! They'd gone. Over the mountains, across the plain and back to their fortified cities. The Philistine push had been broken. Saul rode up and lifted David into his chariot. 'Have this!' he said, and pinned a medal on his chest. 'And this, and this, and this!' Soon David's whole front was covered with medals. 'And do you want to be a general? – I'll make you a general. And you've got to stay at the palace, OK, and have you met my daughters? You'll love them, I know you will. We'll have a great time, a great time!'

As they rode back everyone was cheering and throwing flowers, and the crowd was singing, 'Saul has killed thousands! Saul has killed thousands!'

'Great people, the Israelites,' said the King.

'Da-da has killed tens of thousands!' they sang.

'What was that?' snapped Saul, 'Who's killed tens of thousands?'

'Da-da has killed tens of thousands!' sang the crowd.

'Stop the chariot! Stop the chariot! What exactly are you singing?' he asked the crowd.

'Saul has killed thousands!' they replied.

'No, not that bit, the next bit.'

'David has killed tens of thousands!' they sang.

'Ha ha' laughed Saul. 'Yes, very good. Bit of exaggeration for comic effect. Ha!'

But he didn't say another word for the entire journey.

Tony Robinson

Activity

1 Read both versions aloud and jot down some first impressions about the differences between the two versions – in their words, their sentences, the use of dialogue, the way the characters are presented.

2 Look at the beginning of the verses in the Authorized version. Notice how they begin with connectives like *And, So, Then, Therefore*. What effect does this have on the story? How does Tony Robinson link parts of his story together?

3 Pick out some expressions from the Authorized version which feel archaic (very old) and we no longer use. Then pick out some expressions from Tony Robinson's version which make it feel very contemporary (modern).

4 Look at verse 49 where David kills Goliath. How could you make this verse more dramatic? What does it lack? If you were writing a modern written version of the story, what details would you add to this scene to increase the reader's involvement? Have a go at rewriting the verse in a single, more descriptive paragraph.

Follow-up

- To look at some of the specific influences of the Bible, see the Literature Timeline for the Seventeenth Century on page 204.
- To become more familiar with the language of the Bible, read parts of the Authorized version; compare it with *Good News for Modern Man* (a more recent translation of the New Testament), or Leon Garfield's *Tales from the Bible*. Tony Robinson's *Blood and Honey* is sometimes shown early on Sunday mornings on BBC-TV, and the text is published by BBC Books.

Influential Texts II

Arthurian Legend

At the end of the 20th Century we are still haunted by stories told thousands
of years ago. Films recreate legends, nursery rhymes refer to distant historical
events (for example 'Ring o' Roses', refers to the symptoms of the bubonic
plague; 'Goosey Goosey Gander' may refer to the goose-stepping march of
Cromwell's troops in the 17th Century); advertisers use a long-lost world to
sell their products; writers recreate fantasy worlds rooted in a distant past...

In Britain, no legend has been more influential than that of King Arthur.

From Fact...

Historians agree that although Arthur probably existed, he was probably never
a king. He was perhaps a Celtic cavalry leader whose swift-moving army
drove the Saxons back to the North Sea. The Romans had left Britain at the
beginning of the Fifth Century, leaving the people of Britain to fend for
themselves. At the same time, the Angles, Jutes, and Saxons from the Rhine
and Denmark began to make bloody attacks on the east coast. The Saxons
threatened to overwhelm Britain, but the British rallied. A man called Artos,
or Arthur, begins to emerge as a talented soldier, able to unite the squabbling
petty kings of Britain, and he travelled quickly about the country with an
army on horseback. To the British crouching in isolated hill-top ramparts, he
would have seemed a reassuring and miraculous sight: small wonder that he
was thought of as king.

...To Fiction

Arthur's life first became a literary form in Geoffrey of Monmouth's History
of the Kings of Britain in the 1130s. He makes Arthur a soldier of legendary
status: he conquers Ireland, Iceland, the Orkneys, Norway, and Gaul,
building a sizeable empire which he rules from his court, surrounded by
knights, priests, and astrologers.

...To More Fiction

Twenty years after Geoffrey of Monmouth's version, the poet Robert Wace adds the Round Table to the story – something Arthur devised to ensure that no one knight should have greater influence than any other.

Later in the 12th Century the French poet Chretien de Troyes grafts on the love stories of Launcelot and Guinevere; the quest for the Holy Grail; and the story of Arthur's' famed capital, Camelot. The Quest for the Holy Grail draws on earlier myths about a magic cup and the search for it in the Holy Lands. The magic cup is said to be the chalice used at the last supper and containing Christ's blood – a symbol of purity. And so a story of an English soldier merges with Christian motifs.

...And On

In medieval romance, which produced whole libraries of Arthurian legends, the story merges into a pattern of chivalry – gallant knights on noble quests and doing battle for the pure favours of fair damsels. Sir Thomas Malory's *Morte d'Arthur* (1485) paints a picture of a golden age with a strong United Kingdom ruled by a noble aristocracy – an example to the squabbling kings and barons of the time who were still engaged in the Wars of the Roses.

In Malory's version Arthur becomes King by drawing the magic sword from an anvil in London – something no other man could do. Guided by the magician Merlin, he rules the country in glory. But despite the noble lives of the Knights of the Round Table, Merlin predicts a future time of evil, and Arthur's empire begins to disintegrate into civil war. Mordred – who kills Arthur – is described in the Malory version of the legend as Arthur's son.

Activity The history of Arthur also illustrates how the English language has changed over the centuries and, as the language changes, so does the portrayal of the character of Arthur. Read these two extracts which both present versions of Arthur's final hours.

The first version was written in French in 1940 and translated into English in 1968. The second version was written by the Victorian poet, Tennyson, in 1842.

The Death of Arthur

...thieves combing the field, stripping the dead knights of their precious rings and all their other ornaments. To those who were not quite dead they dealt a death blow, so as to loot their shields and their jewels. Sir Lucan hastily returned to the king, thinking that it would be best to take him to some safe place in a nearby town.

So, between them, he and Sir Bedivere lifted the king who fainted quite away with the pain. But the effort was too much for Sir Lucan, who collapsed, his noble and faithful heart finally being overcome.

When the king regained consciousness and saw Lucan lying dead, he wept bitter tears, while Bedivere too bewailed the loss of his brother.

At last Arthur said: 'My hour is near; the death prophesied by Gawaine approaches. Bedivere, take my sword Excalibur and go to the seashore. There, throw my faithful blade into the water, and return to tell me what happens.'

Sir Bedivere departed and, pausing to contemplate the noble sword – the gift of the fairies – with its rich hilt of precious stones, said to himself: 'Nothing but ill can come from losing such a precious weapon.'

So he hid Excalibur in the hollow trunk of a tree, then returned to the king and told him that he had accomplished his mission.

'What did you see,' asked Arthur, 'and what did you hear'?

'Sire,' answered Bedivere, 'I saw only the dancing of the waves and heard only the sighing of the wind.'

'You are not telling me the truth,' said the king. 'Go back and obey me. If ever you have felt affection for me, throw the sword as far as you can into the water.'

Bedivere returned to the shore but, once again, thought that it would be a pity to throw such a valuable sword into the water, and once again hid it in the tree trunk. Then he returned to the king and told him that he had obeyed his orders.

'What did you see,' asked Arthur, 'and what did you hear?'

'All I saw,' answered Bedivere, 'was the water lapping against the rocks; and all I heard was the lament of the wind.'

'Ah, traitor!' cried the king. 'Twice you have betrayed me! Who would have believed it of you, you who were always so dear to me? Once so noble and valiant, now you betray me for gold and jewels. Return once more, for all these delays are putting me in great danger. If you do not obey me, wounded as I am, I shall still find the strength to kill you with my own hands.'

Bedivere, bitterly repenting his disloyalty, seized the sword, ran towards the sea, and without looking at the weapon hurled it with all his strength as far out as he could. An arm, clothed in white, appeared about the waters, took told of the sword, brandished it three times, and then vanished for ever. Bedivere returned to the king and, with a lighter heart, told him what he had seen.

translated by *Caroline Moorehead*

Idylls of the King

And slowly answered Arthur from the barge:
'The old order changeth, yielding place to new,
And God fulfils Himself in many ways,
Lest one good custom should corrupt the world.
Comfort thyself: what comfort is in me?
I have lived my life, and that which I have done
May He within Himself make pure! but thou,
If thou shouldst never see my face again,
Pray for my soul. More things are wrought by prayer
Than this world dreams of. Wherefore, let thy voice
Rise like a fountain for me night and day.
For what are men better than sheep or goats
That nourish a blind life within the brain,
If, knowing God, they lift not hands of prayer
Both for themselves and those who call them friend?
For so the whole round earth is every way
Bound by gold chains about the feet of God.
But now farewell. I am going a long way
With these thou seest – if indeed I go
(For all my mind is clouded with a doubt) –
To the island-valley of Avilion;
Where falls not hail, or rain, or any snow,
Nor ever wind blows loudly; but it lies
Deep-meadowed, happy, fair with orchard-lawns
And bowery hollows crowned with summer sea,
Where I will heal me of my grievous wound.'

So said he, and the barge with oar and sail
Moved from the brink, like some full-breasted swan
That, fluting a wild carol ere her death,
Ruffles her pure cold plume, and takes the flood
With swarthy webs. Long stood Sir Bedivere
Revolving many memories, till the hull
Looked one black dot against the verge of dawn,
And on the mere the wailing died away.

Alfred, Lord Tennyson

Working on

1 For both versions of the story, pick out words or phrases which:
 • give the story an old-fashioned feel
 • make it feel like a legend or fairy tale
 • show Arthur's character
2 How does the character of Arthur differ in each version – in what he says and does?
3 Which version do you prefer, and why?

Follow-up

• To examine another influential text, see 'The Bible' on page 132.
• To examine the way literature has developed through the ages, see the Literature Timeline (in the 'Reference Section') beginning on page 198.

Shakespeare's Language

Objectives:
- to examine the difference between poetic verse, blank verse, and prose
- to look closely at some of the language of Shakespeare

Enjoy the Rhythm

You will almost certainly have already studied Shakespeare in English.

The National Curriculum for English says:

'During each of Key Stages 3 and 4, pupils should read:
- a range of drama, including a play by Shakespeare'

One reason that Shakespeare's 37 plays continue to be performed, read, analysed, debated, and enjoyed is because of the variety of their language. Shakespeare was a remarkable writer not only because he could tell a good story (though some plots are a bit creaky), but because of his skills with language. To simplify things drastically, Shakespeare has three main written styles:
- poetic verse
- blank verse
- prose

Shakespeare used each of these styles in his play, *Macbeth*.

Poetic verse

Shakespeare's poetic verse contains rhyme and an underlying sense of rhythm.

Act 3 Scene 4

Here, Macbeth has murdered Duncan, two guards, and has the guilt of his friend Banquo's murder on his conscience. He contemplates what he should do next, realizes there can be no turning back, and resolves to revisit the mysterious witches to seek their advice:

Macbeth:
> For mine own good
> All causes shall give way: I am in blood
> Stepp'd in so far, that, should I wade no more,
> Returning were as tedious as go o'er.
> Strange things I have in head that will to hand,
> Which must be acted ere they may be scann'd.

Lady Macbeth: You lack the season of all natures, sleep.

Macbeth:
> Come, we'll to sleep. My strange and self-abuse
> Is the initiate fear that wants hard use:
> We are yet but young in deed.

Poetic verse is often used to reveal characters' most important moments. They may be speaking directly to an audience, or wrestling with their thoughts, as here.

Commentary:
The **rhyme** gives strong emphasis to Macbeth's thoughts, showing us perhaps someone determined to restore order in his life. The fact that the scene ends without a rhyme hints at the uneasiness of Macbeth's position.

The **rhythm** at the start is slow and faltering, broken by punctuation, and this emphasizes the uncertainty of Macbeth's position.

The **vocabulary** is dominated by *I*, *mine*, and *my*, a sign of the obsessive inward-looking thoughts that now dominate his mind.

The key **metaphor** is to create an image of himself standing in a river of blood, reassuring himself that he cannot turn back, whilst emphasizing the horror of what he has done.

Blank verse

Blank verse looks like poetry on the page, and frequently has a poetic rhythm. But it does not rhyme – though the last two lines may be made to rhyme at the end of a key speech or scene to give it emphasis.

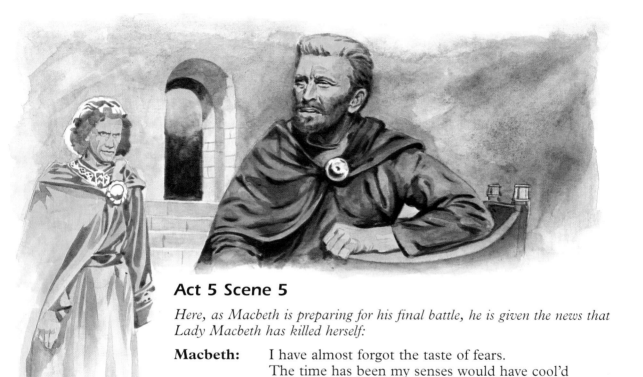

Act 5 Scene 5

Here, as Macbeth is preparing for his final battle, he is given the news that Lady Macbeth has killed herself:

Macbeth: I have almost forgot the taste of fears.
The time has been my senses would have cool'd
To hear a night-shriek, and my fell of hair
Would at a dismal treatise rouse and stir
As life were in't. I have supp'd full with horrors;
Direness, familiar to my slaughterous thoughts,
Cannot once start me.

(*Enter* **Seyton**.)

Wherefore was that cry?

Seyton: The queen, my lord, is dead.

Macbeth: She should have died hereafter;
There would have been a time for such a word.
Tomorrow, and tomorrow, and tomorrow,
Creeps in this petty pace from day to day,
To the last syllable of recorded time;
And all our yesterdays have lighted fools
The way to dusty death. Out, out, brief candle!

Blank verse has a flexible form of iambic pentameters – 5 strong and 5 weak beats to each line:

> I have al-most for-got the taste of fears
> The time has been, my sens-es would have cool'd

Look how Shakespeare uses elisions (*cool'd* rather than *cooled*) to maintain the rhythm. His actors would be very familiar with this underlying rhythm and, at a time when they might be performing a different play each day, it would help them learn and recall their lines. Even across the speech of two characters, Shakespeare is able to maintain the rhythm:

> Wherefore was that cry?
> The queen, my lord, is dead.

Commentary:

The **blank verse** gives the speech the feel of normal conversation, rather than a more formal or more intimate address. The underlying **rhythm** is emphasised by all of the one-syllable words ('To hear a night-shriek; and my fell of hair...'), which makes Macbeth's speech feel weary and plodding – appropriately at this point in the play.

The **vocabulary** is full of menace: *dismal, horrors, direness, slaughterous,* hinting at the bloodiness that is about to end the play, and showing how unnatural Macbeth has become that such horrors no longer disturb him – he has become immune to them.

The **tone** changes. The first part is full of images of horror; the second is more abstract and reflective, thinking about the nature of life and death, how inevitable death is, how trivial life can seem.

The **metaphor** 'Out, out, brief candle' refers to Lady Macbeth's life, now gone, and emphasizes the way death seems to trivialize life.

Prose

We use prose to refer to novels and short stories. It is easily recognizable in Shakespeare's plays because the right hand edge of the text is parallel with the margin, rather than jagged like poetry. Shakespeare frequently gives prose to his comic or minor characters, giving their language a different, less significant feel from the main characters.

Act 5 Scene 1

In this extract, the Doctor and Gentlewoman talk about Lady Macbeth's health:

Doctor: I have two nights watch'd with you, but can perceive no truth in your report. When was it she last walk'd?

Gentlewoman: Since his majesty went into the field, I have seen her rise from her bed, throw her night-gown upon her, unlock her closet, take forth paper, fold it, write upon't, read it, afterwards seal it, and again return to bed; yet all this while in a most fast sleep.

Doctor: A great perturbation in nature, to receive at once the benefit of sleep, and do the effects of watching. In this slumbery agitation, besides her walking and other actual perfomances, what, at any time, have you heard her say?

Gentlewoman: That, Sir, which I will not report after her.

Commentary:

The prose allows Shakespeare to focus on **plot** – what has and is happening to Lady Macbeth. The speech feels informal, straightforward, and is clearer to follow perhaps than the verse. It also shows us less about the speakers or situation because it is short on metaphor or other imagery: the emphasis, simply, is on telling the story.

Activity Choose two contrasting extracts from the Shakespeare play you are studying (for example, a formal speech and an intimate dialogue, or character thinking aloud, i.e. a soliloquy). Then try to write commentaries on them like those above, showing the contrasts. Don't try to be too technical: the important point is to respond to what you notice in the language and relate it to what the character is doing and saying. In other words, every observation you make about the language should answer the question 'So what...?' – it should tell us something about the content of the play.

Try to comment on:
- who is speaking
- who they are addressing
- their purpose
- their tone
- what you notice about their vocabulary
- the use of imagery
- any repetitions
- the style of the verse (conversational, formal, intimate, public...?)
- any changes in the extract – for example, in the main character's attitude

Follow-up
- To learn more about the literature of the 16th and 17th centuries, see the Literature Timeline in the 'Reference Section'.
- To look at ways of responding to drama texts, see 'Reading Drama' on page 154.

Imagery

Objectives:
- to explain the meaning of imagery
- to look at examples of the way it works

A Definition

Imagery is a term we frequently encounter when looking at poetry, though it describes something which occurs in all language – conversation, journalism – as well as creative literature. It is a technique we use to make our meaning more dramatic, more visual and more memorable by **comparing** one thing to another. Insults, for example, frequently use metaphors and similes (two types of imagery) to compare a person we dislike to an object or animal:

> You old cow.
> He's got a face like the back end of a bus.
> She stank like an ash-tray.
> He's very pig-headed.

There's something more colourful about these phrases than simply saying, 'You're horrible', 'He's ugly', 'She smelt badly', and 'He's stubborn'. That's what images do – make our meaning more colourful and often more powerful. They usually involve visual comparison – that's why they are called images – but they can use any of the other senses too. You can see why they are so useful to writers and people who work in advertising.

Three Types

There are three main devices which we call **imagery**:
- simile
- metaphor
- personification

These devices are also sometimes labelled 'figures of speech'.

Simile

A **simile** is simply a comparison of one person or object with another. It allows the writer to draw attention to the qualities (both positive and negative) of the subject. It is frequently found in lyrics of love:

> My love is like a red, red rose.
> Love is like dynamite.
> My lover's eyes are nothing like the sun.

All the writers here are trying to show what love means to them. They want to express a universal human emotion in personal terms – so they try and find a comparison which makes it more individual.

An essential element in a simile is the use of either *as* or *like:*

> I wander'd lonely as a cloud
> That floats on high o'er vales and hills,
> When all at once I saw a crowd,
> A host, of golden daffodils;
> Beside the lake, beneath the trees,
> Fluttering and dancing in the breeze.

Wordsworth's image of himself as a cloud emphasizes his sense of distance from the world around him. It gives an impression of him drifting without purpose, and therefore makes the sudden sight of the daffodils seem more dramatic and unexpected.

Think of original and unexpected similes to bring these subjects to life:
- The fire raged as fiercely as...
- The engines in the distance whined like...
- Their red bulk appeared like...
- The fire-fighters moved like...
- The flames...

Metaphor

A **metaphor** is also a device for comparing one item with another, but it makes itself less obvious because there is no use of *like* or *as*. Often, therefore, it can seem a more powerful device.

> He was a lion in battle.
> Her words were poisonous.
> The waves swallowed him.
> She looked daggers at you.

Notice that comparisons *are* taking place here, but because the words *as* and *like* are not used, it is possible to miss them. Metaphors are more colourful, powerful ways of saying, 'He was brave in battle', 'Her words were intended to hurt', 'He was drowned', and 'Her looks showed she was angry'.

We become so used to using some of these comparisons that we ignore them in our everyday speech: they have become **dead metaphors**.

Ham-fisted means fists like hams = clumsy
'We have done well – we have exceeded our targets' (but, think about firing an arrow at a target. If you exceed the target, it means you miss it!)

Personification

The final form of imagery is used much more in literature than in everyday speech. **Personification** means taking an abstract idea or motion – such as death, beauty, pride, happiness – and treating it as a human being or animal:

> Death was stalking the battlefield.
> The yellow fog that rubs its back upon the window panes.
> Fortune looked kindly upon them.

The effect is to take concepts which could seem abstract and dull, and to breathe life into them, making them seem like people. Think of some metaphors to describe someone who is:
- cowardly
- angry

Take these abstract ideas and see if you can personify them by writing a sentence for each one: ambition, greed, hatred.

Activity   Become more familiar with the use of imagery by examining this poem. Look at the way Craig Raine uses similes and metaphors to create unexpected and original images of the man he is describing:

The Grocer

the Kingdom of God cometh not with observation
(James Joyce to Lady Gregory)

The grocer's hair is parted like a feather
by two swift brushes and a dab of brilliantine.

His cheesewire is a sun-dial selling by the hour.
He brings it down at four and five o'clock,

the wooden T gripped like a corkscrew.
Greaseproof squares curl in diamonds on a hook.

He takes, and orientates the chock of cheese,
swoops his hand away, leaves it on the choppy scales.

Tortoise-necked, he reads the price aloud
and fingers do their automatic origami.

He shakes the air into a paper bag and,
eggs pickpocketed inside, trapezes it.

Coins are raked with trident hand,
trickled into the till – palm out,

with thumb crooked over the stigma
he smiles like a modest quattrocento Christ.

Craig Raine

1 Some of the similes and metaphors used in the poem are listed in the table below. For each one, comment on the effect it creates of the subject that is being described. The first is done for you as an example.

Simile	Effect	Metaphor	Effect
hair is parted like a feather	the parting in the hair appears very obvious – like when one part of a bird's feather is separated from the rest. It might suggest that the grocer is obsessively tidy.	His cheesewire is a sun-dial	
		He brings it down at four and five o'clock	Very exact with his job.
		the choppy scales	makes his job more interesting.
		Tortoise-necked fingers do their automatic origami	long neck, has very rapid and automatic.
the wooden T gripped like a corkscrew	That he holds it very tight.	He shakes the air into a paper bag	He quick
He smiles like a modest quattrocento (14th-Century) Christ	He is a nice guy, peaceful.	eggs pickpocketed inside	deft hand (7 such silent)
		trapezes it	like it makes job interesting as circus
		trident hand	very tidy.

2 Each simile and metaphor is a single image. Read together, they form the **imagery** of the poem (that is, a collection of images). What impression overall do they give of the grocer's character? Be as precise as you can in summing up what we learn about him.

3 Take a similar subject – someone you know well (a teacher, a shopkeeper, a parent) and write a description of them using unexpected images.
In describing them, think of:
• their appearance
• their mannerisms
• their way of speaking (any sayings or phrases associated with them?)
Like Craig Raine, aim to use a vivid variety of images – similes, metaphors, even personification.

A Year 9 student began her description of a friend's journey to school like this:

> Clockwork legs, spinning as if in fast-forward,
> wheels blurred by explosions of mud spray...

See what you can invent.

Follow-up
• To see metaphors used in an extreme way, look at the spread on the Seventeenth Century, on pages 204–205, which contains an account of the Metaphysical poets.
• For advice on close-reading of poetry, see 'Reading Poetry' on the next spread.

Reading Poetry

Problem Poems

Because poetry is *compressed language*, it is often more difficult to follow than prose. Poetry makes the reader work harder to find connections and make sense of the poet's language and ideas. This unit takes a quite baffling poem and traces the way some Year 10 pupils tackled it. To their surprise, they found that they actually enjoyed untangling the poem's difficulties.

Follow the process they went through, and see what you make of the poem.

63

(listen)

this a dog barks and
how crazily houses
eyes people smiles
faces street
steeples are eagerly

tumbl

ing through wonder
ful sunlight
—look—
selves,stir:writhe
o-p-e-n-i-n-g

are(leaves;flowers)dreams

,come quickly come
run run
with me now
jump shout(laugh
dance cry

sing)for it's Spring

—irrevocably;
and in
earth sky trees
:every
where a miracle arrives

(yes)

you and i may not
hurry it with
a thousand poems
my darling
but nobody will stop it

With All The Policemen In The World

The poet e.e. cummings was born in the USA in 1894. His poems are famous for their unexpected use of layout and punctuation.

Activity Read the poem slowly and carefully. Expect to find it difficult to understand. Then jot down first impressions using the questions which follow.

- What is the poem chiefly about – people, places, nature, feelings, himself?
- What do you notice about how it has been written – layout, words, punctuation, patterns, surprises?
- What do you like/dislike about the poem so far?

Working on

So far your notes have focused on:
- what the poem might be about
- first impressions of its style
- your personal response

Now begin to make those first impressions more precise by asking specific questions about the text.

1 Think about the *tone* of the poem. Choose 3 of the following words to help you pin down its tone. Find examples to support your choice of words.
calm excited disturbing strange celebratory spiritual positive negative confusing pointless jerky joyous factual observant descriptive philosophical moody manic comic serious cold

2 Look at these comments from some Year 10 pupils who worked on it. See if their observations help you make more sense of the poem:

> It's a celebration of life.

> It starts with ordinary things and then uses layout to emphasize the way nature is special.

> The layout seems confusing but there's quite a simple idea beneath the surface.

> It's a nature poem, though you can't tell that at first.

> It's about seeing things again for the first time – not taking life for granted.

3 Now ask more difficult, specific questions of the poem. Then try to suggest answers. For example:
- why does it start with a word in brackets?
- why are '(leaves; flowers)' in the centre of the poem?
- why does the poet use dashes in the word 'opening'?

4 When you are ready, write a personal response to the poem, following it through from the first line to the last. As you go through, comment upon:
Meaning: what is it about? Does the subject matter change or develop?
Tone: what is the writer's voice? Does it change?
Words: what patterns do you notice? Any unexpected words?
Layout: what surprises you? What effect does the layout have on the meaning of the poem?
Imagery: what word pictures do you notice?
Overall, what do you make of the poem? What is it about? Why is it written in this way? What do you like or dislike about it?

Follow-up
- Reading poetry becomes more rewarding the more of it you read, because you become familiar with different styles and techniques. See the 'Wider Reading List' on page 216 for suggestions of collections and anthologies you might read.
- To look at the techniques used by poets, see 'Imagery' on page 144.

The Short Story

Essential Ingredients

If someone asked you to define a short story, you might simply answer, 'a story which is short'. That is part of the truth, but a short story has more than just a low word-count. It is to do with the way the story is told. Look at this definition:

> Have you ever suffered from the dismal and embarrassing experience of listening to a joke told by a person who hasn't the slightest idea of how it should be done? Have you been told the 'punch-line' first, so that the whole impact of the story has been lost? Or been told, between uncontrollable guffaws, that this really is something funny that you are being told? You surely have. Awful, isn't it? The 'magic' of the short story – and the joke – is what is invested by the teller. It is the carefully planned intention to catch your attention, and then to take you by the hand and lead you to experience a world which exists only in imagination. It is a technique which is as old as story-telling itself...
>
> *Roy Lomax*

This definition gives the short story an air of mystery, making it a form of magic. Even if you don't agree with that, you will probably see the connection with joke-telling. Like many jokes, short stories have:
• very few central characters (unlike a novel which might have dozens)
• a small amount of background description – but enough to keep the story believable
• usually, a single main event or encounter
• an unexpected or surprising ending

Whilst people have told stories to one another for thousands of years, the short story as a written form only became fashionable in the last century, when American writers like Edgar Allen Poe and Nathaniel Hawthorne used it to create surprising and often shocking endings.

Activity Here are two very short short stories. Before you read each story, try to predict what it might be about, based on the title.

The Weather in San Francisco

It was a cloudy afternoon with an Italian butcher selling a pound of meat to a very old woman, but who knows what such an old woman could possibly use a pound of meat for?

She was too old for that much meat. Perhaps she used it for a bee hive and she had five hundred golden bees at home waiting for the meat, their bodies stuffed with honey.

'What kind of meat would you like today?' the butcher said.

'We have some good hamburger. It's lean.'

'I don't know,' she said, 'Hamburger is something else.'

'Yeah, it's lean. I ground it myself. I put a lot of lean meat in it.'

'Hamburger doesn't sound right,' she said.

'Yeah,' the butcher said. 'It's a good day for hamburger. Look outside. It's cloudy. Some of those clouds have rain in them. I'd get the hamburger,' he said.

'No,' she said. 'I don't want any hamburger, and I don't think it's going to rain. I think the sun is going to come out and it will be a beautiful day, and I want a pound of liver.'

The butcher was stunned. He did not like to sell liver to old ladies. There was something about it that made him very nervous. He didn't want to talk to her any more.

He reluctantly sliced a pound of liver off a huge red chunk and wrapped it up in white paper and put it into a brown bag. It was a very unpleasant experience for him.

He took her money, gave her the change, and went back to the poultry section to try and get a hold of his nerves.

By using her bones like the sails of a ship, the old woman passed outside into the street. She carried the liver as if it were victory to the bottom of a very steep hill.

She climbed the hill and being very old, it was hard on her. She grew tired and had to stop and rest many times before she reached the top.

At the top of the hill was the old woman's house: a tall San Francisco house with bay windows that reflected a cloudy day.

She opened her purse which was like a small autumn field and near the fallen branches of an old apple tree, she found her keys.

Then she opened the door. It was a dear and trusted friend. She nodded at the door and went into the house and walked down a long hall into a room that was filled with bees.

There were bees everywhere in the room. Bees on the chairs. Bees on the photograph of her dead parents. Bees on the curtains. Bees on an ancient radio that once listened to the 1930s. Bees on her comb and brush.

The bees came to her and gathered about her lovingly while she unwrapped the liver and placed it upon a cloudy silver platter that soon changed into a sunny day.

Richard Brautigan

The Explosion in the Parlour

The host poured tea into the cup and placed it on the small table in front of his guests, who were a father and daughter, and put the lid on the cup with a clink. Apparently thinking of something, he hurried into the inner room, leaving the thermos on the table. His two guests heard a chest of drawers opening and a rustling.

They remained sitting in the parlour, the ten-year-old daughter looking at the flowers outside the window, the father just about to take his cup, when the crash came, right there in the parlour. Something was hopelessly broken.

It was the thermos, which had fallen to the floor. The girl looked over her shoulder abruptly, startled, staring. It was mysterious. Neither of them had touched it, not even a little bit. True, it hadn't stood steadily when their host placed it on the table, but it hadn't fallen then.

The crash of the thermos caused the host, with a box of sugar cubes in his hand, to rush back from the inner room. He gawked at the steaming floor and blurted out, 'It doesn't matter! It doesn't matter!'

The father started to say something. Then he muttered, 'Sorry, I touched it and it fell.'

'It doesn't matter,' the host said.

Later, when they left the house, the daughter said, 'Daddy, *did* you touch it?'

'No. But it stood so close to me.'

'But you *didn't* touch it. I saw your reflection in the window-pane. You were sitting perfectly still.'

The father laughed. 'What then would you give as the cause of its fall?'

'The thermos fell by itself. The floor is uneven. It wasn't steady when Mr Li put it there. Daddy, *why* did you say that you...'

'That won't do, girl. It sounds more acceptable when I say I knocked it down. There are things which people accept less the more you defend them. The truer the story you tell, the less true it sounds.'

The daughter was lost in silence for a while. Then she said, 'Can you explain it only this way?'

'Only this way,' her father said.

Bai Xiao-Yi

Working on

Now use these prompts to analyse the way in which each story works.

1 The best short stories make us want to keep reading by making us ask certain questions – about characters, places, and storyline. What questions are raised in these two stories? Add some unanswered questions to this table:

	The Weather in San Francisco	The Explosion in the Parlour
Character questions:	Who is the old woman? Why is the butcher nervous about selling liver to old ladies?	Who are the father and his daughter visiting? Why are they visiting?
Place:		
Storyline:		

2 We have said that four essential ingredients of a short story are:
   • very few central characters
   • limited description
   • usually, a single main event or encounter
   • an unexpected or surprising ending
   Applying each of these points to both stories, which would you say was most typical of the short-story form? Why?

3 Write your short story with these ingredients in mind. Try to keep information back from the reader and so build anticipation. You might want to use one of the following ideas as a starting-point:
   • A practical joke that goes wrong...
   • Someone's revenge...
   • Someone mishearing part of a conversation...
   • Someone giving a warning that is ignored ...

Follow-up

• To examine the way writers create suspense, see 'Building Tension' on page 158.
• To read more examples of the short story form, look at the 'Wider Reading List' on page 216.

Reading Drama

Play Time

Many students like the idea of reading plays in class – they can be much more entertaining than a class novel because of the number of parts they contain. But they can also be difficult to read well. And perhaps the biggest challenge is when you are asked to read a drama-script on your own: here it can be difficult to get a clear sense of what is happening, who the characters are, and how the story is unfolding.

Perhaps the essential feature of a drama text is that we learn about the characters through their words and actions, rather than through what the writer tells us directly.

Alan Bennett's play is about Mr Dodsworth, who has recently retired from Warburton's after a lifetime's service. He has settled contentedly into retirement when his secretary, Miss Prothero, unexpectedly arrives. Her news of the changes at Warburton's gradually disturbs Mr Dodsworth as he begins to sense that everything he had achieved has been overturned... The play begins like this:

A Visit from Miss Prothero

(The living-room of a semi-detached house. A worn, comfortable, cosy place. Dozing in an armchair and similarly worn, cosy, and comfortable is MR DODSWORTH, *a man in his sixties. In a cardigan and carpet slippers with the top button of his trousers undone* MR DODSWORTH *is retired. He is just having five minutes and, unless one counts the budgie, he is alone. A few moments pass, sufficient for the tranquillity of the household to be established, then the door-chimes go.*
MR DODSWORTH *does not respond.*
The chimes go again.
MR DODSWORTH *stirs and fastening the top button of his trousers gets up and addresses the budgie.)*
MR DODSWORTH: Who's this then, Millie? Who's this?
(He goes out, leaving the living-room door open. The front door opens.)
(Off) Is it you, Miss Prothero?
MISS PROTHERO: *(Off)* It is.
MR DODSWORTH: *(Off)* I didn't expect to see you.
(While DODSWORTH *hovers in the living-room doorway the visitor comes in boldly. It is a middle-aged woman, who runs a critical eye over the warm, comfortable, cosy room. She is none of these things.)*
MISS PROTHERO: I was beginning to think I'd got the wrong house.
MR DODSWORTH: Why? Had you been stood there long?
MISS PROTHERO: A minute or two.
MR DODSWORTH: No, it's the right house. Number 59. The Dodsworth residence.
MISS PROTHERO: I rang twice.
MR DODSWORTH: To tell you the truth I was just having five minutes.
MISS PROTHERO: I'm surprised. You were the one who couldn't abide a nap.
MR DODSWORTH: Was I? You'll take your coat off?

MISS PROTHERO: I was waiting to be asked. *(He starts to help her off with her coat.)*

I shan't stop.

MR DODSWORTH: No, but...

MISS PROTHERO: I still have my back, so I'll keep my undercoat on.

(MR DODSWORTH is tugging at her cardigan sleeve, trying to take it off.)

That's my undercoat.

MR DODSWORTH: Sorry, Sorry.

MISS PROTHERO: This time of year can be very treacherous.

(Spring, summer, autumn, winter... to MISS PROTHERO the seasons were all potential assassins.)

And I'd best keep my hat on as well. I don't want another sinus do.

(MR DODSWORTH is about to bear away the fainted form of MISS PROTHERO's swagger coat when she stops him.)

I'm forgetting my hanky.

(She takes it out of the pocket and blows her nose as MR DODSWORTH carries her coat out to the hallstand.)

There's half a dozen people I ought to go and see only I thought you might be feeling a bit out of it. I said to Doreen, 'I know Mr Dodsworth, he'll be wanting to be brought up to date.'

MR DODSWORTH: *(Off)* What on?

MISS PROTHERO: What on? Work! Warburtons!

MR DODSWORTH: *(Off)* Oh, work. No. No.

MISS PROTHERO: *(to herself)* I'm sorry I came then.

(She remains standing on one spot, surveying the room as DODSWORTH bustles back.)

MR DODSWORTH: What I mean, of course, is I do want to be brought up to date but to tell you the truth, Peggy, since I've left I've hardly had time to turn round. What with bowling on Tuesdays and my Rotary thing on Fridays and Gillian and the kiddies bobbing in every five minutes, I honestly haven't given work a thought. Which is amazing when you think I was there all those years. But you know what they say: retirement, it's a full-time job. Ha ha.

(MISS PROTHERO doesn't laugh. She vaguely flinches. MISS PROTHERO is one of those people who only see jokes by appointment.)

Alan Bennett

Activity   1   What can you tell about the two characters from this extract? What do we learn about Mr Dodsworth from his house, the way he speaks, and his reactions to Miss Prothero? Is he pleased to see her or not? What do you think Mr Dodsworth looks like? What about Miss Prothero?

...Some of these questions you may not be able to answer because we are not told by the writer. Characters are revealed through their own and other characters' words. To test the effect, imagine how the dialogue might work in a novel...

> Mr Dodsworth stirred and, fastening the top button of his trousers, got up and addressed the budgie. 'Who's this then, Millie?' he asked. 'Who's this?' He went out, leaving the living-room door open. He opened the front door and saw someone he thought he recognized. 'Is it you, Miss Prothero?' he asked. A stout woman was standing in the doorway peering beyond him into the hall. 'It is,' she said. Mr Dodsworth looked slightly dazed. 'I didn't expect to see you.' While he was hovering uncertainly in the living room doorway, the visitor came boldly in...

2   Pick out the sentences which have been added here. What do they add to the story or our sense of what Mr Dodsworth is like? What do you like or dislike about the way the play has been adapted?

Playrights cannot, in other words, speak directly to the audience (unless they have a narrator or chorus figure, placing greater emphasis on the characters' words and movements.

Screenplays

The same applies in screenplays, except here the writer can control more precisely what the viewer sees, as TV writer Ray Jenkins explains in this extract from the handbook, *Début on Two*.

> Scenes are the building bricks of the script. Whether the scene is a single image, indoor or out, long or short, it will have three components: (i) it has come from somewhere, (ii) it is a stage in the story, (iii) it moves us on...
>
> For example:
>
> INTERIOR. LOUNGE. DAY.
>
> Sandra, thirty, prematurely grey, stands in the middle of the expensive room. Her eyes show apprehension.
>
> **Sandra**: Hello?
>
> No reply.
>
> (Louder.) Hel-lo?
>
> Silence.
She moves slowly towards the closed door to the kitchen and opens it noiselessly.

INTERIOR. KITCHEN. DAY.

She enters –
it is bright, pine-wooded, and empty.
Her eyes check everything –
only the larder door is slightly open.
She crosses to it, puzzled,
and pulls it open.

INTERIOR. LARDER. DAY.

The cat hangs by its neck warmly dead.

What is vital is that scenes move the story on; we are in 'movies' not 'talkies'. Vary the pace, i.e. don't have a necklace of scenes where there's an entrance, something happens, and then an exit – that will produce a dead, hump-backed rhythm to your writing. In the tiny example above, we start with Sandra already in the room, she doesn't come into it. That forces you to concentrate on her and not the furniture, allows me to have an entry for the next scene and avoids duplication.

Ray Jenkins

Activity The best way of getting the feel for the way drama tells stories is to try adapting some prose as drama. Take the opening of a novel you like and have a go at presenting it as the beginning of a stage or TV drama. Or try the opposite: take a play you have studied and write the start of the prose adaptation. Then write a brief paragraph explaining what decisions you made – what to add, what to cut, how you feel you have changed the story or characterization, and how successful you feel your adaptation has been.

Follow-up
- To find out more about use of language and rhythm, see 'Shakespeare's Language' on page 140.
- To look at the way characters are presented in literature, see 'Studying Character' on page 174.

Building Tension

Unputdownable Books!

When they review thrillers, critics sometimes talk about the books as being 'unputdownable'. For example, one reviewer wrote of *Jaws*:

> Pick up *Jaws* before midnight, read the first five pages, and I guarantee you'll be putting it down breathless and stunned – the final climax is even better than the beginning – as dawn is breaking the next day.
>
> Peter Grosvenor, *The Daily Express.*

But what makes a good thriller? What, in a narrative, makes us want to read on? In this spread, examine some of the techniques one expert thriller writer uses to build tension.

Raising Questions

Read this opening section from a novel by Brian Moore called *Cold Heaven*. The secret of creating tension is to make your reader ask questions. Read one section of the story at a time, covering the others with a piece of paper.

Activity

1 At the end of the opening section, jot down some ideas in response to the questions given below.
   - What have you learnt about the setting of the story?
   - What is your response to the characters and the way they relate to each other? Which character is more sympathetic?
   - What clues are there about what will happen next?
   - What questions do you have?
2 At the end of all other sections, look back at the opening questions and, for each one, write about how your impressions and predictions have developed.
3 Then look at the questions on page 161 which some Year 10 students asked when they read the story in this way.

Cold Heaven

1 The wooden seats of the little pedal boat were angled so that Marie looked up at the sky. There were no clouds. In the vastness above her a gull calligraphed its flight. Marie and Alex pedalled in unison, the revolving paddles making a slapping sound against the waves as the pedal boat treadmilled away from the beach, passing through ranks of bathers to move into the deeper, more solitary waters of the Baie des Anges. Marie slackened her efforts but Alex continued determinedly, steering the *pedalo* straight out into the Mediterranean.

2 'Let's not go too far,' she said.
'I want to get away from the crowd. I'm going to swim.'
It was like him to have some plan of his own, to translate idleness into activity even in these few days of vacation. She now noted his every fault. It was as though, having decided to leave him, she had

withdrawn his credit. She looked back at the sweep of hotels along the Promenade des Anglais. Today was the day she had hoped to tell him. She had planned to announce it at breakfast and leave, first for New York, then on to Los Angeles to join Daniel. But at breakfast she lacked all courage. Now, with half the day gone, she decided to postpone it until tomorrow.

3   Far out from shore, the paddles stopped. The *pedalo* rocked on its twin pontoons as Alex eased himself up from his seat. He handed her his sunglasses. 'This should do,' he said and, rocking the boat even more, dived into the ultramarine waters. She watched him surface. He called out: 'Just follow along, okay?' He was not a good swimmer, but thrashed about in an energetic, erratic freestyle. Marie began to pedal again, her hand on the tiller, steering the little boat so that she followed close. Watching him, she knew he could not keep up this pace for long. She saw his flailing arms and for a moment thought of those arms hitting her. He had never hit her. He was not the sort of man who would hit you. He would be hurt, and cold, and possibly vindictive. But he was not violent.

4   She heard a motorboat, the sound becoming louder. She looked back but did not see a boat behind her. Then she looked to the right where Alex was swimming and saw a big boat with an outboard motor coming right at them, coming very fast.

5   Of course they see us, she thought, alarmed, and then as though she were watching a film, as though this were happening to someone else, she saw there was a man in the motorboat, a young man wearing a green shirt; he was not at the tiller, he was standing in the middle of the boat with his back to her and as she watched he bent down and picked up a child who had fallen on the floorboards. 'Hey?' she called. 'Hey?' for he must turn around, the motorboat was coming right at Alex, right at her. But the man in the boat did not hear. He carried the child across to the far side of the boat; the boat was only yards away now.

6 'Alex,' she called. 'Alex, look out.' But Alex flailed on and then the prow of the motorboat, slicing up water like a knife, hit Alex with a sickening thump, went over him and smashed into the pontoons of the little pedal boat, upending it, and she found herself in the water, going under, coming up. She looked and saw the motorboat churning off, the pedal boat hanging from its prow like a tangle of branches. She heard the motorboat engine cut to silence, then start up again as the boat veered around in a semicircle and came back to her. Alex? She looked: saw his body near her just under the water. She swam toward him, breaststroke, it was all she knew. He was floating face down, spread-eagle. She caught hold of his wrist and pulled him towards her. The motorboat came alongside, the man in the green shirt reaching down for her, but, 'No, no,' she called and tried to push Alex toward him. The man caught Alex by the hair of his head and pulled him up, she pushing, Alex falling back twice into the water, before the man, with a great effort, lifted him like a sack across the side of the boat, tugging and heaving until Alex disappeared into the boat. The man shouted, *'Un instant, madame, un instant'* and reappeared, putting a little steel ladder over the side. She climbed up onto the motorboat as the man went out onto the prow to disentangle the wreckage of the pedalo. A small child was sitting at the back of the boat, staring at Alex's body, which lay face-down on the floorboards. She went to Alex and saw blood from a wound, a gash in the side of his head, blood matting his hair. He was breathing but unconscious. She lifted him and cradled him in her arms, his blood trickling onto her breasts. She saw the boat owner's bare legs go past her as he went to the rear of the boat to restart the engine. The child began to bawl but the man leaned over, silenced it with an angry slap, the man turned to her, his face sick with fear. *'Nous y serons dans un instant,'* he shouted, opening the motor to full throttle. She hugged Alex to her, a rivulet of blood dripping off her forearm onto the floorboards as the boat raced to the beach.

Brian Moore

Examining the tension

Tension in narrative relies on questions being raised but not answered. A group of Year 10 pupils read the *Cold Heaven* sections and asked the following questions. They also gave each section a 'tension rating' out of 5.

1   'Who are these people? Are they husband and wife/boyfriend and girlfriend? Why are they not at ease with each other – she's stopping and he's pushing on 'determinedly'? Is the situation going to prove dangerous?' Tension rating: 1

2   'Why has Marie lost courage at breakfast? How long has their relationship been in trouble? Who are these people – their jobs, age, etc? Are they Americans, then? Why do we feel more sympathetic towards Marie, even though she is (probably) going to hurt Alex?' Tension rating: 2

3   'Why are we shown so much about Alex as a weak swimmer? Is he going to drown? Will Marie have to save him, or will she decide not to – a way out of her problem? Why are we told that Alex is not violent – is there going to be some violence? Something is going to happen to Alex in the water – but what?' Tension rating: 3

4   'Will Alex and Marie both be hit by the big boat? Will they survive? Or will she manage to save them?' Tension rating: 4

5   'Brian Moore shows us details about the people on the boat – the man's shirt, for example – is this to build tension by making us wait longer to see what will happen? Will the boat avoid Alex and Marie at the last minute? How seriously will they be hurt if it doesn't?' Tension rating: 5

6   'Why does the boat driver slap the child – to contrast with the earlier comment about Alex not being violent? Why so many references to the blood? Will Alex survive?' Tension rating: 4

Working on

1 Look at this list of some of the techniques Brian Moore uses to create tension. Put them in order of most to least important:
   • holding back information about characters
   • creating conflict between the main characters
   • leaving questions unanswered about character and setting
   • making the storyline difficult to predict
   • giving clues that things will go wrong – Alex's poor swimming, etc.
   • establishing the location without too much descriptive writing
2 What do you predict will happen in the rest of the novel?
3 Continue the chapter from the point where the boat reaches shore.

Follow-up

   • To look more at the plotting of novels, see 'Studying Plot' on page 178.
   • To look at a student's thriller assignment, see 'Creative Writing' on page 110.
   • For suggestions of other thrillers to read, see the 'Wider Reading List' on page 216.

Assessing the Reading of Literature

This is a summary of the kind of criteria used to assess your Literature work. Exact wording will vary from one examination board to another, but the criteria match National Curriculum requirements. Note that more than mere comprehension of storyline is needed: to achieve the highest grades, you need to be able to respond to the subtleties of writers' styles and techniques.

Grade Criteria

Grade G
The candidate can...
- show familiarity with parts of the text – e.g. subject-matter of a poem, sequence of a story, plus some significant details (e.g. setting of a story)
- make a personal response to some characters and situations
- offer simple judgements upon them

Grade F
The candidate can...
- identify significant characters, events, situations
- show awareness that characters speak or authors write in different ways to reveal different personal qualities

Grade E
The candidate can...
- explain and justify preferences through reference to general features and specific details in a text
- describe the effect of certain events or situations on the reader

Grade D
The candidate can...
- offer structured discussions of the content of texts, including feelings and attitudes described in them
- support comments with reference to textual detail
- compare the effects achieved by different writers/texts

Grade C
The candidate can...
- show sustained knowledge of and response to the text
- support ideas on meaning and style with quotations
- respond to different layers of meaning in texts and the way writers use language for different purposes and effects

Grade B
The candidate can...
- successfully communicate insight into texts
- use quotations economically and effectively
- recognize layers of meaning
- show understanding of the structure of texts
- make relevant comparisons between writers' concerns, attitudes, and ideas, and their effect on the reader

Grade A
The candidate can...
- relate detail to broader aspects of the content, meaning and style of texts in clearly-structured responses
- display empathy with writers' apparent and implicit concerns
- show awareness of the social and historical context of a text
- use quotations concisely, in order to evaluate the effect of language and techniques on the reader

Grade A*
The candidate can...
- show consistently high levels of insight
- give convincing and imaginative interpretations of meaning and style, supported by close, concise textual reference and personal response
- show high degree of empathy with writers, using an enthusiastic personal voice, and awareness of the writers' language

Examiner's Comments: Literature Unseen

The following 'Literature Unseen' tests your ability to respond to writers' language. In an examination, it might be followed by questions on another separate text – for example, a poem; or you might be asked to compare two texts at once, looking at the way the authors use language. This sample text allows you to focus on the written style used by one writer. It is the first section of a longer exam.

First read the story and then answer the questions that follow.

Jean Rhys was born and brought up on the West Indian island of Dominica but she spent most of her adult life travelling and working in Europe. The story was written after a return visit to her birthplace in the 1930s.

I Used to Live Here Once

She was standing by the river looking at the stepping stones and remembering each one. There was the round unsteady stone, the pointed one, the flat one in the middle – the safe stone where you could stand and look around. The next wasn't so safe for when the river was full the water flowed over it and even when it showed dry it was slippery. But after that it was easy and soon she was standing on the other side.

The road was much wider than it used to be but the work had been done carelessly. The felled trees had not been cleared away and the bushes looked trampled. Yet it was the same road and she walked along feeling extraordinarily happy.

It was a fine day, a blue day. The only thing was that the sky had a glassy look she didn't remember. That was the only word she could think of. Glassy. She turned the corner, saw that what had been the old pavement had been taken up, and there too the road was much wider, but it had the same unfinished look.

She came to the worn stones that led up to the house and her heart began to beat. The screw pine was gone, so was the mock summer house called the ajoupa, but the clove tree was still there and at the top of the steps the rough lawn stretched away, just as she had

remembered it. She stopped and looked toward the house that had been added to and painted white. It was strange to see a car standing in front of it.

There were two children under the big mango tree, a boy and a little girl, and she waved to them and called 'Hello' but they didn't answer her or turn their heads. Very fair children, as Europeans born in the West Indies so often are: as if the white blood is asserting itself against all odds.

The grass was yellow in the hot sunlight as she walked towards them. When she was quite close she called again, shyly:

'Hello'. Then, 'I used to live here once,' she said.

Still they didn't answer. When she said for the third time 'Hello' she was quite near them. Her arms went out instinctively with the longing to touch them.

It was the boy who turned, his grey eyes looked straight into hers. His expression didn't change. He said, 'Hasn't it gone cold all of a sudden. D' you notice? Let's go in.' 'Yes let's,' said the girl.

Her arms fell to her side as she watched them running across the grass to the house. That was the first time she knew.

Activity

Now examine the text in detail.

1 How does Jean Rhys demonstrate her familiarity with the scenes she observes?

2 Write about the ending of the story.

Once you have completed your own response, look at the examiner's comments on another student's answer below.

Lit Unseen: I Used to Live Here Once

1. The author of 'I Used to Live Here Once,' suggests her familiarity with the scenes she describes by showing the person remembers each detail of the island, 'remembering each one.' She could remember each stepping stone and trees which had always stood along the river, 'The safe stone,' 'Trees had not been cleared.' The author made it clear that she had once lived on the island and therefore knew how it had once been and could recognize particular areas, - for example, 'led up to the house.'

Immediately focusing on details that suggest familiarity.

The author often uses basic language to describe objects which she is remembering – this makes the objects appear more familiar, 'when it showed dry it was slippery.' The author also uses this method to show how many details about the island are not as she remembered. 'A glassy look that she didn't remember.'

Beginnings of appreciation of author's style.

This is important in that the question requires closer focus on the author's 'familiarity'.

2. The ending of 'I Used to Live Here Once' is quite surprising. It is very different to the other section of the story, which has consisted of memories and description. The ending leaves the reader contemplating the rest of the story and would encourage them to continue the story. This

Clear distinguishing between 2 aspects of extract.

Sees the author's feelings and attitude. ———•

ending is showing that all the memories which the author holds are now to be only memories as the island has changed and the people who live there are not as friendly as she had once remembered. 'His expression didn't change.' The author is trying to suggest that she is no longer part of the community. She has become a stranger in her own homeland is no longer recognized or welcomed.' That was the first time she knew.'

Again clearly distinguishing between aspects of text. ———•

Vicky (Year 10)

Question 1
The answer highlights some important details which point to the author's familiarity with the places she is revisiting. However, the answer is too brief and needs to explore the extract further. The answer only focuses on the first three paragraphs of 'I used to live here once'.

Question 2
The answer clearly discriminates between the different parts of the text and recognizes that the writer suddenly realizes that she no longer belongs. This sense of being familiar yet at the same time an outsider needs to be further explored.

Overall there is a clear understanding of the text and the answer is concise and clearly written. There is a need, however, to probe the text further, particularly in response to question 1.

If this standard of work were maintained over a complete exam, the likely grade would be:
Literature grade (C)
Language grade (B-)

Follow-up
- To look at techniques for comparing texts see page 186.
- To examine writers' use of detail, see page 150 and 158.

Creative Responses to Literature

How Creative?

Of course, all responses to literature will be creative if we are fully involved with the text: even when we write in the more impersonal, analytical style of literary criticism, we can still be creative in our thinking and expression. But English at GCSE (as well as at A-level and university) often requires you to respond to literature through creative writing. Here are some of the possibilities:

- Imagine you are Curley's Wife in *Of Mice and Men*. Write about your impressions of Lennie and George.
- Imagine you are Gerald Croft in *An Inspector Calls*. Write your diary for the night of the Inspector's visit.
- At the end of *The Crucible*, Arthur Miller tells us that Elizabeth Proctor remarried. Imagine she looks back on the events in Salem. Write the letter she might send to a friend giving an account of what happened to her and John.
- Imagine you are Lady Macbeth and you have just heard about the possibility of Macbeth's becoming King. Write a monologue revealing the thoughts that are going through your mind.
- Write the front page of a newspaper to report the declaration of the Animals' Republic in *Animal Farm*.

Hints

Notice what is being asked in all of these questions:
- to show close knowledge of the text
- to be able to write in a different form from the original text (diary, letter, monologue, newspaper)

It is also important to know whether the assignment will be assessed just for English Language or also for English Literature. If it is to be assessed for literature, it is vital that you:
- Refer closely to the text, mentioning the events which happen, echoing the language, making sure that your version does not stray too far away from the original story.
- Imagine how a different character would see things and try to write through their eyes. Try your best to imitate the style of their speech.
- Do not simply retell the story. You rarely gain many marks for this – you need to add new insights into what has taken place.

Objectives:
- to examine ways of responding to literature through creative writing
- to explore the possibilities and drawbacks of these approaches

WRITING ON LITERATURE

Activity   Read this example of a creative response and use the prompts which follow to analyse how successful you think it is.

> **Task**
> Write a creative response to Wilfred Owen's poem *Disabled*, imagining that you were in the crowd seeing your old friend return from the War...

Disabled

He sat in a wheeled chair, waiting for dark
And shivered in his ghastly suit of grey,
Legless, sewn short at elbow. Through the park
Voices of boys rang saddening like a hymn,
Voices of play and pleasure after day,
Till gathering sleep had mothered them from him.

About this time Town used to swing so gay
When glow-lamps budded in the light blue trees,
And girls glanced lovelier as the air grew dim, –
In the old times, before he threw away his knees.
Now he will never feel again how slim
Girls' waists are, or how warm their subtle hands.
All of them touch him like some queer disease.

There was an artist silly for his face,
For it was younger than his youth, last year.
Now, he is old; his back will never brace;
He's lost his colour very far from here,
Poured it down shell-holes till the veins ran dry,
And half his lifetime lapsed in the hot race
And leap of purple spurted from his thigh.

One time he liked a blood-smear down his leg,
After the matches, carried shoulder-high.
It was after football, when he'd drunk a peg.
He thought he'd better join. – He wonders why.
Someone had said he'd look a god in kilts,
That's why; and maybe, too, to please his Meg,
Aye, that was it, to please the giddy jilts
He asked to join. He didn't have to beg;
Smiling they wrote his lie: aged nineteen years.

Germans he scarcely thought of; all their guilt,
And Austria's, did not move him. And no fears
Of Fear came yet. He thought of smart salutes;
And care of arms; and leave; and pay arrears;
For daggers in plaid socks; and pay arrears;
Esprit de corps; and hints for young recruits.
And soon, he was drafted out with drums and cheers.

Some cheered him home, but not as crowds cheer Goal.
Only a solemn man who brought him fruits
Thanked him; and then enquired about his soul.

Now, he will spend a few sick years in institutes,
And do what things the rules consider wise,
And take whatever pity they may dole.
Tonight he noticed how the women's eyes
Passed from him to the strong men that were whole.
How cold and late it is! Why don't they come
And put him into bed? Why don't they come?

Wilfred Owen

Home from Victory

(Written in response to Wilfred Owen's, 'Disabled')

When Harold Merton joined the army I thought he was crazy. He was too young to join, but he lied to the sergeant who took down his name, not even asking whether he was lying. Harold was eighteen and you weren't allowed to join until you were nineteen. His family tried to persuade him not to go but he wouldn't listen. I tried to talk him out of it, saying that he was too young to waste his life on the army, but he didn't listen to me either.

The day came when he had to go. Thousands of people were there saying farewell to their sons, husbands, lovers and friends. Some people were cheering and others were crying. I saw Harold go up to his Mum and Dad. He shook his Dad's hand and kissed then hugged his Mum and she started to cry. He came up to me and said goodbye, in a dull, unexcited voice, then he walked away.

I thought to myself then, was it really worth the agony? But I am now at the port where he left off and he is coming back. As thousands of people shout and cheer as the ship gently manoeuvres into the same place from where it departed, now I realize why he left. He left for the shouts and cheers for when he came back.

As the soldiers got off wearily, their faces lit up when they saw their wives. I kept waiting for Harold to come by and walk up to me and say, 'Well, I'm back, and in one piece,' but he didn't. I waited and waited until all the soldiers had come off and then the men in the wheelchairs were brought off. Then I saw him, sitting there with no arms or legs. The shock hit me like a brick wall as I saw this man, this disabled man, being pushed along the road. This man had no triumph in his eyes, no joy to be back and now no reason to live. This once extremely active, fit and inexhaustible man was being condemned to a wheelchair for the rest of his unhappy life. An irreconcilable feeling came into my mind. It was as if we had just had a fight and we had said to each other that we never wanted to see or be friends with each other again.

As my long-forgotten friend passed, I turned and walked home.

Matthew

Working on

1 How well does this creative response work? What do you think of Matthew's style and tone?
2 How successfully does he use the material from the poem? Does he refer closely enough to the poem itself?
3 How could the assignment be improved?

Now see the notes in the 'Feedback' unit on page 223.

Here is what one GCSE student said about Matthew's assignment. Do you agree or disagree with her view?

It's really good, especially when you first read it, because it has real emotional impact. He makes the scene on the dock come to life and presents the events very visually. It doesn't refer very closely to the original poem but it certainly captures the tone of it.

As I started thinking more about Matthew's assignment. I became slightly worried about it. It's the way he presents disability – it's so negative. Wilfred Owen's poem shows the injured soldier's point of view and his negative attitude. But this assignment is written from the point of view of someone who was a friend of Harold Merton. Why should this person jump to the conclusion that Harold had 'no reason to live'? Why does he never want to see or be friends with each other again.

I think it's a really bad view of disability, and I don't think it should go unchallenged. Other people in my class disagreed: they felt the assignment worked well and showed a realistic portrait of what a friend might think. I just hope I'd never think like that.

Lesley, (Year 10)

Follow-up

- To examine the techniques needed to write a more formal literary critical essay, see 'Writing About Literature' on page 170.
- To see an Examiner's comments on a literature assignment, see the end of this section.

Writing About Literature

Types of Tasks

Whether you study GCSE English alone, or together with English Literature, you are required to read and write about books. Writing about literature usually takes place in a variety of styles. You might be asked to:
• continue the story
• write a version of the story from a character's point of view
• write a diary or monologue in role as one character
• write a book review for a newspaper
• rewrite the story for a different audience... and so on
But still the most common way of responding to literature is through an essay in which you are asked to 'Discuss...', 'Compare...', 'Give a personal response ...'. Essays like this are called *literary criticism*, and you need to be able to analyse the text and describe your response. There are certain basic techniques for writing in this way.

Techniques of Literary Criticism

1 Answer the question
2 Write in an appropriate style
3 Support your opinions with evidence

1 Answer the question

Imagine you were asked one of these typical GCSE literature questions:

How are three of the characters in *An Inspector Calls* changed by Inspector Goole's visit?

Discuss whether you agree that Macbeth is responsible for his own downfall and describe the role of Lady Macbeth.

How does Napoleon rise to power in *Animal Farm?*

Compare the characters of Lennie and George in *Of Mice and Men*, saying why you think they depend on one another.

In order to answer the question successfully you need to be absolutely clear about what you are being asked to do. The question will definitely **not** ask you to retell the storyline. This is the biggest mistake GCSE students make – retelling the story rather than answering the question.

Start by underlining or writing out the key words from the question, and then make notes. In your notes you should be writing down the key points you will make in the course of your essay.

Everyone has their own preferred style of note making – some use lists of points; some use spider-diagrams. Whichever format you use, be systematic: try to cover all the main points. Do not write much at this stage – you are simply looking to list the key points of your essay.

Here are two examples of essay plans done by students answering the first question above:

An Inspector Calls

How are three of the characters in *An Inspector Calls* changed by Inspector Goole's visit?

Mr Birling

- older generation changed briefly, but quickly reverts to his old self
- early - Titanic speech, 'no chance of war' shows how arrogant and complacent he is
- only upset about effect on his and family's name
- shocked by final telephone call

Gerald

- early on - he's like Mr Birling - even shares his values
- genuinely upset at first by Eva Smith's death
- then changes back - becomes colder, as he works out how the family are not involved
- by end - he's like older generation

Sheila

- early on - giddy and silly also spiteful, unthinking
- very upset by Eva's death
- blames herself
- tries to warn others
- fascinated and affected by Inspector
- has changed - and doesn't want to change back - is 'frightened' at the end by the older generation's attitudes

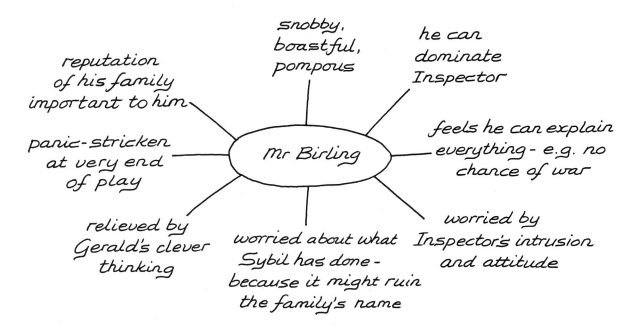

reputation of his family important to him

snobby, boastful, pompous

he can dominate Inspector

panic-stricken at very end of play

Mr Birling

feels he can explain everything - e.g. no chance of war

relieved by Gerald's clever thinking

worried about what Sybil has done - because it might ruin the family's name

worried by Inspector's intrusion and attitude

2 Write in an appropriate style

Literary criticism usually requires a fairly formal style. That means you should:

- Use Standard English.
- Avoid *elisions* (e.g. isn't, aren't)
- Use precise vocabulary – Latinate phrases rather than Anglo-Saxon ones (e.g. *George becomes irritated by Lennie* rather than *George gets fed up with Lennie*).
- Avoid using unfamiliar words from the Thesaurus for fancy effects.
- Write in substantial paragraphs – usually two, three, or four to a side of A4. More than that suggests that you are answering the question superficially.
- Use an Introduction if you need to (a) define the terms of the title, or (b) explain your approach to the question. Otherwise, dive straight into your first point. Writing an introduction can waste time, especially in an exam.
- Generally use an impersonal style – but you do not have to avoid saying 'I' or 'me' altogether.
- Use a variety of sentence types.
- Use cohesive devices to add variety and clarity to your writing: *however, although, therefore, then, at first, later...* and so on.
- Show that you are answering the question by echoing its phrasing at the start of new paragraphs.

Examples:

How does Napoleon rise to power in *Animal Farm*?

When we first encounter Napoleon in *Animal Farm*, he has no more power than the other animals...

A further way in which Napoleon gains power is by...

Later in the story Napoleon seizes the chance to...

---

3 Support your opinions with evidence

One of the most important techniques when writing literature essays is to use quotations to support your ideas.

There are two ways of using quotations:

1 Place long quotations (more than one sentence) in a separate paragraph.
2 Embed short quotations into your own sentences.

There are advantages and disadvantages to each technique:

Separate quotations
- ✓ Useful if you want to analyse the language of a longer extract.
- ✓ Good for quoting poetry and drama, because you can show how the verse or the dialogue works.
- ✗ Can make the essay very disjointed – can feel like you're padding the essay with unnecessary quotations.

Embedded quotations
- ✓ Makes the essay move more fluently – less disjointed.
- ✓ Allows you to quote the key words you need.
- ✗ Too many embedded quotations can clog up the meaning of your essay – the reader finds it difficult to follow your thread.

Look at this extract from a GCSE student's literature assignment and examine the different uses of quotations.

Opening sentence emphasizes the fact that the writer is answering the question

Embedded quotation keeps the pace up whilst also giving supporting evidence

Separate quotation is introduced by a colon

Writer then refers back to the ideas and language of the quotation

Embedded quotation uses / to show line break

> Discuss whether you agree that Macbeth is responsible for his own downfall and describe the role of Lady Macbeth
>
> ...Lady Macbeth's role at this point is to taunt her husband, to mock his lack of courage. She accuses him of being 'Infirm of purpose' and seizes the dagger to undertake the murder herself. At this point she uses language to play down the horror of death, making it seem a childlike concern:
>
> The sleeping, and the dead,
> Are but as pictures; 'tis the eye of childhood
> That fears a painted devil.
>
> She makes death appear trivial here in three ways: partly by comparing it to sleep; partly by comparing it to pictures; and finally by showing that it is children alone who fear such a thing. In doing so, she tries to reassure her husband, but at the same time seems to be mocking his lack of courage, as she did in her previous speech when she said that Macbeth did 'unbend your noble strength, to think/so brainsickly of things'...

Activity Re-read a literature essay you have written, redrafting it using the three techniques outlined in this spread.

Follow-up
- To see a GCSE student's literature essay and the comments of the Examiner, see the end of this section.
- For more information about formal style, see 'Standard English' on page 18.

Studying Character

Objectives:
- to examine ways in which writers create and present characters in texts
- to look at direct and indirect information about characters

Plenty of Character

Every play, novel, or short story you read contains characters – just as soap operas and dramas, films, and radio plays do. With soap operas, viewers sometimes confuse fiction with real life, and this leads them to assume that the wedding, illness, or death of a character in the programme is happening in real life... so they send flowers or cards to the studios.

Like so many of our literary conventions, the idea of characterization derives from the Ancient Greeks. Theophrastus (died 278 BC) wrote *Characters*, a series of sketches of moral types, such as the fop or the country squire, each one a particular type of person. Shakespeare did the same, referring at times to specific characters as Clown, King, Queen – as if they are types, as well as individuals. In literature, there are three broad categories of character.

the hero: (or protagonist)

someone of admirable qualities (e.g. courage, idealism) who is the central focus of the novel or play.

the anti-hero:

this form of character has gained popularity in the 20th Century: it is a hero lacking traditional heroic qualities (such as courage, idealism, wisdom), and instead frequently has vices like drinking or antisocial behaviour. A good example is the type of detective figure found in Raymond Chandler's novels.

the antagonist:

the major character placed in opposition to the hero – usually someone lacking the hero's positive qualities – quite frequently referred to as the 'baddie'.

Character Ingredients

At GCSE you need to become very knowledgeable about the characters in the texts you study. What different ingredients help to make up a character?
- appearance
- behaviour
- what they say
- habits
- what the author tell us directly
- what other characters say about them
- the way other characters react to them
- how they react to events
- how they change during the story

Notice, in other words, how many different clues we can gain about characters from different sources. This information can be divided up into direct and indirect information.

Activity Here is one of the shortest stories ever written. What can you say about the characters?

The Scarlatti Tilt

'It's very hard to live in a studio apartment in San José with a man who's learning to play the violin'. That's what she told the police when she handed them the empty revolver.

Richard Brautigan

Even though there are only two sentences here, we do learn some details about the main character. Look at the information given below and list any more ideas you can think of:

Direct Information	Indirect Information
female she has killed someone	probably American cold-blooded, or at least, cool nerves intolerant accepts her guilt precisely spoken

Now look at a longer extract from the start of a short story by Penelope Lively. This time, for the two main characters, make notes on the direct and indirect information we learn about them.

Bus-Stop

The 73 Bus, plunging from the heights of Islington down Pentonville Road towards King's Cross, put on a burst of speed between the traffic lights. The conductor, collecting fares from the standing passengers, smiled indulgently: a private smile, and hardly detectable in any case below the lush droop of his yellow-white moustache. He was a big man, a shambling figure with a stoop, the London Transport jacket even more ill-fitting than most, hanging lankly on him, the trousers sagging and supported by a broken belt.

'Any more fares then? King's Cross next stop!'

The diction was upper class – Edwardian upper class at that, a whiff of long-retired statesman about it; indeed, his whole head, if you isolated it from the grey uniform jacket and the paraphernalia of the ticket-machine, was that of, say, some city magnate, the kind of face that features in *The Times* above a brief note about an appointment to chairmanship of a bank or building society. Any incongruity, though, attracted no interest; a good many of the bus passengers, indeed, were foreign in any case and perhaps impervious to such subtleties. A Scandinavian couple wanted South Kensington and were redirected on to a 30. The lower deck thinned out at King's Cross and the conductor went to stand for a moment at the end of the aisle, leaning against the driver's window, his very large feet braced against the floor, stooping slightly to keep an eye out of the window and humming to himself. He had an expression of benign detachment, but there was also something faintly *louche*, a suggestion, the merest hint, of afternoon drinking clubs, of the odd flutter on the horses.

At Euston he came loping down the aisle to help a woman with a push-chair. As the bus halted at the Park Crescent traffic lights he restrained an elderly man from getting off – 'Not the stop, watch it! Just hang on till we get across the lights.' In Gower Street he remonstrated with a bunch of teenagers pushing their way up the stairs against the descending passengers. He ran an orderly bus, it was apparent. At the Great Russell Street stop he paused a full minute or so before ringing the bell to direct a party of Japanese to the British Museum; a querulous fist knocked on the panel of the driver's window. 'All right, all right,' he muttered amiably, reaching for the cord. The bus swung round into the seedier wastes of New Oxford Street, leaving behind it the grace of Bloomsbury, its cargo constantly mutating – raincoated map-laden tourists, bright-eyed shoppers, girls with rainbow hair, a West Indian woman with a tiny staring doll-like baby propped over her shoulder.

At the bottom of Tottenham Court Road there was a surge from the waiting queue, sending the conductor racing up the stairs to check empty seats on the upper deck. The lower deck filled up completely. A plump woman in her late sixties, fur-jacketed, forged her way panting to one of the seats up front. The bus proceeded in fits and starts along Oxford Street; the conductor moved down the aisle, collecting fares.

When he reached the fur-jacketed woman she said, 'Barkers, please', delving in her purse. Then she looked up, met the conductor's gaze fair and square, and gave a gasp that caused heads to turn.

'Hello, Milly,' said the conductor. 'Fancy seeing you. Barkers – forty, that'll be.'

The woman found, at last, speech. 'George!' She clutched a pound note in a gloved fist, staring transfixed.

The conductor glanced back at the platform, rang the bell for the request stop. 'How's Philip, then?'

'George...' whispered the woman. 'I don't believe it. Oh my God, how could you...'

'Come on, Milly,' said the conductor with a trace of impatience. 'How could I what? Forty, please.'

The woman closed her eyes for a moment and hugged the jacket about her. She turned to the conductor, spoke in shocked hushed complicity; 'Oh my God, George, what would Shirley say...'

'Look, turn it down would you, Milly.' The bus lurched, stopped. 'Oxford Circus! Anyone for Oxford Circus?' Passengers jostled on and off. 'I'll come back, Milly. Forty, to Barkers.' He made for the platform, gave an arm to a woman with a stick, stowed another pushchair for a mother, swung up the stairs.

Penelope Lively

George		Milly	
Direct	Indirect	Direct	Indirect

Based on your examination of the characters, what do you predict happens later in the story? Now look at the 'Feedback' unit on page 222.

Follow-up
- For advice on 'Keeping a Reading Diary' see page 130.
- To look at the way authors construct plots, see 'Studying Plot' on page 178.

Studying Plot

Objectives:
- to distinguish between stories and plots
- to examine the way authors construct plots in fiction

Stories and Plots

Q: What is the difference between a story and a plot?

A: A story is a sequence of events told in the right order. A plot is a sequence of events which the writer controls, changing the sequence where necessary, giving flashbacks, dropping hints, holding details back. A plot, in other words, shows sign of the writer's mind at work – a structure. A story tells itself.

Perhaps the central ingredient in storytelling is *cause and effect*. Because someone does something, something happens:

> Goldilocks needs to rest... so she sneaks into the bears' house...
> She is hungry... so she tries some porridge... and so on

This is a simple story of cause and effect. Take a novel or play you have recently read and fit it into this structure:

> X does something ⇨ so Y happens ⇨ so ..... ⇨ so ..... ⇨ so ..... ⇨ and finally...

Most stories are built around this structure, with the storyline tracing the progress of a single character through a series of events. The basic pattern of stories is frequently one of these:

Plot type 1

Character X starts off dissatisfied/out of luck ⇨ events take place ⇨ s/he ends up happier than at the start: this is the classic pattern of **comedy** – e.g. *Hobson's Choice, Jack and the Beanstalk.*

- Think about why this is such a popular story format. Is it something to do with our desire to see stories ending positively, with characters coming off better at the end than they began?

Plot type 2

Character X starts off successful/ambitious/arrogant ⇨ events go wrong ⇨ ends in disaster: this is the pattern of **tragedy** – e.g. *Macbeth, An Inspector Calls, Lord of the Flies.*

- What is the attraction of this type of tale? Does it always carry the same moral message – that being over-ambitious, too self-confident, unpleasant will lead to disaster? Do we read these stories for different reasons from those which end more optimistically?

Plot type 3

Character X starts off unsuccessfully ⇨ seems to make progress ⇨ things go wrong – e.g. *A Kestrel for a Knave.*

- This pattern of story is more rare. Why, do you think? Do we find it too disappointing to see someone making progress and then suddenly losing out? How do our feelings for the main characters in these stories differ from those in plot type 2?

Activity Look at the following titles and draw a graph to show their plots, tracing the progress of their main characters:

Little Red Riding Hood *Any Shakespeare play you know*
Cinderella *Of Mice and Men*
Hansel and Gretel *The Snowman*
Sleeping Beauty *Other set-texts*

Subplots

Sometimes writers will keep two storylines going at once, flipping from one to the other. Horror writers such as James Herbert and Stephen King frequently do this, starting their first three chapters with three different sets of characters in three different locations. The rest of their novels shows how these stories converge into a single plot.

Turn the page and discover how Peter Benchley creates a similar effect at the start of his novel *Jaws.*

Jaws

The great fish moved silently through the night water, propelled by short sweeps of its crescent tail. The mouth was open just enough to permit a rush of water over the gills. There was little other motion: an occasional correction of the apparently aimless course by the slight raising or lowering of a pectoral fin – as a bird changes direction by dipping one wing and lifting the other. The eyes were sightless in the black, and the other senses transmitted nothing extraordinary to the small, primitive brain. The fish might have been asleep save for the movement dictated by countless millions of years of instinctive continuity: lacking the flotation bladder common to other fish and the fluttering flaps to push oxygen-bearing water through its gills, it survived only by moving. Once stopped, it would sink to the bottom and die of anoxia.

The land seemed almost as dark as the water, for there was no moon. All that separated sea from shore was a long, straight stretch of beach – so white that it shone. From a house behind the grass-splotched dunes, lights cast yellow glimmers on the sand.

The front door to the house opened, and a man and a woman stepped out on to the wooden porch. They stood for a moment staring at the sea, embraced quickly, and scampered down the few steps on to the sand. The man was drunk, and he stumbled on the bottom step. The woman laughed and took his hand, and together they ran to the beach.

'First a swim,' said the woman, 'to clear your head.'

'Forget my head,' said the man. Giggling, he fell backward on to the sand, pulling the woman down with him... The woman looked at him and smiled. 'Now, how about that swim?' she said.

'You go ahead. I'll wait for you here.'

The woman rose and walked to where the gentle surf washed over her ankles. The water was colder than the night air, for it was only mid-June. The woman called back, 'You're sure you don't want to come?' But there was no answer from the sleeping man.

She backed up a few steps, then ran at the water. At first her strides were long and graceful, but then a small wave crashed into her knees.

She faltered, regained her footing, and flung herself over the next waist-high wave. The water was only up to her hips, so she stood, pushed the hair out of her eyes, and continued walking until the water covered her shoulders. There she began to swim – with the jerky, head-above-water stroke of the untutored.

A hundred yards offshore, the fish sensed a change in the sea's rhythm. It did not see the woman, nor yet did it smell her. Running within the length of its body were a series of thin canals, filled with mucus and dotted with nerve endings, and these nerves detected vibrations and signalled the brain. The fish turned towards shore.

The woman continued to swim away from the beach, stopping now and then to check her position by the lights shining from the house. The tide was slack, so she had not moved up or down the beach. But she was tiring, so she rested for a moment, treading water, and then started for shore.

The vibrations were stronger now, and the fish recognized prey. The sweeps of its tail quickened, thrusting the giant body forward with a speed that agitated the tiny phosphorescent animals in the water and caused them to glow, casting a mantle of sparks over the fish.

The fish closed on the woman and hurtled past, a dozen feet to the side and six feet below the surface. The woman felt only a wave of pressure that seemed to lift her up in the water and ease her down again. She stopped swimming and held her breath. Feeling nothing further, she resumed her lurching stroke.

The fish smelled her now, and the vibrations – erratic and sharp – signalled distress. The fish began to circle close to the surface. Its dorsal fin broke water, and its tail, thrashing back and forth, cut the glassy surface with a hiss. A series of tremors shook its body.

For the first time, the woman felt fear, though she did not know why. Adrenalin shot through her trunk and her limbs, generating tingling heat and urging her to swim faster. She guessed that she was fifty yards from shore. She could see the line of white foam where the waves broke on the beach. She saw the lights in the house, and for a comforting moment she thought she saw someone pass by one of the windows...

Peter Benchley

Activity Use this opening from *Jaws* to experiment with the way plots work. Try rewriting part of it as a single narrative – just telling the story of the woman going swimming. Or try retelling the story from the woman's point of view, using first-person narrative. And what happens if you rewrite the storyline so that every new sentence rather than every new paragraph switches from woman to shark?

Follow-up
- To look at the way writers build suspense, see 'Building Tension' on page 158.
- To read some examples of horror and detective fiction, see the 'Wider Reading List' on page 216.

Poetry Unseens

To See or Not to See

GCSE Literature exams quite often require students to read an unseen poem and to respond to it. Sometimes they may give you points to focus on; at other times you may simply have to structure ideas yourself.

Some people find the idea of responding to an unseen poem a terrifying activity. Others enjoy the challenge. Perhaps the key point to remember is that there is no single correct answer. You should have the confidence to describe what you notice.

Does this mean that you can say anything you like about a poem and it will be right?

No. If you read a poem about love and say that it is about car parks, and you can provide no evidence, you are clearly wrong! But you should not feel that there is some mysterious hidden meaning lurking inside the poem which only a genius can find. With practice, you will easily find things to say. There are a few techniques which will help you in responding to unseen poems:

The Techniques of unseens

1 If possible, annotate the poem as you read it – that is, circle, underline, and make notes of patterns, hints, ideas it reminds you of, other texts you have read, changes you notice, what the narrator seems to be like, how the subject is being treated, what the tone is like... and so on.
2 Expect to read any poem three times before you begin to feel any level of confidence in writing about it. Poetry is compressed language: you should expect to have to work at it.
3 Analysing poetry will become easier the more you read. Get a good anthology (see the Wider Reading recommendations on page 216) and get in the habit of reading a variety of poems by different authors.
4 When writing about poetry, give your personal response, but be sure that you support your ideas with quotations.
5 Follow the structure of the poem, writing about it as it unfolds, starting with the title, then the first line, and ending with the last line. Be sure to organize your ideas into paragraphs – a brief plan is vital.

What to Say

This checklist of points might help you to gain confidence in writing poetry. But it is important that you don't simply work your way mechanically through it every time, or else your response will lack heart...
- Look at the title – what does it suggest/remind you of? What do you predict the poem will be about?
- Look at each line of the poem – what is it saying? What unexpected words or images do you notice? Is there rhythm or rhyme and how does this add to the meaning?
- How does the poem develop – are the ideas at the end different from the ideas at the beginning? Has the writer's attitude changed?
- What is your impression of the writer? What creates this?
- What is the tone of the poem – serious, comic, ironic, bitter...?
- Which parts of the poem do you most like/dislike? Why?

- Which parts of the poem seem most memorable? Why?
- Which parts of the poem are most straightforward or difficult?
- What, overall, does the poem say to you about its theme? What have you learnt from it?

Activity   Now read Seamus Heaney's poem *Mid-Term Break* and make notes on what you notice about it. Then look at the response of Adele in Year 9 and the questions which follow.

Mid-Term Break

I sat all morning in the college sick bay
Counting bells knelling classes to a close.
At two o'clock our neighbours drove me home.

In the porch I met my father crying –
He had always taken funerals in his stride –
And Big Jim Evans saying it was a hard blow.

The baby cooed and laughed and rocked the pram
When I came in, and I was embarrassed
By old men standing up to shake my hand

And tell me they were 'sorry for my trouble';
Whispers informed strangers I was the eldest,
Away at school, as my mother held my hand

In hers and coughed out angry tearless sighs.
At ten o'clock the ambulance arrived
With the corpse, stanched and bandaged by the nurses.

Next morning I went up into the room. Snowdrops
And candles soothed the bedside; I saw him
For the first time in six weeks. Paler now,

Wearing a poppy bruise on his left temple,
He lay in the four foot box as in his cot.
No gaudy scars, the bumper knocked him clear.

A four foot box, a foot for every year.

Seamus Heaney

Mid-Term Break by Seamus Heaney

The title 'Mid-Term Break' seems very straightforward and clearly announces what the poem is about. It seems to mean that it is about a mid-term break for the person the poem is about, who is obviously of school age. As you read through, there could be another, slightly different meaning, a contradiction to what you immediately think of. The boy who has this mid-term break is sent home because his little brother is dead and he goes home for the funeral, so instead of the holiday or break you immediately think of as a 'mid-term break', it is actually not a holiday or anything good, but is a time of sadness and sorrow.

The first verse is very simple and straightforward; the boy who is about to be sent home has to sit in the sick-bay at school, whilst waiting for his neighbours to come and pick him up and take him home. They finally come at two o'clock, but before, the boy sits waiting in the sick-bay counting the school bells that end the classes, as they seem to be his only means of telling the passing of time. That is the only thing he has to do in the sick-bay. This way of counting the hours while the boy waits also shows how childish the boy is, just to sit patiently counting the bells. This seems to be a very childish reaction, and Heaney's way of hinting at childishness.

The next verse also seems to be straightforward. When the boy gets home he meets his father crying. This seems to be unusual and unexpected, as the boy says, 'He had always taken funerals in his stride'. This means that this particular death must have hit the father harder than any there had been before. The boy also meets 'Big Jim Evans', who is possibly a neighbour or friend of the family, who also seems to be sad and says it was a hard blow, although I don't know whether it's supposed to be a hard blow especially for the boy. It doesn't make it clear. So far the poem seems to be very straightforward.

I have been referring to the person in the poem as a boy. This is because of the general impression that the poem gives me. There are also several clues in the poem; the way the boy reacts and tells the poem, and also, when the boy goes into the room the old men 'shake his hand', an unusual thing to do to a girl. He also says that he is the eldest, as though he is the eldest of a couple of boys. It is also easier to refer to the person as a 'he' or a 'she', rather than an 'it' or a 'person'.

In the third verse the boy describes the scene when he comes in; the baby, obviously younger than the boy who was killed, laughing and cooing in the pram, whilst old men stand up when he comes in, to shake his hand and tell him they were 'sorry for my trouble.' He was embarrassed at this, although it doesn't make it clear whether this is by the shaking of the hand, the principle behind the action, or just the action. 'His trouble' is this brother dying and him having to leave school, I think. The men whisper that he is the eldest away at school, while his mother hangs on to his hand tightly. She's already lost one child, and it seems to me that by hanging on to him she's trying to make sure she doesn't lose him as well. He's also probably a comfort to her. It says she 'coughed out angry, tearless sighs.' This shows that she is too sad to cry, is welled up with all the emotion and this is the only way she can show her emotion without totally breaking down.

When he finally sees him, he is surrounded by candles and snowdrops. The boy hadn't seen his brother for six weeks, which means the school he's at must be a boarding school. He describes the scene naturally, as though it wasn't a dead body he was looking at but, for example, a chair, with a poppy red bruise on his left temple (forehead), while the rest of his face is pale. This is the only metaphor in the entire poem; comparing the red bruise to a poppy. This shows it must be bright. We now learn how he died; a car hit him, but cleanly, without cuts, as the bumper hit such a small body clear. As the boy gazes at his brother, he says 'he lay in the coffin as in his cot.' This suddenly makes you realize he was only a baby. I think the last line is very good; it really sums up the sadness and unfairness of the death that the whole poem has been getting at.

This poem is about childhood. The boy in the poem is very childish; the way he deals with the situation and tells the poem, and the way he deals with his emotions, and sees others do the same thing. Even his actions are very childish and the way at the beginning he sits in the sick-bay just counting the bells.

The language Heaney uses is very simple, matching the childish aura of the poem and the ideas, and is easy to understand. This is quite different to some other poems he has written, where he relies a lot on metaphors, similes, on the senses, and on descriptive writing. I think he has done this because the poem is told as seen through a boy's eyes, with a boy's mind.

Adele (Year 9)

1 How successful is Adele's commentary on the poem? Say whether you agree or disagree with each statement and find evidence from the essay or poem to support your view.
   A The essay responds well to the storyline in the poem.
   B It makes the poem seem clearer to follow.
   C It is short of quotations.
   D It does not focus sufficiently on the language of the poem.
   E It could say more about the narrator's character.
   F The vocabulary is not precise enough.
   G The essay does not recognize the complexity of the poem.
   H It is a very good response to the poem.
2 Write your own response to *Mid-Term Break*, in which you move through the poem describing what you notice and commenting upon Seamus Heaney's use of language.

Follow-up
• For advice on comparing poems, see 'Comparing Texts' on page 186.
• For ways of using quotations to support your ideas, see 'Writing About Literature' on page 170.
• For advice about problem poems and compressed language, see 'Reading Poetry' on page 148.

Comparing Texts

Objectives:
- to look at ways of comparing texts
- to suggest ways of organizing a written response

Shall I Compare Thee... ?

English at GCSE sometimes requires you to compare two unseen texts – possibly two poems, or a poem and short story. In itself this is not so different from doing a poetry unseen – but how should you organize your response so that it deals with each text systematically and creatively?

Reading paired texts

Paired texts usually have some shared theme – they might both deal with childhood, or crime, or love. Or they might deal with a similar theme in a different way – one celebrating love, one showing bitterness. Or they might have a similar theme but a different style – one a monologue spoken by the person involved, the other a piece of impersonal descriptive writing. The possibilities are numerous. The secret is to be systematic as you study the texts in spotting similarities and differences.

Activity Use the prompts in the chart which follows texts A and B to group your notes about the similarities and differences between these.

A: Response

When you wrote your letter it was April,
And you were glad that it was spring weather,
And that the sun shone out in turn with showers of rain.

I write in waning May and it is autumn,
And I am glad that my chrysanthemums
Are tied up fast to strong posts,
So that the south winds cannot beat them down.
I am glad that they are tawny coloured,
And fiery in the low west evening light.
And I am glad that one bush warbler
Still sings in the honey-scented wattle...

But oh, we have remembering hearts,
And we say 'How green it was in such and such an April,'
And 'Such and such an autumn was very golden,'
And 'Everything is for a very short time.'

Mary Ursula Bethell

B: The Voice

Woman much missed, how you call to me, call to me,
Saying that now you are not as you were
When you had changed from the one who was all to me,
But as at first, when our day was fair.

Can it be you that I hear? Let me view you, then,
Standing as when I drew near to the town
Where you would wait for me: yes, as I knew you then,
Even to the original air-blue gown!

Or is it only the breeze, in its listlessness
Travelling across the wet mead to me here,
You being ever dissolved to wan wistlessness,
Heard no more again far or near?

Thus I; faltering forward,
Leaves around me falling,
Wind oozing thin through the thorn from norward,
And the woman calling.

Thomas Hardy

	Similarities	Differences
subject matter		
narrator's character		
narrator's attitude to love		
narrator's attitude to passage of time		
images of nature		
structure of poem		
language of poem		

Writing about paired texts

You might be given specific questions which will help to structure your response. For example:

1 Write a paragraph comparing what we learn about the narrators of the two poems.
2 How do the writers differ in their attitude to love? ...and so on.

But if not, you will need to organize your response around the notes you have made. There are two possible ways of approaching this:

Model 1
- Write entirely about text A tracing its development from title to last line.
- Then write about text B referring back to text A and comparing the two.

Model 2
- Write about one theme of text A and text B.
- Write about the next theme of text A and text B.
- Write about the next theme...comparing the two as you go along.

Model **1** is easier to write because the structure is more straightforward. But model **2** is usually better because it doesn't leave all the comparison of the texts to the end of the essay – it compares the two more actively throughout.

A **plan** for model **2** might look like this:

similarities and differences in...   the poems' themes
                                      the poets' attitude to love
                                      the poets' attitude to ageing
                                      the poets' references to nature
                                      the poets' use of structure
                                      the poets' use of language
personal response: which I prefer and why...

Notice how the essay moves from more general points (themes) to more specific points (examples of language). Each of these points would represent a paragraph, supported by brief quotations. One important hint for writing the essay is to avoid using subheadings (e.g. *themes, attitude to love*), which could make the essay read like a set of notes. Instead, use topic sentences at the start of each new paragraph to indicate the subject-matter that you will be covering in the paragraph. For example:

> There are also differences in the two writers' attitudes to the theme of love. For example...
> The references to nature in both poems show...
> In terms of language, the two poems are...

Working on   Read and annotate the poems carefully again. Then have a go at writing the essay, based on this question:

Write a comparison of the two poems saying which you prefer. Refer to their treatment of the theme of love and ageing, as well as their use of structure and language.

Follow-up
- For ways of reading and responding to poetry, look at 'Reading Poetry' on page 148.
- For advice on using quotations, see 'Writing About Literature' on page 170.

Planning Coursework

Are You Prepared?

English at GCSE has two important components: preparation for examinations and preparation of a coursework folder.

Coursework generally counts for less of the overall mark (usually 40% for English Language and 30% for English Literature). All syllabuses require students to compile a folder of coursework assignments containing usually between three and six pieces of work. Of course, during the two-year GCSE course you will produce more than that basic number, so that you can then choose your best assignments within different categories.

Some people perform best under coursework conditions.

Coursework types

- spend a lot of time getting their ideas into the right order
- research background to the texts
- find the appropriate quotations
- redraft
- get the phrasing and style just right.

These students frequently put in many hours on each assignment and gain satisfaction from seeing their folder of assignments develop and progress.

Examination types

- like the pressure of examination conditions
- do not like spending hours on each assignment
- have confidence (sometimes too much) in their ability to perform well on the day of the exam
- enjoy working close to deadlines

Most people are probably a mixture of these two types. What is important is to realize that coursework gives different opportunities from exam study. Your coursework folder gives you the opportunity to look at a text in depth, to pursue a particular interest or enthusiasm, to show evidence of wider reading, to get your style carefully crafted... Perhaps most importantly it allows you to show the full range of your abilities in English and English literature.

A well-balanced GCSE folder might look like this:

Literature assignments

This contains two contrasting responses to literature. For example:

1 **Analytical response**
   - Trace the decline of *Macbeth*.
   - Look at one scene from *Romeo and Juliet* and write about what we learn from the language about the characters.
   - How do the characters in *An Inspector Calls* change during the Inspector's visit?
   - How does John Steinbeck maintain our sympathy for Lennie throughout *Of Mice and Men*?

2 Creative response
- Imagine you are Mr Farthing in *A Kestrel for a Knave*. Describe the way your attitude to Billy has changed since you learnt about his skill with Kes.
- Imagine you are Elizabeth Proctor in *The Crucible*. Describe your relationship with John, showing how it has developed during your marriage.

This range of literature assignments might also include a wider reading, personal response essay, such as:
- Write about two detective/horror novels you have enjoyed reading, comparing the main characters and the authors' styles.

Whatever combination of essays you finally choose for your folder of literature assignments, the important point is that the folder should contrast with and complement your examination work. Coursework essays should therefore be:
- more developed (but not excessively lengthy – around 6 sides of A4 is the top limit)
- more detailed
- more varied in approach

Language assignments

Your language coursework will probably consist of between one and three assignments, such as:

Response to non-literary material
For example:
- take facts and figures about smoking and represent them in a leaflet for young people
- look at arguments about animal rights and create a speech aimed at persuading your audience...

Creative assignment
For example:
- write a narrative
- write a personal account

Factual assignment
For example:
- write a work experience report

Remember that you will not be able to include all of these types of assignments – your English teacher will give you more guidance on the exact choices. But the important point to note is that your coursework folder should provide a variety of styles and topics, and work on an assortment of texts.

Follow-up
- To revise your use of quotations, see 'Writing about Literature' on page 170.
- For more about writing lively and persuasive assignments, see 'Discursive Assignments' on page 118.

Revision Advice

Objectives:
- to look at ways of revising set-texts actively and creatively
- to suggest how to cope with examination panic!

Revision Checklist

Here are six hints on revising your set-texts for final examinations:

1 Re-read the texts before the examination, but do not leave it until the day before. Read them in the month before the examination and, as you do so, keep a page in your reading diary to note down new ideas that occur to you, quotations that seem especially relevant, etc.

2 Check whether your examination allows you to annotate, or mark, the texts. If you are allowed to, beware: highlighting key quotations and important incidents from the storyline is useful as a way of speeding-up your examination performance, but it does not replace knowing the text inside out.

3 Make your reading active by using charts and tables, doodles, pictures, lists – anything which will help you to recall important information. Many students feel happier and more confident if they have learnt some quotations before they go into the exam. Ideally, choose quotations which will prove useful for a number of purposes – e.g. to back up points about a character and a particular theme.

4 Be able to say more about your texts than what happens. Have a clear idea about the role and development of the main characters; of the main themes; and become familiar with the writer's style. A useful way of testing your detailed knowledge of the text is to choose an opening page from a new chapter or section; read it through; and then list the kinds of points you would make in an examination, using questions like these:
   - what is significant about the storyline at this point?
   - what is significant about the characters?
   - which important themes does the extract contain?
   - how is the style characteristic and uncharacteristic of the book as a whole?

5 In revision, keep reducing your notes using key words so that a single prompt conveys strings of information to you. To do this you need to be able to keep testing yourself at each stage to ensure that you are memorizing details effectively.

   For example: a set of key words for John Steinbeck's novel, *Of Mice and Men*, might look like this:

Characters
George, Lennie, Curley, Curley's wife, Slim, Candy

Themes
ambition, relationships, place

Style
structure, language, images

This would be the top 'layer' of your revision. Looking at each key word would trigger a list of main points and quotations. So a postcard of notes based on the key word **ambition** might say:

<u>Ambition</u>
Most characters have a 'dream'. None ever achieves it

<u>George and Lennie:</u>
To own their own ranch and 'live off the fatta the land'
Important to have control of their own lives: 'if there was a circus, we'd just say to hell with work'
Begin to compromise their ideal - sharing with others
George hasn't got the self-discipline - goes drinking with others

<u>Curley's wife</u>
Thinks she could have been an actress: 'I could have worked in movies'
But Steinbeck hints that she would not have been good: lifts her little finger in a very hammy way

<u>Candy</u>
Fear of being canned- wants to share G+L's dream

6 Do not panic: as you will have sensed from Martyn Thorpe's advice (he is the examiner writing in this book), questions are not there to catch you out. They are written with the aim of allowing you to show what you know about a text, rather than what you don't know. Most people get very nervous at the start of exams: plough your energy into quick, precise planning of your answer. It will build your confidence as you begin to organize your thoughts and quotations. If you can't remember an important quotation, and you can't find it quickly in your set text, simply paraphrase it (put it into your own words) without using quotation marks – like this:
George says: 'Without you I could live so easy'
… to paraphrase it…
George says that without Lennie he could live so easily…

Follow-up
- For advice on active reading, see 'Keeping a Reading Diary' on page 130.
- For advice on organizing your ideas, see 'Note-making' on page 124.

Examiner's Comments: Literature Essay

A Year 11 student has written the *Macbeth* essay that appears on page 194 for his coursework folder. Even if you have not studied *Macbeth*, you will still be able to learn about essay technique from reading the essay. It may help, however, to read the following short plot summary.

Macbeth – William Shakespeare

Macbeth wins honour in battle for Scotland and King Duncan decides to reward him with the title, Thane of Cawdor. Macbeth and fellow officer Banquo meet the witches who prophesy Macbeth's new title and that he shall be king. King Duncan visits Macbeth's castle; he has just declared his own son, Malcolm, as his heir. Macbeth is driven on by his wife to kill the king and immediately regrets it. The murder is discovered by Macduff who, along with Banquo, begins to suspect Macbeth.

Macbeth becomes king. He then arranges the murder of Banquo without his wife's knowledge. At the ceremonial banquet which follows, Banquo's ghost appears to Macbeth and the meal is disrupted. Macbeth meets up with the witches who make further prohecies to reassure him he will remain king.

Macbeth has Lady Macduff and her child killed and Macduff himself becomes Malcolm's ally. Lady Macbeth dies deranged at Dunsinane and Malcolm's troops advance towards the besieged castle. All the witches prophecies are overturned and Macbeth's head is brought to Malcolm by Macduff. Order is restored.

Activity

1 As you read the essay, cover the examiner's comments and make some brief notes about:
   - how well the student answers the question
   - how well he organizes his answer
   - how clear his style of writing is
   - how effectively quotations have been used
   - what works particularly well
   - what could be improved
2 Then look at the comments alongside the essay from the GCSE examiner who read it.

<u>To what extent do you think Macbeth is in control of his own destiny and therefore responsible for events in the play?</u>

The essay begins well, immediately focusing on the idea of destiny.

It quickly establishes an argument, using a well-chosen quotation.

Before we meet Macbeth a certain image is portrayed to us. This is mainly where the Captain describes Macbeth's prowess in battle. He is described as 'brave Macbeth' and was like 'valour's minion'. This all builds up an image of a heroic Macbeth. Also, importantly, we are informed that Macbeth 'disdains fortune'. It is interesting to note, even early on, how this connection appears. At this instant we are seeing Macbeth not believing in fortune but entrusting his destiny into his own hands.

The first group of people who really begin to put a strong influence on Macbeth's actions are the witches. They tell Macbeth of their prophecy yet in a very cryptic way. In doing so they in fact set Macbeth's mind working. Therefore although the thoughts are his own they have been triggered by the mystery of the witches. The three predictions are interesting to note. We know already that Macbeth is Thane of Glamis. We know also that he will become Thane of Cawdor because of his actions. It wasn't chance that gave him the honour it was his own bravery and courage. Finally to achieve this title he had to spill blood. Macbeth's brutal capacity is described plainly when he is told 'Nothing afeard of what thyself didst make, Strange images of death.' This ability of Macbeth's to be unaffected by death has gained him the title Thane of Cawdor. Therefore at this point Macbeth is in total control. Similarly if this is the way Macbeth acquired this title, then it would seem inevitable, although he doesn't realize it yet, purely because of his character. If he were to become king it would be by similar acts of butchery.

The second paragraph maintains the focus but becomes confused at the end.

The key point to note at this stage is when Macbeth says 'If Chance will have me king, why, Chance may crown me.' This summarizes Macbeth's current attitude. Although fascinated by the witches prophecies he is not going to take control, preferring to allow fate to dictate his life. This seems confusing. Macbeth is saying that he is not in control and yet in most aspects he is. His actions are not being dictated by any outside influences. So the witches themselves, except for stirring Macbeth's inner ambitions, did nothing to affect his later behaviour.

The third paragraph wrestles with the idea of Macbeth's 'control', but the expression suffers and the essay loses its way.

Lady Macbeth provides a far stronger influence on Macbeth. As his wife she has developed a knowledge of his weaknesses, mainly emotional.

Straight away, Lady Macbeth is overcome by the idea of being royalty. In fact it is she who first contemplates the idea of murder. She says how she feels he is too considerate to 'catch the nearest way' - kill Duncan. She decides she will 'chastise with the valour of my tongue all that impedes them from the golden crown.' Adding to this she says, 'I may pour my spirits in thine ear,' again considering strong persuasion.

The writer exaggerates the importance of Lady Macbeth and the essay loses its focus.

Throughout the play until her death Lady Macbeth appears to be the driving force behind her husband. Macbeth's own ideas centred purely on fate but Lady Macbeth is the one who convinces him he must seize his own destiny. Even Lady Macbeth however feels superstitious. We know this because she frequently calls on the spirits to help her.

Later in the play we have the death of Lady Macbeth, which also affects the way Macbeth acts. Its seems to be the final straw of his sanity. From this point onwards he slowly loses control.

All through the play Macbeth creates his own opportunities. It is he that kills the Thane of Cawdor thus gaining the title. It is he who kills the king, thus gaining the throne. All of these actions were his own, he was in total control over them. Although the ideas did come from outside influences, finally it was he that chose the path to take. Therefore it would seem he was in control of his own destiny.

The reference of Macbeth's return to the witches needs much more detail.

Later on in the play Macbeth does display a dependency. He revisits the witches to seek advice. Although it could be argued that he chose to go to the witches therefore he was in control, I believe it shows more of a dependency like a smoker addicted to cigarettes is not in control.

At the very end of the play Macbeth believes he is invincible. He says 'I bear a charmed life' and even adds 'But swords I smile at, weapons laugh to scorn.' This again shows he has lost control. He is acting upon the witches' advice that he cannot be killed by any man of woman born. Without the witches he would probably have hidden or fled instead of remaining to be killed.

The conclusion is good.

Therefore, in conclusion, I believe that the question of whether or not Macbeth controlled his own destiny is a complex one. It can easily be said that he was influenced significantly in certain decisions yet he still had the final word. Certainly the murder of Banquo and others later on was not prompted by anyone. Finally I believe that at the outset Macbeth was in control of his destiny, but as more murders occurred events got out of hand and finally he lost control leading to his death.

Overall: some strong points of style; a fairly systematic use of quotations; but the thread of the essay, and supporting detail, are not clear enough.

Language B+
Literature A-

Follow-up • For more on researching and planning coursework see 'Planning Coursework' on page 189.

Examiner's Question & Answer

In this spread, Examiner, Martyn Thorpe, answers students' questions about English at GCSE...

Speaking and Listening

1 Does my spoken English *have* to be assessed at GCSE? If so, why?

Yes, it is required by the National Curriculum, which has statutory power. It also makes sense that your ability to communicate through talk should be assessed alongside your reading and writing skills.

2 What kinds of activities will I be expected to do?

A range of formal and informal activities, including group discussion and individual performance. Some examples: discussing a poem, taking part in a debate, performing some drama, chairing a meeting.

3 What if I'm very shy about speaking in front of others?

Almost everyone feels the same at times and teachers can minimize the stress. But as the course progresses, you'll see your confidence develop.

4 Does it matter if I speak in a strong accent?

No – everyone has an accent of some sort. Speaking clearly is the most important thing.

5 How will I be assessed?

It is teacher-assessed, with teachers following criteria to guide their marking (see 'Assessing Speech' on page 68). For example, a good candidate will express a point of view clearly to a range of audiences; an exceptional candidate will express a point of view on more complex subjects persuasively and clearly. It is remarkable in practice how closely the marks reflect overall ability in English.

English Language

6 How is English Language different from English Literature?

There are no set-books, and a different range of skills is tested, with some overlap in reading. English Language requires you to read non-literary materials – such as magazines, newspapers, and advertisements.

7 Doesn't English Language involve reading?

Yes, it's a compulsory part of the coursework and examinations, but the material you need to read is not the same as for Literature.

8 What kinds of assignments count as Language assignments?

Essays, letters, reports, creative writing, plus response to non-literary materials such as newspapers, magazines, and so on.

9 What kinds of tasks will be set in the exam?

These vary from one examination board to the next. Some use pre-release anthologies, which you read in advance and then work on in the exams. Usually there is a comprehension of literary and non-literary materials, plus a range of writing tasks (write a report, letter, story, and so on).

10 How important are spelling, punctuation, and grammar in my overall grade?

Very. All three elements are taken into account in the final grading of your work. It is impossible to write clearly and effectively without having good control of writing, accuracy, and style.

11 Can I word-process my coursework assignments?

Yes, but there has to be evidence of handwritten work as well.

English Literature

12 Is English literature totally separate from English Language?

There is some overlap in the coursework folder – your literature assignments will also be assessed for language grades. You would need to look more closely at the syllabus your school or college is following.

13 What kind of work will it involve?

Study of set books, plus 'unseens' on most syllabuses in which you answer questions on an unfamiliar text. You will study a range of poetry, prose, and drama, some for coursework, some for the final examinations. The focus of your work will include characters, themes, plot, style, and language.

14 How does coursework and examination work differ?

The types of questions will usually differ. Coursework assignments provide opportunities to explore texts more fully and sometimes to negotiate possible essay titles with your teacher. Examination questions will, of course, be constrained by time limits.

15 Are spelling, punctuation, and grammar important when writing literature assignments?

Firstly, examiners need to be able to follow what you have written! The quality of writing inevitably influences the quality of your response. There is a 5% mark allocation for spelling, punctuation, and grammar.

16 Would it help me to buy study aids – books of notes on specific texts, etc?

No. Reading the set-texts thoroughly is essential. It is also useful to read other works by the same author. But the text you are studying is the most important one to know well.

17 What are the most important things I need to be able to do to succeed in Lit?

Read the books carefully and get to know them inside out. Write clearly and support what you say by textual reference and quotation. Develop a clear view of the book – major themes, characters, style, and so on. Remember, many different interpretations of a text are possible so long as your views are based on careful reading, discussion, and close reference to the text.

Good luck!
Martyn Thorpe.

Literature Timeline

Objectives:

- to learn more about the history of English literature
- to develop a sense of the main developments in each century

Warning: Danger Zone

This section has to start with some important words of warning because it is attempting the impossible: to give a history of English Literature in just 18 pages. So you must handle it with care and realize that:

- each spread is designed to give you some of the 'headlines' from each century – not the news in full
- the idea behind each spread is to show you how literature has developed – so you need to read it actively, not imagine that you can just drop any facts into your own essays
- the idea of a history of literature is controversial, and there are many writers not mentioned here who are just as good and just as readable as the 'star names'. Histories like this one tend to neglect women writers and writers from other cultures
- the idea of key events is to give a flavour of the century, not to identify the most important things that happened.

Each spread has the following elements:

1 historical background
2 a timeline of some of the century's key writers
3 examples of some of the most significant texts from each period
4 activities designed to get you familiar with each century's literature

Fifteenth Century

Some key events:

1400   Chaucer dies
1420   Henry V conquers France
1452   metal plates are used for printing
1459   English civil war begins again
1492   discovery of the New World (the Americas)

Historical Background

In this painting Richard II leans forward in praise of the new-born Christ. This is a world in which royalty has the divine right to rule – the gift of God – and Richard is presented as in perfect harmony with the religious elements. The angels even wear his insignia – the white hart – and Jesus leans forward, perhaps to bless the king. The message is as clear as the flag of England flying above: there is a set pattern to the universe, with everything in its exact, unmoving place. All is reassuring, unthreatening, and right.

As the key events of the century show, this is a time of excitement abroad and disruption at home. But as one of the major events in human history begins to be felt – the invention of the printing press – social life is in the grip of war. Meanwhile the 15th Century has a clear sense of the human position in the universe, which had existed since Classical times. It looked like this:

The 'Ptolemaic' Universe.

At the centre of the diagram is the Earth, or Terra, surrounded by the orbits of various planets. At the top is God, surrounded by the angels. And at the four corners are the four winds. Everything is in its right place, with God on top and human beings at the centre. This map of the universe would be overturned in the next century.

Poetry:

In the previous century Geoffrey Chaucer had written his massively influential *Canterbury Tales*. They used the South East Midlands dialect and were written in the iambic pentameter form which Shakespeare would use so creatively in the 16th and 17th centuries. Chaucer established English as a powerful medium for poetry, with his epic story of a pilgrimage to Canterbury by a host of riotous characters. Here the Wife of Bath gives a warning about marriage: 'You'll hear of all the tribulations man and wife can have,' she says, and promises to give at least ten examples. See if you can catch the gist of what she says from Chaucer's language.

Around 1470 Sir Thomas Malory publishes *Le Morte D'Arthur*, a prose translation from the French and one of the first books ever printed. But remember that most people are illiterate at this time and popular communication takes place not through the written word, but through performance...

The Wife of Bath's Prologue

'Abide!' quod she, 'my tale is nat bigonne.
Nay, thou shalt drinken of another tonne,
Er that I go, shal savoure wors than ale.
And whan that I have toold thee forth my tale
Of tribulacion in mariage,
Of which I am expert in al myn age –
This is to seyn, myself have been the whippe –
Than maystow chese wheither thu wolt sippe
Of thilke tonne that I shal abroche.
Be war of it, er thou to ny approche;
Fro I shal telle ensamples mo than ten.
'Whoso that nil be war by othere men,
By him shul othere men corrected be.'

Geoffrey Chaucer

Drama:

Mystery plays dominate the century, as they did the 14th Century. Mystery means 'mastery' or 'craft', because these plays were performed on carts in the streets of towns and cities like York, Coventry, and Wakefield by guilds of local craftsmen. The mysteries took Bible stories and retold them. Their ambitious aim was to explain the entire history of the universe.

Look at this extract from the York Mysteries which tells the story of Adam and Eve being tempted by the Serpent:

SEPRENS: Take of this fruite and assaie.
It is good meate, I dare laye.
And but thou fynde yt to thy paye,
Say that I am false.
Eate thou on apple and no moe,
And yow shall knew both wayle and woe,
And be lyke to goddess, both twoo,
Thou and thy housband also.

EVA: Ah, lord, this tree is fayre and bright,
Greene and semelye in my sighte,
The fruyte swete and much of mighte,
That goddes it may us make.
An apple of it I will eate,
To assaye which is the meate;
And my housband I will get
One morsell for to take.

Adam, husband, life and deere,
Eate some of this apple here –
It is fayre, my leeif fere,
It may thou not forsake.
ADAM: That is sooth, Eve, without weere.
The fruite is sweete and fayre in feere;
Therefore I will doe thy prayer,
One morsell I will take.

Out! Alas! What eales me?
I am naked, well I see;
Woman, cursed must thou be
For bothe now we be shente.
I wotte not for shame whether to flee,
For this fruite was forbydden me;
Now have I broken, through red of the,
My Lordes commaundement.

EVA: Alas! This adder hath done me nye.
Alas! Her red why did I?
Naked we bene bothe for-thye,
And of our shape ashamed.
ADAM: Yea, soothe said I in prophesie,
When thou wast taken of my body,
Mans woe thou woldest be witlie;
Therefore thou wast so named.

EVA: Adam, husband, I red we take
Thes figg-leaves, for shame sake,
And to our members a hillinge make
Of them for thee and me.
ADAM: Therewith my members I will hyde,
And under this tre I will abyde;
For sickerlie come God us beside
Owt of this place shall we.

DEUS: Adam, Adam, where art thou?
ADAM: Ah, Lord, I hard thy voyce right now;
I am naked, I make a vowe,
Therefore nowe I hyde me.
DEUS: Whoe tolde the, Adam, thou naked was,
Save onelie thyne owne trespasse,
That of the tree thou eaten hase
That I forbade thee?

ADAM: Lord, this woman that is here,
That thou gave me to my fere,
Gave me part: I did [att] her prayer;
Of it I did eate.
DEUS: Woman, why hast thou done soe?
EVA: This adder, Lorde, shee was my foe,
And sothelie deceaved me thoe,
And made me eate that meate.

This text was probably first copied in 1378, and then added to and revised in the 15th Century. Use the prompts which follow to compare it with a very modern account of the same story on page 201:

'Where are you, Adam?'
'I'm behind this tree, Lord.'
'What are you doing there?'
'Nothing, Lord. I'm naked is all.'
'Who told you you were naked?'
'I noticed it, Lord.'
'Naked, shmaked, what does it matter?'
'You can get six months for indecency, Lord.'
'What's six months to you, you're immortal.'
'It might give the animals funny thoughts.'
'My animals don't have funny thoughts.'
'The best people wear suits, Lord.'
'You were the best people, Adam.'
'The weather might change, Lord.'
'Too right. It will.'

D.J. Enright

- Which parts of the Mystery play have similarities to D.J. Enright's modern version?
- How do the characters of Adam, Eve, and God, seem similar and different in the two versions?
- How does the Mystery play feel different from any modern drama scripts you have read?

By the late 15th Century these had developed into Morality Plays, in which there is a clear presentation of vices and virtues – drama with a more moralistic purpose. A sign of the developments: in 1490, Henry Medwall writes *Nature*, a play which is not based on the Bible and in which personifications of vices and virtues are given contemporary features.

Sixteenth Century

Some key events:

1509 Henry VIII becomes King
1517 Martin Luther clashes with Catholic Church – beginning of Protestantism
1528 major plague outbreak in England
1531 the 'Great Comet' (Haley's) terrifies Britain and brings wave of superstition
1576 first public playhouse established – The Theatre by James Burbage

Historical Background

Compare this portrait of Henry VIII with the depiction of Richard II in the last century. Where that presented an idealized picture of a king bowing to Christ, Henry is a figure of ruthless self-confidence, prepared to take on religious authority and get his own way.

The Polish astronomer Nicolaus Copernicus published his theory of the universe in 1543. For him the universe looked like this.

The Copernican Universe

Look at how this differs from the vision in the last century. Now the Sun rather than the earth is at the centre. The place of human beings, in other words, has suddenly shifted: their importance suddenly seems less definite.

In the 16th Century science needed new mathematical concepts to explore and explain the cosmos. An age of new discoveries requires a new mode of expression, and so the prose style of writers is in flux, as scholars begin to express themselves in English rather than Latin.

Prose:

Feel the excitement of the discovery of the New World from this prose account of San Francisco, written by Sir Francis Drake:

Drake's Diary

In this bay we anchored the seventeenth of June, and the people of the country, having their houses close by the water's side, showed themselves unto us, and sent a present to our general.

When they came unto us, they greatly wondered at the things which we brought, but our general, according to his natural and accustomed humanity, courteously entreated them, and liberally bestowed on them necessary things to cover their nakedness, whereupon they supposed us to be gods, and would not be persuaded to the contrary. The presents which they sent unto our general were feathers and cawls of network.

Their houses are digged round with earth, and have from the uttermost brims of the circle clifts of wood set upon them, joining close together at the top like a spire steeple, which by reason of that closeness are very warm.

Their bed is the ground with rushes strawed on it, and, lying about the house, they have the fire in the middest. The men go naked, the women take bulrushes and kemb them after the manner of hemp, and thereof make their loose garments, which being knit about their hips, having also about their shoulder a skin of deer, with the hair upon it. These women are very obedient and serviceable to their husbands.

After they were departed from us, they came and visited us the second time, and brought with them feathers and bags of tobacco for presents. And when they came to the top of the hill, at the bottom whereof we had pitched out tents, they stayed themselves, where one appointed for speaker wearied himself with making a long oration, which done, they left their bows upon the hill and came down with their presents.

Drama:

Three main types of plays mushroom in this century:

Interludes: small-scale plays devised by amateurs to perform at the local Lord's manor

University Plays: used as a vehicle for philosophical or religious thought

Inns of Court Plays: performed by law students... leading to the most important play of all: *'Everyman'*

Drama is now less concerned with telling the stories of the Bible, and instead dramatizes Everyman's journey from birth to death. Everyman represents the ordinary person in the audience, tempted and haunted by the Devil's false promises.

Poetry:

Famous names: Thomas Wyatt; the earl of Surrey; Sir Philip Sidney; Edmund Spenser... Poetry takes on a smaller, more personal scale, concerned in particular with the emotion of love. Many poems are set to haunting melodies – the idea of a lyric, in fact, is a reference to the lyre (string instrument of the violin family) that would accompany the words. The focus is strongly human, as this favourite of the period, shows. Chidiock Tichborne was a conspirator against the Queen who has been sentenced to death: here he thinks about his life and death.

Elegy for Himself

Written in the Tower before his execution, 1586

My prime of youth is but a frost of cares;
My feast of joy is but a dish of pain;
My crop of corn is but a field of tares;
And all my good is but vain hope of gain;
The day is past, and yet I saw no sun;
And now I live, and now my life is done.

My tale was heard, and yet it was not told;
My fruit is fall'n, and yet my leaves are green;
My youth is spent, and yet I am not old;
I saw the world, and yet I was not seen;
My thread is cut, and yet it is not spun;
And now I live, and now my life is done.

I sought my death, and found it in my womb;
I looked for life, and saw it was a shade;
I trod the earth, and knew it was my tomb;
And now I die, and now I was but made;
My glass is full, and now my glass is run;
And now I live, and now my life is done.

Chidiock Tichborne

- Look at all the images of nature (crop, field, fruit). What picture of his life does Chidiock Tichborne present?
- How does he create a strong sense of waste?
- What effect does the rhythm and repetition of the poem have?
- What do you like or dislike about the poem?

Seventeenth Century

Some key events:

1605   Gunpowder Plot – an attempt to blow up Parliament
1611   Authorized Version of the Bible published
1619   first Negro slaves taken to America
1642   Puritans close all theatres in England (to 1660)
1665   Plague kills 68,596 people in London

Historical Background

Some people have seen in this portrait of Charles I an expression of gloom and foreboding, as the King foresees his own execution. Others might see a hint of arrogance. Certainly Charles continued to believe in the divine right of kings to rule, even though his decision to rule without parliament led to civil war in England and resulted in his death.

The early years of the century (1603 to 1625) are known as the Jacobean period, named after King James I. He was a supporter of the arts, and Shakespeare probably wrote plays specially for him.

Prose:

Prose is the form used for philosophical writing and science (this is a century fascinated by scientific discoveries) – for example, Francis Bacon. Some works of fiction are written (John Bunyan), and brilliantly vivid diary accounts which are to lead into the growth of journalism in the next century...

John Bunyan (1628–1680) writes *The Pilgrim's Progress in* 1684.

Bunyan's religious tale is sometimes described as the first novel in English. It draws on the Everyman tradition of the 16th Century, telling the story of a dream vision of Christian's pilgrimage from the City of Destruction (the present world) to the Celestial City (heaven). Unsurprisingly, the language is heavily Biblical in its style and tone.

- What, in the words and punctuation, hints that this text is old?
- Which parts of the text indicate its religious nature?
- How would you write the extract in modern Standard English? What is lost in doing so?
- On a scale of 1 (easy) to 5 (difficult), how did you find reading this brief extract?
- Some people have called *Pilgrim's Progress* a novel. But it has no strong characterization; it follows the storyline of the Bible; it uses its storyline to criticize the modern world. Can you think of a better definition than a novel?

Pilgrim's Progress

As I walked through the wilderness of this world, I lighted on a certain place where was a den, and I laid me down in that place to sleep: and as I slept I dreamed a dream. I dreamed, and behold I saw a man clothed with rags, standing in a certain place, with his face from his own house, a book in his hand, and a great burden upon his back. I looked and saw him open the book and read therein; and, as he read, he wept, and trembled; and not being able longer to contain, he brake out with a lamentable cry, saying, What shall I do?

Although not written for public audience, Samuel Pepys' diaries give us a brilliant picture of life at the end of the 17th Century. Take for instance his account of the Great Fire of London (1666):

Pepys' Diary

Having seen as much as I could now, I away to White-hall by appointment, and there walked to St James's Park, and there met my wife and Creed and Wood and his wife and walked to my boat, and there upon the water again, and to the fire up and down, it still increasing and the wind great. So near the fire as we could for smoke; and all over the Thames, with one's face in the wind you were almost burned with a shower of Firedrops – this is very true – so as houses were burned by these drops and flakes of fire, three or four, nay five or six houses, one from another. When we could endure no more upon the water, we to a little alehouse on the Bankside over against the Three Cranes, and there stayed till it was dark almost and saw the fire grow; and as it grew darker, appeared more and more, and in Corners and upon steeples and between churches and houses, as far as we could see up the hill of the City, in a most horrid malicious bloody flame, not like a fine flame of an ordinary fire.

- What clues can you find that this is factual writing, rather than fiction? – Are there examples of where it feels less polished and more spontaneous than fiction?
- Pick out three examples of words and punctuation which give the writing an archaic (old) feel.
- How does Pepys make the description of London burning immediate and powerful?

Poetry:

In the early part of the century, Metaphysical Poetry was popular – poetry full of outrageous ideas, clever word-play, unexpected comparisons. Metaphysical poets include:

John Donne (1572–1631)
George Herbert (1593–1633)
Andrew Marvell (1621–1678)

Look, for example, how Marvell tries to seduce his lover using all the powers of his intellect:

To His Coy Mistress

…But at my back I always hear
Time's wingèd chariot hurrying near;
And yonder all before us lie
Deserts of vast eternity.
Thy beauty shall no more be found,
Nor, in thy marble vault, shall sound
My echoing song; then worms shall try
That long-preserved virginity,
And your quaint honour turn to dust,
And into ashes all my lust:
The grave's a fine and private place,
But none, I think, do there embrace.

- What is the gist of the speaker's argument – about time and their love?
- How would you describe his tone of voice – sincere? sarcastic? How can you tell?
- What effect does the rhyme-scheme of the poem have – the rhyming couplets? Do they make the speaker's argument more or less persuasive? Write it out in modern prose to test the effect.

Later in the century the key figures in poetry are:

John Milton (1608–1674) – lengthy, powerful religious and personal verse
John Dryden (1631–1700) – described by Doctor Johnson as 'the first who joined argument with poetry' – difficult, intellectual, often writing about the important events of his day

Drama:

Remember that Shakespeare was writing his most powerful plays in the first dozen years of the century, as was his great rival Ben Jonson (1572–1637). Early drama was dark and disturbing, obsessed with secrecy and sex. Thomas Middleton's *The Changeling* ends in a series of murders. When the theatres reopened at the end of the century, comedy was on the menu – like our modern bedroom farces, Restoration comedies delight in confused identities, lusty older men, and a light, frothy tone. Key writers: William Wycherly (1640–1710), William Congreve (1670–1729), and Aphra Behn (1640–89).

Eighteenth Century

Some key events:

1704   first newspaper, *the Review*, begun by Daniel Defoe

1731   Ten Downing Street, residence of British Prime Minister, built

1761   Bridgewater Canal from Liverpool to Leeds opens

1766   first paved footpath laid in Westminster

1775   Britain at war with America: War of Independence

1789   French Revolution begins

Historical Background

Look at this painting by Thomas Gainsborough (1727–88). Notice how everything is in its right place – corn newly harvested, nature under human control, dog obedient to its master. Through the trees is the spire of a church. This is the 18th Century – a place of order, balance, and harmony.

Poetry:

The century falls into two halves. Early on poetry is formal, balanced, almost symmetrical–Augustan in style. The rhyming couplet gives a strong sense that the world of feelings and emotions are controlled and in their right place. Key writer: Alexander Pope (1688–1744).

Look at Pope criticizing human beings for their

An Essay on Criticism

Of all the causes which conspire to blind
Man's erring judgement, and misguide the mind,
What the weak head with strongest bias rules,
Is *pride*, the never-failing vice of fools.
Whatever Nature has in worth denied,
She gives in large recruits of needful pride;
For as in bodies, thus in souls, we find
What wants in blood and spirits, swelled with wind;
Pride, where wit fails, steps in to our defense,
And fills up all the mighty void of sense.
If once right reason drives that cloud away,
Truth breaks upon us with resistless day;
Trust not yourself; but your defects to know,
Make use of every friend – and every foe.

Alexander Pope

arrogance and pride, and notice the balanced way in which the language works.

- Explore the way Pope creates a sense of balance using antithesis (opposites). For each of these words, find its opposite counterpart:
  weak   bodies   fills   friend
- Nature is described as a person – 'She'. What picture of Nature's character does Pope give? Why do you think he 'personifies' nature?
- How does Pope's punctuation add to the meaning of his lines and to the sense of order?

From the mid-century, poets are beginning to place more emphasis on emotions and the importance of the heart as well as the intellect. Key writer: Thomas Gray (1716–1771).

Gray's *Elegy in a Country Churchyard* reflects upon the people of a village who have now died. He celebrates their lives, suggesting that even though they did not become famous, their lives were valuable and worth remembering:

- Note the use of 'polite' words (euphemisms) – no mention here of death, for instance, even though it is the theme of the poem. For each of

Elegy in a Country Churchyard

Beneath those rugged elms, that yew-tree's shade,
Where heaves the turf in many a mouldering heap,
Each in his narrow cell forever laid,
The rude forefathers of the hamlet sleep.

The breezy call of incense-breathing morn,
The swallow twittering from the straw-built shed,
The cock's shrill clarion or the echoing horn,
No more shall rouse them from their lowly bed.

For them no more the blazing hearth shall burn,
Or busy housewife ply her evening care;
No children run to lisp their sire's return,
Or climb his knees the envied kiss to share...

Thomas Gray

the words listed, write a more direct alternative: narrow cell, sleep, rouse, sire.
- Although we see pictures of animals and people in the poem, they cannot really be described as individuals. They are doing activities which might be expected. Pick out the adjectives and verbs which describe each of these characters: swallow, children.

Poetry like Gray's led directly to the Romantics – such as Blake, Wordsworth, Coleridge. See the 19th Century spread to trace the development.

Prose:

Early prose consisted of journalism by writers like Richard Steele (1672–1719) and Joseph Addison (1672–1719). Journalist Daniel Defoe turned his hand to fiction with *Robinson Crusoe* (1719) and *Moll Flanders* (1722), which by tracing the lives and loves of a single character are sometimes thought to be the origins in Britain of the novel. Key writers in the development of the novel: Jonathan Swift (1677–1745) *Gulliver's Travels*; Henry Fielding (1707–1768) *Tom Jones*; Laurence Sterne 1713–1768 *Tristram Shandy*; Samuel Richardson (1689–1761) *Pamela*.

Because there was no fixed idea of what a novel should be like, writers made up the rules as they went along. At its most experimental, the novel resembled some of Dickens' most eccentric writing (see 19th Century spread). Here, at the start of his book *The Life and Opinions of Tristram Shandy, Gentleman*, the narrator criticizes his parents for not concentrating when their future son was being conceived.

I wish either my father or my mother, or indeed both of them, as they were in duty both equally bound to it, had minded what they were about when they begot me; had they duly considered how much depended upon what they were doing; – that not only the production of a rational Being was concerned in it, but that possibly the happy formation and temperature of his body, perhaps his genius and the very cast of his mind; – and, for aught they knew to the contrary, even the fortunes of his whole house might take their turn from the humours and dispositions which were then uppermost.

- How easy (1 to 5) or difficult did you find the extract? What made it more problematical – the vocabulary or sentence structure?
- What do you notice about how Laurence Sterne creates a bond between himself as writer and his reader?
- If you were to summarize the extract in Standard English, what would your summary say?

Drama:

More than a hundred years after Shakespeare's death and his plays are being rewritten to make them more suitable and, where necessary, less vulgar for social taste. Frothy comedies dominate the theatre, often containing criticism of the upper classes. Key writers: Oliver Goldsmith (1728–74) *She Stoops to Conquer* and Richard Brinsley Sheridan (1751–1816) *The Rivals*.

Nineteenth Century

Some key events:

1817: riots in Derbyshire against low wages

1825: first passenger-carrying railway opens

1847: Factory Act limits working day for children aged 13–18 to 10 hours

1855: Florence Nightingale introduces hygienic standards into hospitals at Crimean War

1870: Education Act establishes education for all

1879: First telephone exchange established

Historical Background

Look at this painting by J.M.W. Turner (1775–1851). It shows the 19th Century as a time of change, speed, and progress. It is a century in which working people are sucked from their lives in villages and transplanted into the newly-growing towns and cities, where the mills, mines, and factories need human labour. With progress comes suffering and appalling housing and sanitation conditions. Whilst Turner's painting shows us speed and progress, it is also murky, unclear, worried.

Just as Turner's painting reflects the mixed attitude of many Victorians towards the idea of 'progress', so many writers of the period see industrial cities as disturbing and threatening. In his novel *Hard Times* (1854), Charles Dickens (1812–1870) paints a grim picture of Coketown. Notice how his imagery suggests danger ('red', 'painted face of a savage') and evil ('serpents of smoke') and life-throttling routine ('every year the counterpart of the last and the next'):

Hard Times

It was a town of red brick, or of brick that would have been red if the smoke and ashes had allowed it; but, as matters stood it was town of unnatural red and black like the painted face of a savage. It was a town of machinery and tall chimneys, out of which interminable serpents of smoke trailed themselves for ever and ever, and never got uncoiled. It had a black canal in it, and a river that ran purple with ill-smelling dye, and vast piles of buildings full of windows where there was a rattling and a trembling all day long, and where the piston of the steam-engine worked monotonously up and down, like the head of an elephant in a state of melancholy madness. It contained several large streets all very like one another, and many small streets still more like one another, inhabited by people equally like one another, who all went in and out at the same hours, with the same sound upon the same pavements, to the same work, and to whom every day was the same as yesterday and tomorrow, and every year the counterpart of the last and the next.

Charles Dickens

The Prelude Book 1

I dipp'd my oars into the silent Lake,
And, as I rose upon the stroke, my Boat
Went heaving through the water, like a Swan;
When from behind that craggy Steep, till then
The bound of the horizon, a huge Cliff,
As if with voluntary power instinct,
Uprear'd its head. I struck, and struck again,
And, growing still in stature, the Huge Cliff
Rose up between me and the stars, and still,
With measur'd motion, like a living thing,
Strode after me. With trembling hands I turn'd,
And through the silent water stole my way
Back to the Cavern of the Willow tree.
There, in her mooring-place, I left my Bark,
And, through the meadows homeward went, with grave
And serious thoughts; and after I had seen
That spectacle, for many days, my brain
Work'd with a dim and undetermin'd sense
Of unknown modes of being; in my thoughts
There was a darkness, call it solitude,
Or blank desertion, no familiar shapes
Of hourly objects, images of trees,
Of sea or sky, no colours of green fields;
But huge and mighty Forms that do not live
Like living men mov'd slowly through the mind
By day and were the trouble of my dreams.

William Wordsworth

Poetry:

The early part of the century is dominated by the Romantic poets, for whom the formal, balanced style of Augustan poetry is too limiting. They believe strongly in the power of the human imagination, in exploring feelings, in glorifying nature, and in recognizing the mind-forming importance of childhood. Here, William Wordsworth (1770–1850) writes about stealing a boat and rowing at night across a lake. Notice the way nature seems alive and breathing all about him:

- What clues are there in the poem that the narrator is uneasy and nervous about what he is doing?
- How does nature seem alive and threatening? Pick out three examples.
- What makes the poem seem to belong to the past? Pick out any words or spellings which give clues about the age of the poem.
- What has the writer learnt from the experience on the lake? Look again at the end of the extract and try to work out what effect the episode has had.

Nineteenth-Century poetry is dominated by the long narrative poems of Wordsworth and Tennyson. Much of the poetry of the century was religious, but increasingly suggested a sense of unease about God's relationship to humans. By the end of the century Gerard Manley Hopkins (1844–1889) was writing agonized, dark sonnets (as well as celebratory religious verse) in which he described nights spent mentally wrestling with God. His tortured emotional state is echoed in the complexities of his language. For example, look at these last lines of *Carrion Comfort:*

> ... That night, that year
> Of now done darkness I wretch lay wrestling with (my God!) my God.

Prose:

The novel dominates the century, as publication in instalments and the establishment of lending libraries bring books into the reach of ordinary people. Levels of literacy are rising and do so especially after the 1870 Education Act, which establishes universal education.

Many novelists recognize the power which writing in instalments can give to their narratives, enabling tension to be built and prolonged in the way that writers of soap operas do today. Dickens, Thackeray, Charlotte and Emily Brontë, Elizabeth Gaskell, Thomas Hardy – these are the most widely-read novelists of their day. Writing to tight deadlines, they produce novels for an avid reading public. The pressure of the writing cycle is demonstrated by this recollection of Charles Dickens'. One day in a stationer's shop in Kent he overheard a woman ask for the latest instalment of *David Copperfield*. The assistant said that it would be available at the end of the month. Dickens panicked. He knew that he had not yet written a word of it. 'Once, and but once only in my life, I was – frightened!' he admitted.

Social issues dominate many of the great novels of the Victorian age: the need for better education, improved prison conditions, compassion for the poor. There is also an emphasis on childhood, as if the future lies in the hands of society's youngest members. Charlotte Brontë's *Jane Eyre* is more than an account of one woman's journey through life; it also exposes the cruelty of the church school to which Jane is sent by her foster parents:

Jane Eyre

Meantime, Mr Brocklehurst, standing on the hearth with his hands behind his back, majestically surveyed the whole school. Suddenly his eye gave a blink, as if it had met something that either dazzled or shocked its pupil; turning, he said in more rapid accents than he had hitherto used:
'Miss Temple, Miss Temple what – *what* is that girl with curled hair? Red hair, ma'am, curled all over?'
And extending his cane he pointed to the awful object, his hand shaking as he did so.
'It is Julia Severn,' replied Miss Temple, very quietly.
'It is Julia Severn, ma'am! And why has she, or any other, curled hair? Why, in defiance of every precept and principle of this house, does she conform to the world so openly – here in an evangelical, charitable establishment – as to wear her hair one mass of curls?'
'Julia's hair curls naturally,' returned Miss Temple, still more quietly.
'Naturally! Yes, but we are not to conform to nature; I wish these girls to be the children of Grace: and why that abundance? I have again and again intimated that I desire the hair to be arranged closely, modestly, plainly. Miss Temple, that girl's hair must be cut off entirely; I will send a barber to-morrow: and I see others who have far too much of the excrescence – that tall girl, tell her to turn round. Tell all the first form to rise up and direct their faces to the wall.'
Miss Temple passed her handkerchief over her lips, as if to smooth away the involuntary smile that curled them; she gave the order, however, and when the first class could take in what was required of them, they obeyed. Leaning a little back on my bench, I could see the looks and grimaces with which they commented on this manoeuvre: it was a pity Mr Brocklehurst could not see them too; he would perhaps have felt that, whatever he might do with the outside of the cup and platter, the inside was further beyond his interference than he imagined.
He scrutinized the reverse of these living medals some five minutes, then pronounced sentence. These words fell like the knell of doom:
'All those top-knots must be cut off.'
Miss Temple seemed to remonstrate.
'Madam,' he pursued, 'I have a Master to serve, whose kingdom is not of this world: my mission is to mortify in these girls the lusts of the flesh; to teach them to clothe themselves with shamefacedness and sobriety, not with braided hair and costly apparel; and each of the young persons before us has a string of hair twisted in plaits which vanity itself might have woven; these, I repeat, must be cut off.

- What are your first impressions of the school's owner, Mr Brocklehurst?
- What is his objection to the girl's long hair?
- How does Charlotte Brontë make us feel critical of him, and sympathetic towards Miss Temple?

Drama:

The century is largely dominated by melodrama (as the name suggests, drama + music) which presented crude character types, often as simple as heroes and villains, and used music to intensify the audience's response. The effect would have been rather like watching a silent movie today. Overseas, the startling realism of Henrik Ibsen (1828–1906) and Anton Chekov (1860–1904) will have their effect on drama in the Twentieth century.

Norwegian playright Henrik Ibsen was remarkable at the end of the 19th Century for writing about issues which startled the public and led to riots in his home-town: the right of a woman to leave her husband and create her own life... suicide... public men in private scandals...

His realism can feel a little stilted today, with echoes of the tradition of melodrama which preceded it. People talk in a way that sounds a bit too formal, too tidy. Here Nora's desperate husband, Helmer, tries to convince her that she should stay, that life can be normal.

If this feels a little stagey, remember that it was written in 1879 and, as one critic put it, 'exploded like a bomb into contemporary life' (Halvdan Koht). Seen on stage, it retains its powerful impact, revealing marriage as far from being 'an automatic provider of bliss' (Michael Meyer) and suggesting that women do have power within a relationship.

A Doll's House

Try to calm yourself and get your balance again, my frightened little songbird. Don't be afraid. I have wings to shield you. How lovely and peaceful this little home of ours is, Nora. You are safe here; I shall watch over you like a hunted dove which I have snatched unharmed from the claws of the falcon. Your wildly beating little heart shall find peace with me...

Henrik Ibsen (translated by Michael Meyer)

Twentieth Century

Some key events:

1905   Einstein's 'Special Theory of Relativity' creates a new map of the universe
1914   World War I begins
1921   British Broadcasting Company (BBC) founded – first radio station (2LO) in the following year
1932   Amelia Earhart crosses Atlantic by plane in 13.5 hours
1939   World War II declared when Hitler invades Poland
1957   USSR launches first earth satellites (Sputnik I & II)
1968   Martin Luther King assassinated in Memphis
1969   Neil Armstrong is the first human being on the Moon

Historical Background

Paul Nash's landscape shows war – a dominant theme of the 20th Century. If Turner's portrayal of the future was full of worry, this presentation of the human effects of war is full of horror – a barren waste pocked with shell holes and criss-crossed with barbed wire. The lake bubbles unnaturally from bombs. By the 20th Century human beings have lost confidence in themselves – certain only of the human capacity to destroy...

Poetry:

Early in the century the Imagists used poetry to create clear, precise pictures. H.D. (Hilda Doolittle) was typical of the movement, as her poem *Oread* illustrates:

Oread

Whirl up, sea –
whirl your great pointed pines,
splash your great pines
On our rocks,
hurl your green over us,
Cover us with your pools of fir.
                                 H.D.

But a criticism of Imagist poetry is that it is all about technique and has little to say – that it can be self-indulgent. Whilst Imagism was being developed by T.S. Eliot into some of the most original and experimental poetry of the century,

another group of poets were responding to the unimagined horrors of the First World War. Most famous is Wilfred Owen, a young poet of real promise who was killed in the last weeks of the war. More bitter and angry in tone is the work of Siegfried Sassoon. This tender poem reminds us that one horror of war is the persistent fear of losing someone close:

The Dug-Out

Why do you lie with your legs ungainly huddled,
And one arm bent across your sullen, cold,
Exhausted face? It hurts my heart to watch you,
Deep-shadow'd from the candle's guttering gold;
And you wonder why I shake you by the shoulder;
Drowsy, you mumble and sigh and turn your head...
You are too young to fall asleep for ever;
And when you sleep you remind me of the dead.

                                 July 1918
                                 Siegfried Sassoon

- What can you tell about the relationship between the writer and soldier being addressed?
- What image does the poem create of the sleeping soldier?
- Does the poem feel modern or old-fashioned? Look in particular at the vocabulary Sassoon uses.

In the late 20th Century, poetry maintains its link with the Imagists, and the influence of T.S. Eliot remains strong. But the poets respond to different themes: the lurking threat of nuclear war; the human relationship with nature; the changing roles of women and men; loss of religious faith; social breakdown. Some poets give deeply personal reflections – Thom Gunn's moving poems on hearing of his friend developing the AIDS virus. In general, the tone is one of anxiety and lack of confidence. Technological progress has been immense – think of the developments in science, medicine, and the media. But, judging by contemporary poetry, the technological age has not brought emotional security.

Anne Stevenson's poetry takes personal, reflective themes but responds also to wider, social concerns. This poem takes one of the most pressing social issues of the late 20th Century - the destruction of the natural environment.

The Fish are All Sick

The fish are all sick, the great whales dead,
the villages stranded in stone on the coast,
ornamental, like pearls on the fringe of a coat.
Sea men, who knew what the ocean did,
turned their low houses away from the surf.
But new men, who come to be rural and safe,
add big glass views and begonia beds.

Water keeps to itself.
White lip after lip
curls to a close on the littered beach.
Something is sicker and blacker than fish.
And closing its grip, and closing its grip.

Anne Stevenson

- What is actually happening in Anne Stevenson's poem?
- Do you think it is a poem about the future or the present? Why?
- How does Anne Stevenson use simple language to create a powerful effect? Which lines do you find most effective and why?

Prose:

The novels of D.H. Lawrence start as a documentary of life amongst working-class people, but increasingly seem concerned with the fundamental relationship between women and men, an attempt perhaps to find certainty in a harsh world. William Golding's *Lord of the Flies* is perhaps the central novel of the post-war period because it shows how
innocence is never far removed from savagery. Look at this extract in which the sensitive Simon is haunted by the head of a pig on a wooden stake – the Lord of the Flies:

Lord of the Flies

Simon stayed where he was, a small brown image, concealed by the leaves. Even if he shut his eyes the sow's head still remained like an after-image. The half-shut eyes were dim with the infinite cynicism of adult life. They assured Simon that everything was a bad business.

'I know that.'

Simon discovered that he had spoken aloud. He opened his eyes quickly and there was the head grinning amusedly in the strange daylight, ignoring the flies, the spilled guts, even ignoring the indignity of being spiked on a stick.

He looked away, licking his dry lips.

A gift for the beast. Might not the beast come for it? The head, he thought, appeared to agree with him. Run away, said the head silently, go back to the others. It was a joke really – why should you bother? You were just wrong, that's all. a little headache, something you ate, perhaps. Go back, child, said the head silently.

Simon looked up, feeling the weight of his wet hair, and gazed at the sky. Up there, for once, were clouds, great bulging towers that sprouted away over the island, grey and cream and copper-coloured. The clouds were sitting on the land; they squeezed, produced moment by moment, this close, tormenting heat. Even the butterflies deserted the open space where the obscene thing grinned and dripped.

Simon lowered his head, carefully keeping his eyes shut, then sheltered them with his hand. There were no shadows under the trees but everywhere a pearly stillness, so that what was real seemed illusive and without definition. The pile of guts was a black blob of flies that buzzed like a saw. After a while these flies found Simon. Gorged, they alighted by his runnels of sweat and drank. They tickled under his nostrils and played leap-frog on his thighs. They were black and iridescent green and without number; and in front of Simon, the Lord of the Flies hung on his stick and grinned. At last Simon gave up and looked back; saw the white teeth and dim eyes, the blood – and his gaze was held by that ancient, inescapable recognition. In Simon's right temple, a pulse began to beat on the brain.

William Golding

- How does William Golding make the landscape vivid?
- How does he show Simon's reactions to what he sees?
- How does he make the scene seem full of foreboding – as if it must lead to something worse? Pick out a sentence which illustrates this.

From the 1970s the novel is powerfully influenced by new writers from the wider English-speaking world, reinventing the English language to express their experiences. Compare these two opening paragraphs – the first from Salman Rushdie's *Midnight's Children*, the second from Ben Okri's *The Famished Road*.

Midnight's Children

The perforated sheet

I was born in the city of Bombay . . . once upon a time. No, that won't do, there's no getting away from the date: I was born in Doctor Narlikar's Nursing Home on August 15th, 1947. And the time? The time matters, too. Well then: at night. No, it's important to be more... On the stroke of midnight, as a matter of fact. Clock-hands joined palms in respectful greeting as I came. Oh, spell it out, spell it out: at the precise instant of India's arrival at independence, I tumbled forth into the world. There were gasps. And, outside the window, fireworks and crowds. A few seconds later, my father broke his big toe; but his accident was a mere trifle when set beside what had befallen me in that benighted moment, because thanks to the occult tyrannies of those blandly saluting clocks I had been mysteriously hand-cuffed to history, my destinies indissolubly chained to those of my country. For the next three decades, there was to be no escape. Sooth-sayers had prophesied me, newspapers celebrated my arrival, politicos ratified my authenticity. I was left entirely without a say in the matter. I, Saleem Sinai, later variously called Snotnose, Stainface, Baldy, Sniffer, Buddha and even Piece-of-the-Moon, had become heavily embroiled in Fate – at the best of times a dangerous sort of involvement. And I couldn't even wipe my own nose at the time.

Salman Rushdie

The Famished Road

In the beginning there was a river. The river became a road and the road branched out to the whole world. And because the road was once a river it was always hungry.

In this land of beginnings spirits mingled with the unborn. We could assume numerous forms. Many of us were birds. We knew no boundaries. There was much feasting, playing, and sorrowing. We feasted much because of the beautiful terrors of eternity. We played much because we were free. And we sorrowed much because there were always those amongst us who had just returned from the world of the Living. They had returned inconsolable for all the love they had left behind, all the suffering they hadn't redeemed, all that they hadn't understood, and for all that they had barely begun to learn before they were drawn back to the land of origins.

There was not one amongst us who looked forward to being born. We disliked the rigours of existence, the unfulfilled longings, the enshrined injustices of the world, the labyrinths of love, the ignorance of parents, the fact of dying, and the amazing indifference of the living in the midst of the simple beauties of the universe. We feared the heartlessness of human beings, all of whom are born blind, few of whom ever learn to see.

Ben Okri

- What other stories do the two extracts remind you of?
- How do you predict the stories will continue?
- Pick out an example from each text of the way the writer uses language in a creative, unexpected way.

Drama:

George Bernard Shaw dominates the early century, with comedies and satires of ideas. Ibsen and Chekov's realism has replaced melodrama, and the theatre is now presenting plays which disturb as well as entertain. But by the war, the 'well-made play' has become safe, middle-class, and predictable. Again, a fresh influence from overseas – Samuel Beckett, Ionesco – brings disturbing 'absurdist' ideas into drama – all with the bleak message that life is pointless: all we can do is hope to survive it.

Wider Reading List

Students at GCSE sometimes say that they know they ought to be reading more, but they are uncertain what to read. This brief list makes some suggestions, listing them in approximate order of difficulty (the first texts in each category are usually more accessible; the last are usually the most challenging). It contains texts from other centuries and other cultures, as well as contemporary writing. All titles are in paperback.

FICTION

Detective stories/Thrillers

Brian Moore, *Lies of Silence* (Paladin)
Raymond Chandler, *Murder is My Business and Other Stories* (Penguin)
Sarah Paretsky, *Indemnity Only* (Penguin)
Ruth Rendell, *The Fever Tree and Other Stories* (Arrow)
Maxim Jakubowski, *Murders for the Fireside* (Pan)
Michael Dibdin (ed.), *The Picador Book of Crime Writing* (Picador)

Horror fiction/Ghost stories

Lisa Tuttle (ed.), *Skin of the Soul* (The Women's Press)
Doris Lessing, *The Fifth Child* (Paladin)
Edgar Allen Poe, *Collected Stories* (Penguin)
Mary Shelley, *Frankenstein* (Penguin)
Robert Westall, *Ghost Stories* (Kingfisher)
Robert Phillips, *The Omnibus of Twentieth Century Ghost Stories* (Robinson)
Richard Dalby, *The Virago Book of Ghost Stories* (Virago)

Science fiction

Brian Aldiss, *The Penguin Science Fiction Omnibus* (Penguin)
Ray Bradbury, *Something Wicked This Way Comes* (Penguin)
H.G. Wells, *The War of the Worlds* (Corgi)

Fictional autobiography

Peter Benson, *The Levels* (Penguin)
Jane Gardam, *God on the Rocks* (Abacus)
Harper Lee, *To Kill a Mockingbird* (Mandarin)
Charles Dickens, *David Copperfield* (Penguin)

Short stories

Roald Dahl, *Collected Short Stories* (Penguin)
Susan Hill, *The Albatross and Other Stories* (Penguin)
Ian Murray (ed.), *The New Penguin Book of Scottish Short Stories* (Penguin)
Robert Shephard and James Thomas (eds.), *Sudden Fiction International* (Paladin)
Penelope Lively, *Pack of Cards* (Penguin)
Daniel Halpern (ed.), *The Penguin Book of International Short Stories* (Penguin)

POETRY

Look either at some poetry collections, where you can explore a range of authors from a range of centuries; or read some single authors in depth:

Collections

Seamus Heaney and Ted Hughes, *The Rattle Bag* (Faber)
Gerard Benson, Judith Chernaik, Cicely Herbert, *100 Poems on the Underground* (Cassell)
Fleur Adcock, *The Faber Book of Twentieth Century Poetry* (Faber)

Single authors

Been Okri, *An African Elegy* (Jonathan Cape)
Gillian Clarke, *Selected Poems* (Carcanet)
Seamus Heaney, *Selected Poems 1965–1994* (Faber)
Emily Dickinson, *Collected Poems* (Faber)

DRAMA

Plays can be difficult to read on the page, and your best introduction to drama is to go regularly to the theatre. But the following texts are recommended:

Alan Bennett, *Talking Heads* (BBC Books)
Arthur Miller, *A View from the Bridge/All My Sons* (Penguin)
Marshall Cassady, *An Introduction to Modern One-Act Plays* (National Textbook Company)
Geoff Barton (ed.), *Ten Short Plays* (Longman)

NON-FICTION

Autobiography

Roald Dahl, *Boy* and *Going Solo* (Penguin)
Paul Zindel, *The Pigman and Me* (Penguin)
Alice Thomas Ellis, *A Welsh Childhood* (Penguin)
Barry Humphries, *More Please* (Penguin)

Travel writing

Bill Bryson, *The Lost Continent* (Abacus)
Jonathan Raban, *Hunting Mr Heartbreak* (HarperCollins)
Eric Newby, *A Book of Traveller's Tales* (Picador)
Georgina Harding, *In Another Europe* (Sceptre)
Christina Dodwell, *A Traveller on Horseback* (Sceptre)
Robyn Davison, *Tracks* (Granada)
Mary Morris, *The Virago Book of Women Travellers* (Virago)

Reportage

John Carey, *The Faber Book of Reportage* (Faber)
Geoff Barton, *Reportage* (OUP)
Tom Wolfe, *The New Journalism* (Picador)
E.J. Taylor, *Shock Horror!* (Black Swan)
Margaret Busby (ed.), *Daughters of Africa* (Vintage)

Diaries

Janina Baumann, *Winter in the Morning: A Young Girl's Life in the Warsaw Ghetto and Beyond* (Virago)
Ronald Blythe, *The Penguin Book of Diaries* (Penguin)
Alan Bennett, *Writing Home* (Faber)
Dorothy Wordsworth, *Journals* (OUP)
Ruth First, *117 Days* (Bloomsbury)
Anne Hughes, *The Diary of a Farmer's Wife 1796–97* (Penguin)

Miscellaneous

Brian MacArthur, *The Penguin Book of Twentieth Century Speeches* (Penguin)
Dhineweizu (ed.), *Voices from Twentieth Century Africa* (Faber)

To keep up-to-date with the bext contemporary fiction and non-fiction writing, look out for *Granta*, edited by Ian Jack (Granta Books/Penguin), which is published four times a year.

LANGUAGE REFERENCE

John Ayto, *The Oxford School A-Z of English,* (OUP)
Bill Bryson, *Mother Tongue: The English Language* (Penguin)
David Crystal, *The Cambridge Encyclopedia of Language* (CUP)
Graham King, *The Sunday Times Wordpower Guide* (Heinemann)

Glossary

The Glossary provides quick definitions of words you are likely to encounter during your GCSE course. Where appropriate, the end of each definition refers you to the spread in which the term is used or discussed, so that you can see it in context.

accent the way we pronounce words. Everyone talks with an accent of some kind and we frequently make judgements about people based on their accent. For example, Northern accents are often considered by people in the south to suggest honesty and reliability – and these attitudes to accent are often exploited in commercials. Bread and beer are frequently sold using regional accents; insurance, up-market cars, after-dinner mints, often use an accent called RP (BBC English).
(See 'Attitudes to Accents' on page 61 and 'Received Pronunciation' on page 64.)

apostrophe a form of punctuation used to indicate two things: elision (did + not = didn't) and possession (the casserole belonging to Sam = Sam's casserole). Rules for its use and awkward customers are explained in 'Apostrophes' on page 28.

clause a group of words containing a verb which cannot stand on its own – e.g. who had just arrived; Having already eaten...; After watching the TV...
(See 'Complex Sentences' on page 16.)

cliché a well-worn phrase – e.g. they gathered round her *like flies; stunned silence; About as exciting as watching paint dry*. The advice in this book about clichés is: Avoid them like the plague!

cohesion the way texts are organized so that we can follow their meaning. One way of speeding up your reading efficiency is to be alert to discourse markers which indicate how the writer has structured their text. Discourse markers include phrases like: *firstly, in contrast, therefore, on the other hand, another idea...* and so on.
(See 'Advanced Reading Skills' on page 94.)

colloquial informal language, usually suited to conversation between friends rather than to writing. In colloquial English we might compress words (*is not* becomes *isn't*) and we might pronounce words less precisely (*butter* becomes *bu'er*, with a glottal stop, a kind of swallow, in the middle).
(See 'Formal v Informal Speech' on page 56.)

dialect a variety of English with its own vocabulary and grammar. In some dialects it is normal to say *there aren't none;* in others, *there aren't any*. Some dialects will use the word *scarecrow;* others will use *bogle* or *mawkin* or *shuft*. Most people will move between dialects according to the situation, using their own regional dialect in less formal situations, and reverting to Standard English for writing.
(See 'Standard English' on page 18 and 'Dialects' on page 58.)

euphemism a polite term used to refer to something which is embarrassing or even taboo (a forbidden topic). We use many euphemisms for subjects like death – e.g. *passed away, kicked the bucket*, and going to the toilet – e.g. *WC, bathroom, spend a penny*.
(See 'Formal v Informal Speech' on page 56.)

grammar the rules that make it possible for you to communicate. Children know most of the rules of English at a very early age. A five-year-old would know, for example, that this sentence is ungrammatical – it breaks the basic rules of English: *My table on the foot smelly.* (See 'The Tools of English' on page 6.)

homophone a word which sounds the same as another word but has a different spelling and meaning – e.g. *there/their/they're.*

idiom an expression which does not mean exactly what it says. Even though you might understand each individual word in an idiom, you may still not recognize its overall meaning – e.g. *split my sides* = laughed a lot, *pull the wool over your eyes* = deceive you.

jargon specialized language with its own vocabulary. The jargon of cricket includes *googly, third man, silly mid off.* Jargon can make communication more precise between two specialists: it saves them having to say 'a type of bowling in which... But too often jargon is used to confuse outsiders or to hide the truth. To call 'killing the enemy' *servicing the target* is an attempt to hide the brutality of war.

metaphor a comparison of one idea with another, often for dramatic effect. In insults we use metaphors all the time, comparing people to something we dislike ('you *silly cow*', 'what a *filthy pig*'). Writers use metaphors to help us visualize people, places, and ideas more powerfully: 'The fire *attacked* the top floor of the house'. Using the word 'attacked' makes the fire seem aggressive and calculating: it becomes more menacing than saying 'the fire reached the top of the house'. Dead metaphors are metaphors which have lost their power. To say 'I have *exceeded my targets* this month' doesn't make sense: think of a round target which you might fire arrows at. If you were to exceed your target, you would actually be missing it. The metaphor is dead – it no longer conjures up a strong visual image. (See 'Imagery' on page 144.)

mother tongue the language you learned to speak first. In many cultures, people's first language is their local language, the one they use most; but they might also speak a second language – such as English – in school, parliament, etc.

narrative a story. Writers use different narrative techniques in telling stories: *first person* mode has a character narrating the story like this: 'Walking through the forest that day, *I* began to wish *I* hadn't travelled so far. *I* began to notice how dark it was becoming...'. It is the style used for autobiographies, and has the effect of showing us events from the perspective of one character. *Third person* mode is the traditional style of any legends and fairy tales: the narrator is outside the events of the story, describing them: 'Little Red Riding Hood suddenly realized how tired *she* was...'. It allows the writer to show us what different characters think and do. *Second person* narrative mode is very rare. It has a narrator who writes like this: '*You* didn't realize how tired *you* were until *you* had travelled deep into the forest. Then *you* looked for a place to stop...'. It is sometimes used in horror, fantasy fiction, and thrillers to give a sense of one person watching another. (See 'Creative Writing' on page 110.)

onomatopoeia a word whose sound echoes its meaning – e.g. *Slurp! Moo! Crash!* Writers sometimes use onomatopoeia to create an underlying sense of mystery or tension. In *Death of a Naturalist*, Seamus Heaney writes: 'Bluebottles / Wove a strong gauze of sound around the smell'. The repetition of 's' and 'z' sounds and the long vowels ('ou') recreate the sounds of the flies.

parody   an imitation of a writer's or speaker's style for humorous effect.

parts of speech   Refer to 'Word classes' entry. (See 'Grammar Grounding' on page 10.)

passive mode   the passive is used in impersonal, formal writing and is frequently found in newspaper reports, where phrases like *it was announced* conceal who did the announcing. To convert a verb from active to passive, simply place the verb *to be* in front of it and use the past participle. For example: *eat* becomes *is eaten/was eaten/were eaten*, etc. The writer George Orwell advises: 'Never use the passive where you can use the active'. But it can be useful where the person who did the action is irrelevant – e.g. 'Miss Graham *mixed* hydrogen and oxygen...' (active) becomes 'Hydrogen and oxygen *were mixed...*' (passive).

personification   making an abstract idea more vivid by comparing it to a person or animal – e.g. 'Death stalked the battlefields'; 'Beware the green-eyed monster Jealousy'. (See 'Imagery' on page 144.)

phrase   a group of words which make sense on their own but cannot stand alone as a sentence – e.g. in the middle, the old house, on the other hand. (See 'Simple Sentences' on page 12.)

prefix   one or more letters which can be added to the start of a word to change its meaning – e.g. *un*+pleasant = unpleasant.

Received Pronunciation   a neutral accent of English sometimes called BBC English. It is often associated with upper-class speakers and is an influential accent. In fact, it is only used by around 3% of English speakers. (See 'Received Pronunciation' on page 64.)

sentence   a group of words, beginning with a capital letter and ending with a full stop, question mark or exclamation mark, which make sense on their own. The three types of sentences are: **simple sentences** (express one idea: 'I like cheese-on-toast), **compound sentences** (express more than one idea by linking simple sentences using conjunctions like *and, but, or*: 'I like pickled onions *but* I hate gherkins'), **complex sentences** (express more than one idea by including subordinate clauses – e.g.: *Although I like pickled onions*, I hate gherkins; The dog, *which I think is revolting*, licked my face and neck.). (See 'Simple Sentences', 'Compound Sentences', 'Complex Sentences' on pages 12–17.)

simile   comparison of two ideas using the words *as* or *like* – e.g. 'He walked into the room *like* a frightened poodle' (he is being compared to a dog). (see 'Imagery' on page 144.)

slang   informal spoken language, often used between people with common interests. Slang words have more standard equivalents for use in more formal situations – e.g. footy = football, technicolour yawn = vomiting. (See 'Formal v Informal Speech' on page 56.)

Standard English   a dialect which has become established as the language of education, government, and trade, and the form used for most written contexts. It is considered by some as 'correct' English and is the dialect understood by most English speakers throughout the world.

stem the basic identity of a word when stripped of its prefixes and suffixes (it is also known as the root). For example, *decompression* is made up like this: de+com+*press*+ion: the root of the word is press. Some words have two roots *(blackboard, carrycot)* and are called **compound words**. (See 'Spelling Matters II' on page 32.)

suffix one or more letters which are added to the end of a word to change its meaning – e.g. peace+*ful* = peaceful.
(See 'Spelling Matters II' on page 32.)

synonym a word with the same general meaning as another word – e.g. large – big – gigantic – enormous – huge. English has a huge number of synonyms, allowing us to vary the shades of meaning in what we say – e.g. house – home – residence – domicile – pad.

syntax the organization of the words in a sentence and the study of the relationship between them.

tense the form of the verb which indicates when an action took place – present *(we go or we are going)*; past *(she walked; she was walking; she had walked)*; future *(they will eat; I am going to eat; I might eat)*.

theme the key ideas of a text – e.g. the themes of *Macbeth* include ambition, the supernatural, and evil.

tone the writer's attitude in a text – e.g. humorous, angry, neutral, concerned.
(See 'Poetry Unseens' on page 182.)

transcript an exact written copy of something that was spoken. (See 'Speech v Writing' on page 66.)

word classes **noun**: the name of an object or person.
Different types of nouns include:
common (or concrete) – e.g. table, computer, book – items you can touch
proper – e.g. Emily Dickinson, Martyn, Luton – names of specific people and places
collective – e.g. family, the government – nouns that are singular (one family) but refer to a collection of individuals
abstract – e.g. happiness, wealth, evil – nouns that are concepts rather than concrete things

verb: a word describing what someone or something *does* or *is* – e.g. she *likes* ice-cream; they *were* cold. It also indicates tense – that is, when the action happened (past, present, or future) – e.g. he *sang*; she *will decide* tomorrow.

adjective: a word which adds detail to a noun – e.g. the *enormous* table; the *revolting* soup.

adverb: a word which adds detail to the verb – e.g. he sang *tunelessly*; she will *hopefully* decide tomorrow.

preposition: a word which indicates position – e.g. *under, through, in, on, between*.

conjunction: a word which joins phrases, clauses and sentences – e.g. *and, but, or, when*.

pronoun: a word which can stand in place of a noun – e.g. The woman saw the cat = she saw *it*. Other pronouns include: he, you, they, them, I, me, us.
(See 'Grammar Grounding' on page 10.)

Feedback

Language Skills

Apostrophes (page 29)

 1 the cat's litter-tray (1)
 2 the cats' litter-tray (more than 1)
 3 the writers' meeting (more than 1)
 4 the teacher's strange habits (1)
 5 the light bulbs' bright beams (more than 1)

 6 the boy's bad temper
 7 the farmers' bad language
 8 the rocking chair's unreliable legs
 9 the cooks' revolting soup
10 the potter's peculiar sculptures

11 I saw that we weren't going to arrive on time. (E)
12 The turtle raised its head above the waterline. (No apostrophe needed)
13 Both computers' memory chips failed. (P)
14 I couldn't believe my eyes when I saw the price of the potatoes. (E)
15 I have decided that it's now or never. (E)
16 I hope that Jessica's mother is okay. (P)
17 I hate discos. (No apostrophe needed)
18 Francis's friends seem like a nice bunch to me. (P)
19 When shall we eat those tomatoes? (No apostrophe needed)
20 There's too much to do here. (E)

Spelling Matters II (page 32)

ghoti = fish

 gh = f, as in cou*gh*
  o = i, as is w*o*men
  ti = sh, as in na*ti*on

Speaking and Listening

Storytelling (page 38)

1 The speaker adds tension by making it the babysitter's first time – it gives a hint of her not being entirely confident. The reference to 'short notice' also feels a little unnerving – suggesting that things have not gone according to plan.

2 The speaker is perhaps in danger of overdoing the detail, but you can see what the effect is: isolation, cold weather, long waits – all add to the general feeling that there is something wrong.

3 Same again!

4 Notice how the speaker changes the tone – trying to give a sense of reassurance – that there's nothing much to the baby-sitting, that it should be straightforward. But the word nightmares gives a hint of trouble. It's one of the speaker's false clues perhaps – hinting that all will be well, whilst we sense that it won't be.

5 Notice how the speaker uses questions to help us to see inside the girl's mind – it makes us sympathize with her situation, baffled and worried.

6 Same again!

Dialects (page 58)
All the words mean 'to beat'.

Speech v Writing (page 66)
Hamza's account was written; Lindsay's was spoken.

Reading for Information

Non-fiction: Autobiography (page 70)
text A = auto; text B = fiction; text C = auto

Reading for Meaning II (page 88)
The comprehension question types in the activity are as follows:
- A
- A
- B
- C
- A
- C
- B
- C
- B
- A

Advanced Reading Skills (page 91)
Sunrise with Sea Monsters is a book of travel writing, autobiography, and journalism. The most helpful clues in the contents list were probably the specific dates (showing that these were events from during a person's life) and the references to particular places (suggesting travel).

Writing on Literature

Creative Responses to Literature (page 166)
Matthew's response is impressive, though there are problems. 'The shock hit me like a brick wall' is a simile which doesn't work – walls can't hit people. Its attitude to disability is highly negative. And it is a little too removed from the text to count as a literature assignment. With revisions, it could be an excellent language assignment.

Studying Character (page 174)
Milly becomes more and more outraged at the job George is doing, especially when she finds that the bus-driver is female. She leaves the bus vowing that she won't be able to sleep for nights. The bus drives off into the distance.

Acknowledgements

The author and publisher are grateful for permission to reprint the following copyright material:

Peter Benchley: extract from *Jaws* (1974), reprinted by permission of the publishers, André Deutsch Ltd; **Alan Bennett**: extract from 'A Visit from Miss Prothero' in *Office Suite* (1981), reprinted by permission of the publishers, Faber & Faber Ltd; **Peter Benson**: extract from *The Levels* (1987), reprinted by permission of the publishers, Constable & Company Ltd; **Mary Ursula Bethell**: 'Response' from *Collected Poems* (OUP, 1985), reprinted by permission of Oxford University Press, Australia and New Zealand; **Elizabeth Bowen**: extract from *Death of the Heart* (Cape, 1938), reprinted by permission of Random House UK Ltd; **Raymond Carver**: extract from 'Boxes' in *Elephant and Other Stories*, first published in Great Britain by Collins Harvill, © Raymond Carver 1988, reprinted by permission of The Harvill Press; **Geoffrey Chaucer**: extract from 'The Canterbury Tales', text from *The Riverside Chaucer* edited by Larry D Benson, Copyright © 1987 by Houghton Mifflin Company, reprinted by permission of the publisher; **E E Cummings**: '(listen)' is reprinted from *Complete Poems 1904-1962*, by E E Cummings, edited by George J Firmage, by permission of W W Norton & Company Ltd. Copyright © 1963, 1991 by the Trustees for the E E Cummings Trust; **D J Enright**: extract from 'Paradise Illustrate: A Sequence' in *Selected Poems* (OUP, 1990), reprinted by permission of Watson, Little Ltd; **William Golding**: extract from *Lord of the Flies*, reprinted by permission of the publishers, Faber & Faber Ltd; **Georgina Hammick**: extract from *Spoilt* (Chatto & Windus, 1992), reprinted by permission of Random House UK Ltd; **HD** (Hilda Doolittle): extract from *Red Roses for Bronze* (Chatto & Windus, 1931), courtesy of Perdita Schaffner and the Estate of Hilda Doolittle, used by permission of New Directions Publishing Corporation, New York, agents, and of Laurence Pollinger Ltd; **Seamus Heaney**: 'Mid-Term Break' from *Death of a Naturalist*, reprinted by permission of the publishers, Faber & Faber Ltd; **Barry Hines**: extract from *A Kestrel for a Knave* (Michael Joseph, 1968), Copyright © Barry Hines 1968, reprinted by permission of Penguin Books Ltd; **Ray Jenkins**: extract from *Début on Two: A Guide to Writing for Television* (BBC Books, 1990), reprinted by permission of MBA literary agents on behalf of the author; **James Joyce**: extract from 'Ivy Day in the Committee Room' in *The Dubliners* (Cape), reprinted by permission of Random House UK Ltd on behalf of the Estate of the author; **Neil Kinnock**: speech reprinted by permission of Neil Kinnock; **Penelope Lively**: extract from 'Bus Stop' in *Pack of Cards* (Heinemann, 1986/Penguin), reprinted by permission of Murray Pollinger; **Michael Meyer**: extract from his translation of 'The Doll's House' by H Ibsen in *Ibsen: Plays 2* (Methuen, 1980), reprinted by permission of David Higham Associates; **Brian Moore**: extract from *Cold Heaven* (Cape, 1983), reprinted by permission of Random House UK Ltd; **Caroline Moorehead**: extract from her translation of *Legends of Britain* by S Clot, C Quinel, and A de Montgon (Burke Books, 1968), reprinted by permission of Chambers Harrap Publishers Ltd; **Ben Okri**: extract from *The Famished Road* (Cape, 1991), reprinted by permission of David Godwin; **Samuel Pepys**: extract from *Pepys Diaries* edited by Robert Latham & L E Matthews (HarperCollins), reprinted by permission of the Peters Fraser & Dunlop Group Ltd; **Harold Pinter**: extract from 'The Lover' in *Plays: Two*, reprinted by permission of the publishers, Faber & Faber Ltd; **Jonathan Raban**: lines from *Hunting Mr Heartbreak*, first published in Great Britain in 1990 by Collins Harvill, © Jonathan Raban 1990, reprinted by permission of The Harvill Press; **Craig Raine**: 'The Grocer' from *The Onion, Memory* (OUP, 1978), reprinted by permission of Oxford University Press; **Jean Rhys**: extract from 'I Used to Live Here Once' in *Sleep It Off Lady* (Penguin, 1979), first published by André Deutsch 1976, Copyright © Jean Rhys 1976, reprinted by permission of Penguin Books Ltd; **Tony Robinson**: extract from *Blood and Honey*, reprinted by permission of BBC Worldwide Limited; **Salman Rushdie**: extract from *Midnight's Children*, reprinted by permission of Aitken, Stone & Wylie; **May Sarton**: extract from *As We Are Now* (Norton, 1973), Copyright © The estate of the late May Sarton, reprinted by permission of A M Heath & Co Ltd; **Siegfried Sassoon**: 'The Dug-Out' from *Collected Poems* (Faber, 1947), reprinted by permission of George Sassoon; **Anne Stevenson**: 'The Fish Are All Sick' from *Selected Poems 1956-1986* (OUP, 1987), reprinted by permission of Oxford University Press; **Paul Theroux**: contents page of *Sunrise with Sea Monsters* (Hamish Hamilton, 1985), reprinted by permission of Penguin Books Ltd; **Tom Wolfe**: extract from *The New Journalism* by Tom Wolfe and E W Johnson (Picador, 1990), reprinted by permission of the Peters Fraser & Dunlop Group Ltd; **Irene Zahava** (ed): extracts by Canyon Sam, Shay Youngblood and Terri de la Peña, from *Finding Courage* (1989), reprinted by permission of The Crossing Press.

Also for:

Advertisement for *BBC Wildlife* magazine reproduced by permission of BBC Worldwide Publishing;
Extracts from the Authorized Version of the Bible (The King James Bible), the rights in which are vested in the Crown, reproduced by permission of the Crown's Patentee, Cambridge University Press;
Extract from *There's More To Meat* leaflet reprinted by permission of British Meat and Livestock Commission;
Article from the *Daily Mail*, 6.11.87, reprinted by permission of Associated Newspapers;
Extract from advertisement for Neutradol reproduced by permission of M S George Ltd;
Extract from article by Andrew Culf in *The Guardian*, 28.22.94, Copyright © The Guardian 1994, reprinted by permission of The Guardian;
Extract from *Hutchinson Dictionary of World History*, Copyright © Helicon Publishing Ltd 1993, extract from the *Hutchinson Encyclopedia*, Copyright © Helicon Publishing Ltd 1995, and extract from article from *Hutchinson Gallup Info 1992*, reprinted by permission of Helicon Publishing Ltd;
'The Baby Sitter' cited in *Inside Stories 4*, edited by Peter and Susan Benton, (Hodder & Stoughton, 1990), reprinted by permission of Hodder Headline plc;
Extract from *A Dictionary of 20th Century Biography* edited by Asa Briggs (OUP, 1992), reprinted by permission of Market House Books Ltd.
Article from the *Daily Mirror*, 1.11.56, reprinted by permission of Mirror Group Newspapers.
Extract quoted in chapter by Bernard Clare from *A Rest from Shakespeare*, (NATE, 1994), reprinted by permission of Bernard Clare and the National Association for the Teaching of English, 50 Broadfield Road, Broadfield Business Centre, Sheffield, S8 0XJ;
'Fit for What?' from sample English GCSE paper reprinted by permission of the Northern Examinations and Assessment Board;
Extract from Italy: *The Rough Guide* by Belford et al (Harrap Columbus, 1990) reproduced by permission of The Rough Guides;
Extract from leaflet 'Easy Ways to Eat More Fruit and Vegetables' by permission of J Sainsbury plc;
Extract from article by John Askill and Lenny Lottery in *The Sun*, 28.22.94, reprinted by permission of The Sun;
Extract from an article from *The Times*, 12.11.92, © Times Newspapers Limited, 1992, reprinted by permission of Times Newspapers Ltd.

Illustrations by:

Gary Andrews p 95; **Martin Cottam** pp 80, 187, 203, 209; **John Dunne** pp 42, 43, 44, 51, 77, 140, 141, 142, 157; **Rosamund Fowler** pp 6, 25, 72, 84, 144, 145, 146, 186, 213; **Paul Hunt** pp 152, 167, 183; **Conny Jude** pp 45, 46; **Alexis Liosatos** pp 39, 66; **Steve Noon** pp 15, 36, 73, 83, 124, 198; **Chris Price** p 151 **Robert Price** pp 64, 201; **William Rowsell** pp 19, 67, 112, 113, 148; **Linda Schwab c/o Pennant Illustration Agency** pp 21, 72, 82, 136, 137, 138, 193, 211; **Darrell Warner** pp 75, 111, 159, 160, 176, 177; **Colin Woolf c/o Linda Rogers Associates Ltd** p 58
All the handwriting is by **Kathy Baxendale**

The publishers would like to thank the following for permission to reproduce photographs:

Cover photograph by **Zefa**.
British Broadcasting Corporation p 155; **Kenneth Earle representing Hugh Lloyd** p 155; **Format Photographers/Stephanie Henry** p 120; **Imperial War Museum London** pp 76, 212; **Marmont Management Ltd representing Patricia Routledge** p 155; **Garry O'Brien** pp 56, 70; **John Walmsley Photo Library** p 96; **Rex Features Ltd** pp 48, 61, 180; **SCALA Istituto Fotografico Editoriale S.p.A.** p 202; **The Bridgeman Art Library** pp 92, 199, 204, 206, 208